An Educative
Approach to
Behavior Problems

1995
-5

An Educative Approach to Behavior Problems

A Practical Decision Model for Interventions with Severely Handicapped Learners

by

Ian M. Evans, Ph.D.
Department of Psychology
SUNY-Binghamton
Binghamton, New York

and

Luanna H. Meyer, Ph.D.
Division of Special
   Education and
   Rehabilitation
Syracuse University
Syracuse, New York

·P A U L·H·
BROOKES
PUBLISHING Cº

Baltimore · London

Paul H. Brookes Publishing Co.
Post Office Box 10624
Baltimore, Maryland 21204

Copyright © 1985 by Paul H. Brookes Publishing Co., Inc.
All rights reserved.

Typeset by Brushwood Graphics, Baltimore, Maryland.
Manufactured in the United States of America
by The Maple Press Company, York, Pennsylvania.

Library of Congress Cataloging in Publication Data

Evans, Ian M.
  An educative approach to behavior problems.

  Bibliography: p. 163
  Includes index.
  1. Handicapped children—Education.   2. Behavior modi-
fication.   I. Meyer, Luanna H.   II. Title.
LC4019.E9   1984   371.9′043   84-19980
ISBN 0-933716-44-3

Contents

List of Tables

List of Figures

Preface

Because we have been involved in services for severely handicapped children and adults throughout our professional careers, the perspectives and strategies in this book are derived from our interactions with many individuals and programs across the years. Some of the ideas were formalized in the context of the Behavioral Systems Intervention Project (BSIP), which was supported by a field-initiated research grant from the Office of Special Education and Rehabilitative Services in the U.S. Department of Education. We conducted this project from 1979 through 1982 in the state of Hawaii. Our research involved monitoring a state-wide sample of young children with severe handicaps and behavior problems, and conducting a series of intervention studies in collaboration with professionals serving these children in public schools and preschool programs.

Various members of the BSIP staff were crucial to these efforts. Cynthia Azama, Sally Donellon, Kristine Derer, Rae Hanashiro, Terry Annon, Gordon Bauer, Ken Freedland, Jerry Brennan, and David Lipton all provided valuable assistance at various stages. In addition, Kris Derer and Rae Hanashiro co-authored the formal decision model with us (Chapters 3 and 4), and Gordon Bauer and Ken Freedland contributed valuable suggestions for the cost-benefit analysis procedures, among many others. We are also very grateful for the consistent support we received from several leading administrators of Hawaii's health and education systems, particularly Miles Kawatachi and Alan Oglesby. James Hamilton, who served as our project officer in the U.S. Department of Education, was helpful both in directing us to relevant work going on in other parts of the country and in stimulating our ideas through several discussions of assessment issues and concerns.

Our formal research investigations in BSIP, however, were but one of many sources of influence. In Hawaii we were extremely fortunate in having so many students, professionals, and parents willing to try new ideas (theirs as often as ours!). There are too many valued contributors to mention each one by name, but their aloha for us and for their children and pupils was common to all.

Ultimately, of course, it is to the rigor of the scientific community that we are answerable; the research literature is just bursting with new appreciation for the meaning of excess behaviors and for severely handicapped children's educational needs. We asked three academic colleagues to serve as major reviewers for the first draft of this manual: Anne Donnellan, Assistant Professor of Behavioral Disabilities at the University of Wisconsin; Robert Gaylord-Ross, Associate Professor of Special Education at San Francisco State University; and Martha Snell, Associate Professor of Special Education at the University of Virginia. Their excellent critiques and suggestions for revision have, we feel, greatly improved the content and format of this book.

Finally, we wish to thank the many children who have participated in our clinical and educational research studies. We have learned much from each of them, and it is our hope that their contribution to the design of the intervention approach described in the following pages will be reciprocated by our continuing sensitivity to their status as individuals rather than simply representing handicapping conditions and problem behaviors.

To Gia and Kim

Introduction

This book is about educational decision making as it relates to behavior problems in the classroom. We have written the volume primarily for teachers of severely handicapped, school-age children, but it should have considerable relevance for any clinician confronted with behavior problems in students for whom the critical educational need is the enhancement of skills. The presence of behavior problems in handicapped students places considerable demands on the judgments of any professional, especially those primarily involved in the educational process. In general, of course, the problem of dealing with disorders of conduct in classroom settings will not be new to any teacher or psychologist. Schools require at least some conformity of behavior to those rules and principles that allow pupils and teachers to interact in academically productive ways. The opportunities for students to engage in inappropriate behavior—from minor, high-spirited infractions to more seriously deviant incidents of disruption and violence—are considerable. With severely handicapped learners in the classroom, the types of behavior problems confronting the teacher are likely to be of a rather different nature, and yet just as damaging to teacher effectiveness as the more organized, antisocial acts of delinquent and behaviorally disturbed pupils.

Like any other children, severely handicapped children can display oppositional, aggressive behavior (biting or hitting when scared or angry), or try to escape aversive situations by negative means (e.g., throwing materials off the table when the task is too difficult or boring). They may try to control their environment through coercive behaviors (scream and tantrum to get their own way). However, children who have not yet acquired complex repertoires of skilled, self-directed behavior are also likely to display other forms of behavior that we judge as negative but which do not often occur in regular education settings. These are typically described as self-stimulatory or stereotypic behavior (rocking, head weaving, finger flicking, etc.), self-injurious behavior (biting self, head banging, picking and gouging body parts, etc.), and behaviors that are socially negative and basically represent a lack of behavioral control or skill (drooling; being incontinent; having erroneous, age-inappropriate social behaviors such as greeting strangers or wearing clothes that are left unzipped or unbuttoned, etc.).

The procedures and ideas presented in this book represent instructional based strategies for dealing with all of the above behaviors in educational settings, including community-based and vocational training programming. Most readers will know that the predominant approach to such problem behaviors has been behavior modification—the systematic application of principles of learning and motivation designed to reduce and hopefully eliminate undesirable behavior. Behavior modification techniques are now so widely known, have been described in so many textbooks, and form

1

such a core component of graduate training in special education and school or clinical psychology, that we will not attempt to review them. Readers who do wish to consult a basic text in this area as background for the material presented here will find Gaylord-Ross and Holvoet (1984) most helpful. Our approach involves an extension and elaboration of standard behavior modification methods. It is a "second generation" of behavior modification in which the focus is no longer simply on the derivation of techniques from learning principles, but on how these principles may be most effectively adapted to the instructional situation and extended to deal with the total educational needs of the child. This volume is about educational programming, not just the design of isolated behavioral interventions; about clinical strategies and the values that influence clinical decisions, not just techniques that produce behavior change.

When we say "our" approach, we do not wish to imply that the ideas behind this book are in some way uniquely our own. What we are trying to do is represent, in a useful way, the most recent developments in behavioral psychology and special education–notions that can be thought to represent, or to be consistent with, the accepted "best practices" for professional involvement with handicapped children and youth. As an illustration of how this synthesis extends beyond what might be called "traditional" behavior modification, consider the following issues. Most of the original work in behavior modification with children's problem behaviors was developed by psychologists working in mental health, institutional, or other clinical contexts. Without in any way diminishing the importance of this contribution, it is rather clear that the needs of teachers in today's integrated educational settings require systematic elaboration of the basic strategies developed for implementing an intervention. An obvious example is that various types of physical punishments were utilized in early clinical demonstrations of applied behavior analysis; for instance, the early pioneering work of Lovaas and his colleagues and students

at UCLA (Lovaas, 1967) involved slapping children contingent upon inappropriate behavior. However, regardless of other ethical and humanitarian concerns, such punishments are in most places strictly illegal in school for use by teachers (Martin, 1975). Thus, the *implementation* of a principle of learning (behavior followed by an aversive consequence will tend to be reduced in frequency) has to be radically changed if it is to be appropriate to the school context.

Another closely related example can be seen by considering the choice of the target behavior for intervention. In the original behavior modification studies, the target responses were selected because they were clearly inappropriate, but there was no consideration of other, longer range implications. It might seem very sensible to intervene with a behavior such as throwing objects *unless* the student happened to be a severely multiply handicapped child who has only recently mastered grasping objects and is beginning to release those objects but will only do so by throwing them. Would one as an educator be quite so willing to simply reduce this throwing behavior and risk reducing in the process the acquisition of an important manual skill? Or would it be preferable to structure the context and gradually shape the behavior into a more appropriate release action? Issues such as these will be addressed in detail in the following chapters.

One of the major innovations in contemporary behavior modification is a focus on decision making processes—the judgments that clinicians and teachers must make when identifying, analyzing, and evaluating abnormal behavior (Evans & Wilson, 1983; Kanfer & Nay, 1982). Think for a moment how the importance of the decision process is reflected in the procedures for designing individualized education programs (IEPs). The need to weigh and consider the concerns of parents, teachers, and other professionals is carefully protected in the federal guidelines for IEP conferences. Thus, our first chapter orients the reader to the view that the special education teacher (or other professional) is an *active decision maker* in the day-to-day educational happenings as well as in the longer term planning and evaluation of intervention procedures. Because intervention decisions are closely related to curricular decisions, we also review those approaches to educating severely handicapped students that have insufficiently recognized the child's needs in relationship to present and future environments. An overview of procedures currently recommended to teach the functional skills necessary for participation in community (or least restrictive) environments, that is, those guided by the "criterion of ultimate functioning" (Brown, Nietupski, & Hamre-Nietupski, 1976), is provided at the end of Chapter 1 of this volume.

The second chapter focuses specifically on the judgments we make about excess behaviors and what these behaviors actually mean. "Excess" is a more neutral and objective term for inappropriate or undesirable behaviors that need to be reduced in frequency. There are various ways of conceptualizing excess behavior, and these viewpoints have significant implications for the design of intervention tactics. For instance, we would probably approach a behavior like "mouthing hands" very differently if we judged it to be a self-stimulatory behavior that gave the child some enjoyment, rather than as a means of avoiding the task demands of a self-help instructional program. The realization that even excess behaviors can serve important functions for a student has a very dramatic and positive influence on the rational planning of effective interventions. Several possible functions of excess behavior are presented, each of which suggests the need to teach a more positive behavior to accomplish that particular function.

In the third chapter we discuss some detailed suggestions regarding the choice and selection of target behaviors. Listing the criteria and justifications for deciding which behaviors are most changeworthy focuses attention on the implicit assumptions that determine clinical and educational priorities. We have tried to articulate our own assumptions, all of which

reduce to the general belief that interventions with excess behaviors must be subordinate to, or at least serve, the primary purpose of education, which is the acquisition of new skills to enable the child to participate as fully as possible in society. Since there is evidence that such behaviors signify the absence of an "alternative" skill, this position is also empirically defensible. These notions are integrated into a logical decision model that we have designed. The model is presented in general outline form in Chapter 3. By following the model systematically, you will be able to incorporate all of the previously defined best practices into a cohesive strategy for judging excess behavior and planning interventions.

The following chapter, Chapter 4, takes a detailed look at the steps in the decision model by systematically working through an actual example of a child's needs. To encourage you to extend the model to the students you are familiar with, sample work sheets have been provided in Appendix A, The Flowchart Task Book. In addition, various practical exercises are included throughout the text.

In the decision model we suggest certain standard behavioral techniques. As mentioned earlier, we did not feel it was necessary to describe these procedures; we expect readers will be quite familiar with procedures like the differential reinforcement of an alternative/incompatible response, brief physical restraint, and so on. However, when such interventions are implemented in classrooms, they interfere with the normal routines of instruction. Think, for instance, how disruptive timeout can be, and what valuable instructional time is lost during the timeout period. How should interventions that were originally designed in clinical "treatment" settings be adapted so they can be incorporated naturally into the ongoing activities of the classroom? Staffing in schools is limited, and any intervention that requires intensive and extended use of a professional's time must be closely related to the purpose of the educational environment. Schools are also being increasingly held accountable for the progress of the students served, and an intervention that reduces a pupil's learning time has important implications for what the student can be expected to learn in a given area. Alternative interventions that do not require extensive staff time or subtract from a student's learning opportunities might include ecological strategies such as the simple rearrangement of the classroom environment. Changes in physical organization help reduce, for example, conflict between two students, or distractibility in a child who is positioned too close to tempting toys. Decisions about how to continue an intervention plan when carrying out a nonschool instructional program are even more complicated. What sorts of consequences can be programmed when you have a group of students in a grocery store to practice shopping skills? In Chapter 5, we attempt to provide strategies to answer these and other questions concerning the integration of interventions in natural instructional sequences and environments.

Finally, in Chapter 6 we propose certain ways of evaluating both the efficacy and appropriateness of behavioral interventions. Again, thanks to the heritage of interventions evolving from rather formal single-case experimental studies in clinical psychology, the importance of keeping systematic and objective data on behavior in order to change it is a well-established principle. All reliable texts on behavior modification spend a good deal of time teaching procedures of record keeping, graphing, and other data gathering methods. Special education teachers will generally have been trained in single-subject experimental methodology and taught important principles of research design in order to evaluate the effectiveness of an intervention. While having this background is critical for the special educator as a consumer of research, we doubt that the most feasible way for practicing professionals to evaluate their behavioral interventions is by carrying out experiments that rigorously control for extraneous variables—even if these studies were clinically practical. There are more informative and valuable methods for evaluating one's activities in this

critical area. For example, how could you, fairly quickly, check that you are implementing an intervention plan the way you originally designed it? Think how many times you have watched another teacher, or an aide, or a practicum student, and instantly recognized some feature of their interaction with the pupil that had not been planned but that could affect the quality of instruction. This perceptiveness could be reversed, and you could quite easily have a trusted colleague observe your own interactions with pupils, thus establishing the "treatment integrity" of your intervention efforts. As another example, reflect on how this book is about decision making and clinical judgment. What judgmental criteria would be most important in determining the success of an intervention: a statistically significant decrease in your baseline from preintervention to postintervention, or a note from the student's parents saying they have been really pleased to see how much the behavior has improved this semester? Of course, objective data are very important; parents, like the rest of us, can be overly optimistic or so accustomed to their child's behavior that they do not really notice change. But objective improvement must be accompanied by recognition of improvement from the people who really matter in the child's life: parents, neighbors, employers. These and other outcome evaluation issues are covered in the final chapter.

We hope that from this brief overview of the book you will have realized that we are interested in ideas and principles as opposed to formal techniques. Although we try to present very practical, easily implemented suggestions, we do not see this volume as offering technical prescriptions. Anyone in a position to be designing intervention programs that will substantially determine the repertoire that severely handicapped children will bring to their adult lives does not typically apply procedures described in instructional manuals exactly as written, from child to child. Different environments engender different needs, and individual students present unique problems. Teachers, we believe, operate as problem solvers, adapting their academic knowledge and clinical experiences to produce unique, often highly creative programs for their students. We cannot possibly anticipate the multitude of unique situations that students create for us.

The purpose of this book is to encourage the development of these creative, flexible strategies in accordance with principles reflecting the most recent advances in our field.

chapter 1

The Teacher as Decision Maker

Decision making is a pervasive feature of our everyday behavior. Waiting at a stop sign and deciding that there is enough time to drive across the road safely is just as much a decision as deciding that it is time to buy a new car, or which model to buy. Cognitive psychologists have long been interested in how people make such decisions and the degree to which these processes violate the idealized, rational model of how decisions could be most effectively made. One method for investigating decision making is called process tracing, whereby through questioning and thinking-aloud techniques we try to trace the decision maker's thought processes. If you were asked why you bought the new car that you did, you might be able to describe how you read *Consumer Reports,* thought about costs, long-term maintenance, and so on. Actually, your decision might have been influenced by the look of the car, or the persuasiveness of the salesperson. So, another strategy in decision making research is to develop mathematical models that try to recapture the degree to which various considerations are weighted and then combined to form a judgment. Some factors have *absolute* values: it is unlikely that even the most persuasive salesperson could convince you to buy a pickup truck if you wanted a family-type car. Some variables that influence your choice have *conditional* weights: a general desire to buy a car with front-wheel drive

may depend on finding a model that has attractive styling. Personal decision making is also complicated by emotional involvement: deciding to end a relationship or change jobs are both notoriously difficult decisions because of the conflicting feelings involved. One can weigh various pros and cons, but as the preferred alternative becomes clearer, anxieties and doubts may increase and change the values you gave to the various factors.

Emotional conflict influences professional decisions as well. In special education, placement and diagnostic decisions are sometimes influenced by what should be irrelevant factors such as the likeability or cultural background of the student. In the next chapter we mention the way that clinical and educational judgments of excess behavior can be biased by background knowledge of the student or prior theories about behavior. Decisions about students' behaviors are influenced by individual attitudes, principles, and ideas acquired during training, and subsequent personal experiences. Part of professional training is designed to reduce the impact of purely personal ideas and to instill a set of general principles. The difference between a professional and a technician is that the technician's decisions are made on the basis of predetermined rules, whereas the professional's decisions are based on the application of abstract principles. Technicians, of course, would know a great deal about how to do certain things once a decision was made as to what should be done, but a technician would not play a major role in making the decision. The purpose of this chapter is to examine both the *processes* of professional judgment and the principles that we believe are of greatest importance for the design of effective behavioral interventions.

THE PROFESSIONAL ROLE IN SPECIAL EDUCATION

Teachers undoubtedly think of themselves as professionals. Yet certain approaches to educational programming and behavior management for handicapped children clearly cast the teacher in a *technician* role. Models and materials that de-emphasize the decision making components often use terms such as "teacher-proof" to signify that directions are so explicit and the activities so well programmed that anyone, with minimal background preparation, could implement them effectively by adhering closely to the guidelines (e.g., DISTAR). Other packages permit the decisions to be negotiated by the IEP team, but once goals have been selected through an essentially democratic process, the "comprehensive" curriculum provides all the detail needed to produce student skill acquisition (e.g., Nishioka-Evans et al., 1983). Some materials are represented as being appropriate for all students with a particular diagnosis, such as autism, so that once the teachers know that the student is autistic, they need only follow the printed page, chapter by chapter, to remediate that pupil's educational and behavioral deficts (e.g., Lovaas, 1981). Most of the so-called "test-train" assessment instruments, including computerized skill inventories within the various curricular domains (motor, language, etc.) are quite explicit in their recommendation that the teacher (or psychologist) has only to ascertain the student's present level of performance. Once this has been done, the appropriate goals would be automatically identified by their position as next-appearing items in the sequence provided (e.g., Sanford, 1971). Closely related to this

approach to goal selection is the notion that once an excess behavior (e.g., finger flicking) has been observed in a student's repertoire, the most appropriate intervention for that behavior can be identified through an index of the published behavioral intervention research (see Nelson, in press, for a rationale for this approach, and Derer & Hanashiro, 1982, for an example of such an index).

In each of the programs and approaches noted above, teachers are reassured that the major decisions are made for them, based upon checking off a skill inventory, knowing the student's diagnosis, or observing an inappropriate behavior. Yet teachers must do far more than this in order to provide effective programs. Our knowledge base is not so well developed that we know in advance what should be done to help an autistic 8-year-old become a competitively employed, socially competent, and happy 21-year-old. Actual handicapped pupils often present so overwhelming a variety of behaviors, skills, and individualized reactions to "tested" intervention programs as to render the concept of a "teacher-proof" package meaningless.

We advocate, of course, continued efforts to design and field test general assessments and curricula. There is a continuing need for the *guidance* that such instruments and programs provide to teachers, parents, related professionals, and policy makers. But they should not be represented as a replacement for professional decision making. They assist professionals and parents in making optimum decisions, but cannot make those decisions for them. The most useful materials for teachers and others providing programs to handicapped learners will be those that focus upon providing choices, questions to be addressed in making one choice rather than another, and a systematic format to guide this process. Both the choices and the format for selecting options would be based upon educational practices generated by empirical findings in pupil outcome studies as well as certain fundamental philosophical principles such as normalization, quality of life, integration, and so forth. Where data are not yet available to validate one choice rather than another, Donnellan's (1984) "criterion of the least dangerous assumption" requires that priorities be established based upon activities most likely to facilitate community competence (this is discussed in more detail in Chapter 6).

It is important to recognize that the teacher (or any other involved professional) does not make *unilateral* decisions. We suggest that others participate as actively as the special education teacher in the various decisions discussed in this volume. First, other professionals will be needed to assist in those decisions. This is particularly so when the emphasis is upon teaching *functional* skills in the context of actual sequences of behavior and activities in the environments where those skills must be performed. For example, very few of the skills that a teacher might target for a child who has a severe motor impairment could be taught without the input of an occupational or physical therapist. For such a child, each instructional activity (as well as the rest of the school day, breaks, etc.) requires that the learner be optimally positioned for performance and learning on that particular task. The behavior itself also nearly always requires the performance of some motoric response (e.g., pointing to something, vocalizing, etc.) that should be defined for that learner with input from a specialist who can identify feasible and developmentally facilitative motions for that student.

Second, parents are clearly in a good position to judge which skills and behaviors are most needed at home and in the neighborhood. They are also likely to have invaluable information on what works well (or doesn't work at all) with their child. Furthermore, the parents are, quite frankly, the ones who must live with the consequences of any programming decisions. But even though the parents' role in these decisions is complete and important, the teacher's role must not be reduced to that of a negotiator among competing opinions or a technician who simply implements whatever decisions are made by the family. For example,

we assume that the teacher is in a position to develop the expertise for identifying the individualized sequence of goals, objectives, and instructional activities most likely to enhance the graduate's future opportunities. We would also argue that teachers become proficient over the years at intuitively diagnosing difficulties in existing programs as well as individualizing new ones for optimum pupil improvements. Based upon their training, experience, and clinical knowledge of a particular student, teachers can predict that a written program is not appropriate and/or would require particular modifications prior to implementation in order to be successful in their classrooms. They can also quite accurately determine on a day-to-day basis that immediate changes are needed without consulting graphed data or waiting for a subsequent intervention phase in a controlled experiment. Such procedures and tools are very important for providing objective information that facilitates decision making, but they are not substitutes for the judgment process itself. In the following section we consider some of the formal and informal judgments that must be made when excess behaviors occur in instructional contexts.

MAKING EDUCATIONAL DECISIONS

There are several major levels of decision making in the educational management of problem behavior. First, and perhaps most neglected, are the moment-to-moment, day-to-day decisions that are made in any program. Take a moment the next time you are in your own classroom, or when you are visiting a colleague's class, or watching your educational assistant, to try to identify a brief decision of this type. You might notice something like the following scenario: A student who is somewhat uncoordinated moves too close to your coffee pot that is in its regular place near the sink in the corner of your classroom. Your immediate reaction is to call out a warning, "Michael, come away from there, please." Because this response is so instinctive it is not always recognized that it is based on a rapid decision—you would not have reacted that way if Michael were deaf. Then, but with more deliberation depending on Michael's subsequent behavior, the following series of informal decisions might be made.

Decision 2: Although you quickly appraised the situation as potentially dangerous and decided on a response, you make the judgment that it is not a recurrent problem and therefore do not attempt to otherwise consequate the behavior.

Decision 3: After having to warn Michael three times that day about not knocking over the coffee pot, you propose a new rule to the class that students may not wander around the classroom without your permission.

Decision 4: Because this still results in you making a series of warnings, you decide to move your coffee pot to a safer place that is well out of reach, leaving no electrical cords dangling.

Decision 5: Because you see Michael approach other harmful objects, you decide to introduce a curriculum change. In a lesson later that week you will present concepts like "hot," "hurts," "dangerous," and so forth, and you go to the school nurse to obtain some poison control stickers of "YUK" faces to use in your lesson plan.

The immediate decisions in such situations are very important because they are based on *implicit* rules and procedures, and, because the teacher reaction tends to be impulsive and hasty, there is less opportunity to base them on a predetermined plan. After a number of instances of similar types of behavior, it is likely that one would identify the occurrences as indicating a problem and begin to devise a more formal type of plan. This is a second level, short-term decision such as the rearrangement of the classroom, the introduction of a specific concept into a lesson plan, or the setting of a new, informal classroom rule. Many times these decisions are made almost unconsciously. For instance, you will probably plan and set up your classroom's structure and layout before you even know exactly which students you will have that semester. General, informal rules about what behavior will or will not be permitted in your class have typically been thought to be dependent on your personality style as a teacher. There is a great deal of educational research surrounding the concept of the teacher as democratic, authoritarian, permissive, and so forth.

We do not advocate any particular style, but we do think it constructive if teachers recognize the degree to which these personal styles are, in fact, individual decisions and could have a profound effect on one's outcomes. By recognizing them as conditions that you establish and that are therefore under your control, you greatly expand your problem solving capabilities. This allows you to design interventions that are relatively subtle and unstructured. For example, suppose you are accustomed to beginning each day with formal introductions in which each child states his or her name and places a name label on your "good morning" board. If two of your students produce a great deal of excess behavior while having to sit and wait for you to go around your class each morning, it may be preferable to dispense with this practice (if it is needed at all) until later in the year when the two students are able to tolerate longer waiting periods. These informal, stylistic decisions will also influence such important variables as whether you use a discrete trial format, how you respond to errors, whether instruction is conducted in criterion settings, and so forth. Later in this chapter we comment on the ways in which these instructional design issues have an important impact on the occurrence and management of excess behavior.

The third level of decision making in instructional settings relates to longer term objectives. These decisions are typically much more formally made, partly because they have become equated with the IEP planning of annual goals and objectives. The IEP process is most interesting from the decision making perspective because it is a group decision, not an individual one. Groups make decisions in even more complicated ways than do individuals because each participant presents new information and different perspectives that must be accommodated by the others. There is also a social influence variable in which one member of the IEP team may be able to strongly influence others by virtue of a more forceful personality, or having great status or power. Gilliam and Coleman (1981) reported that special education teachers were ranked first in importance and first in contribution at IEP conferences by the other participants, with parents ranked tenth in postmeeting importance. By observing actual IEP meetings, Goldstein, Strickland, Turnbull, and Curry (1980) also found that the resource teacher assumed primary responsibility for the conferences, that the regular classroom teachers attended only 43% of the conferences, and that the parents often had a very passive role. The parents were frequently presented with an already developed IEP and they were the resigned recipients of comments made. As Turnbull (1983) emphasizes, parents may have differing abilities and interests regarding participation in this process. Nevertheless, some practical ways of including their opinions and values in the decision making process regardless of their interest in formal participation are described later in this chapter.

Plans to reduce excess behavior may also be developed at IEP conferences but we have concerns for the use of this educational plan as a formalization of methods for decelerating or reducing behavior. Our model represents a way of identifying the need for intervention plans at a formal level but not, thereby, specifying deceleration goals as instructional priorities. Although our model is a formal one, we wish to emphasize how increased attention must be paid to the two other levels of decision making: moment-to-moment responses by the teacher toward the student, and the general, implicit styles of classroom management.

Process of Decision Making

It is likely that the same principles of effective decision making are involved at all three levels we have outlined above. The first step is to review as carefully as possible the alternative options. We know from clinical studies of personal decision making (Janis & Mann, 1977) that being able to derive a range of possible options is one of the most difficult things to accomplish when emotional variables are involved. People who are stuck in problem situations cannot generate a reasonable number of alternatives, so that running away from home, quitting college, and other drastic actions are often the only possibilities considered to be feasible. Sometimes we see professionals act equally rigidly—the teacher who feels extremely frustrated with a particular student might imagine that the only solution to severe behavior problems is to have the child removed to another class or placement. In fact, it is often the case that by the time a consultant is called in to "assist" with a severe problem, the staff are actually seeking external support for their personal frustrations with that child and their often unacknowledged preference to refer the child *out* rather than consider additional strategies. The general recommendation in the problem solving literature is to consider this stage of decision making to be strictly "brain storming," in which the task is to think up as many potential solutions as possible without any regard for their practicality. Possible solutions should not be dismissed at this stage just because they seem like they would not work or could not be implemented. One clear sign that staff are not responding adaptively to a problem is the ready dismissal of all such suggestions with statements like, "Well, I know that won't work," or "But Tommy is too low, too difficult, etc."

The next step in formal decision making is to list the pros and cons that seem related to each solution. Thus, if your proposed solution to a severe behavior problem is to call a case conference and request outside consultation, the list of pros might include: (a) getting additional new ideas, and (b) gaining some professional colleague support for your coping with difficulties presented by the student; and your cons might include: (a) the delay in actually initiating an intervention plan, (b) diffusion of responsibility for the student's educational progress, and (c) being stuck with an intervention plan you may not like. Try to list the various pro and con statements more or less in order of their priority, but there is little point in assigning formal weights to the importance of each. Sometimes, it is useful to have a rule that certain con statements automatically eliminate one of the possible options. If you decide you cannot afford a car that costs over $7,500, any car priced over that amount would automatically be eliminated from consideration regardless of other benefits. There are a number of such absolute criteria in educational decisions with severely handicapped children. For example, no option could be entertained that results in a restrictive environment, or the loss of significant educational programming time, or is strongly disapproved of by parents or other primary caregivers. We have suggested a stage type of decision model (see Chapter 3) in which the most critical of the considerations are weighed first.

The pro and con statements require information that is factually accurate and also directly relevant to the decision to be made. If the estimated highway gas mileage of your preferred choice of car is incorrectly given, this item will affect your decision erroneously; if you are not interested in excessively fast driving, the advantages of a particular type of suspension are irrelevant. Psychologists interested in assessment have, in the past, paid more attention to its accuracy than to its usefulness. Regrettably, we know that much psychological test information is not perceived as valuable by teachers and thus is often neglected in instructional decision making. It is important to keep in mind the criterion of usefulness for a decision whenever you request additional assessment information on a student or gather that information yourself. If I ask for an OT evaluation, exactly *how* is this information going to have impact on what I am now doing? How do I intend to *use* baseline data on a pupil's excess behavior? Will it *help* me do a functional analysis (see next chapter), or help me decide when to modify my program? Thus,

it is essential to evaluate test data and other objective information in terms of your needs as a decision maker. This issue is examined in more detail in the next section.

The Use of Data and Research Findings in Decision Making

Have you ever used overcorrection or brief physical restraint as an intervention procedure? If so, where did you learn about such methods? In one of our studies of educational decision making, teachers described how their strategies for dealing with excess behavior came from a variety of sources (Voeltz, Evans, Freedland, & Donellon, 1982). Often, they had learned of the procedure in a formal university course, sometimes they had read about it directly in a journal, or had picked up the method from a colleague or at a workshop. This is an important aspect of applied science, as advances in the field must obviously be transmitted as rapidly as possible to the teachers and clinicians who are most likely to be using these methods developed by researchers. Most training programs for teachers of severely handicapped students teach research methodology to graduate students, partly on the assumption that this is a good model for teachers to adopt in order to be objective in their own work, and partly because as consumers of research findings special education teachers must be able to appraise the adequacy of the studies and the information on which they will base their new procedures (Snell, 1983). Similarly, clinical psychologists are typically trained at the doctoral level to be able to conduct research, despite the evidence that few practicing clinicians actually do carry out significant original research subsequent to their dissertation. Both behavioral clinical psychology and most major teacher training programs in severe handicapping conditions emphasize their data orientation and the growth of these fields as applied sciences, and we assume that this view is essential to dealing constructively with difficult problems.

While we strongly share the value of science as a model for thinking, we do feel that a slightly more liberalized view of basic research should be adopted if we are to make the most of research findings. Many research studies are conducted as though a demonstration of a valid relationship between the treatment and the outcome will be fully generalizable and will essentially prove the validity or worth of the method studies. Thus, an experiment in which overcorrection successfully reduced an excess behavior in a few severely handicapped students may be cited as support for the use of overcorrection with similar behaviors in other students—and by anyone who can follow the procedures used by the investigators of those studies. At various places in this book, we make clear how misleading we feel this notion is.

We have argued that traditional evaluation strategies—particularly developmentally based outcome measures and single-subject experimental designs—are inadequate for meeting the clinician's need to make intervention decisions based upon data on pupil performance and behavior (Voeltz & Evans, 1983). Decision making by clinicians is not simply *summative*. In the summative model, an evaluation is made as to whether or not the intervention worked only after it has ended. In contrast, clinicians must observe and respond to nearly moment-to-moment information on each individual pupil's performance in a *formative* way. This view is quite close to the interactive program evaluation model recommended by Cronbach and his colleagues who stressed that the primary importance of program "outcome" data ought to be for fine tuning individualized interventions so that they are most relevant to the particular ongoing needs of each situation (Cronbach et al., 1980).

Cost-Benefit Analysis for Making and Evaluating Decisions

Another limitation of the more traditional instructional evaluation procedures is that they generally fail to consider the effects of an intervention upon other behaviors and skills in the pupil's repertoire and upon the environment (Voeltz & Evans, 1982). Teachers and clinicians must judge the appropriateness and effectiveness of an intervention strategy based upon overall "costs and benefits" to the child, not simply on the basis of observed changes in the frequency or duration of a single, targeted excess behavior. There are absolute (empirical validity) and relative (social validity) value judgments that have to be made regarding collateral behavior changes (e.g., side effects) and the use of limited program resources and time. After these factors have been taken into account, one might reconsider a decision to intervene with an excess behavior despite demonstrable "success" in changing that single behavior.

You can see from this discussion that we are particularly interested in monitoring more than simply the target behavior; a major feature of our approach is that behavior represents a *system* in which many different responses are all interrelated. In any system, the changing of one element produces changes in others because they are interconnected. A school is a good example of a system. If you were trying to enhance the integration of severely handicapped students in your school by arranging that they eat their meals in the school cafeteria along with everyone else, you might quickly discover what a complex system is like. Introducing your pupils into the system might result in cafeteria lines that move more slowly, the improvement of your students' eating skills (whether through modeling or through some sense of increased performance standards), an increase in social contact between your students and regular education students throughout the school day, greater interest and understanding regarding people with handicaps by the cafeteria staff, and more complaints by some parents of regular education students to your principal. Actually, the more you know about the system and its interactions, the more you could plan the intervention to prevent any of the "costs," that is, the negative consequences such as the disruptively slow cafeteria lines or the parental complaints. The same is true of individual behavioral repertoires. When we intervene to change one behavior in a student, the actual consequences of that "one" change are considerably far-reaching in affecting other areas as well.

One of the most interesting consequences are the ripple effects (Evans, in press) that might result from a successful intervention. Like the ripples on a pond, one event becomes a setting event for another. Two reasons for changing behavior are that it has long-term benefits for the students, and it is useful to think of behavior change as always being a means toward an end. It is very useful in planning interventions to think of the ripples in the system. In the exercise in Figure 1.1, we would like you to fill in the empty boxes in terms of the types of consequences you *could expect* from the described behavior changes. By considering very carefully the *implications* of any behavior change for the long-term benefits to the child, we begin to confront the issue of whether a behavior is important in its own right or because of the hoped-for influence its change would have on other important behaviors. In the first example given, it is obvious that reducing hand flapping is having its hypothesized benefits only because it increases object manipulation. Thus, a program that had one positive outcome (reduced hand flapping) but not the other (increased object manipulation) might not get rated very highly in an

evaluation. Decreasing teeth grinding, on the other hand, would have the immediate consequence of saving the child's teeth from further damage, which in turn would reduce later pain, trips to an orthodontist, and so on. Those two consequences might not be the ones that you thought of for inclusion in the empty boxes, but that does not mean your ideas were erroneous. One of the major strengths of the decison making approach is that it recognizes there are few right or wrong assumptions. It is easier to judge how a decison was arrived at (e.g., logically, using all available information) than to judge whether the outcome of the decision was successful. Decreasing yelling or aggression at work will have the *possible* consequences of ensuring the student is kept on the job, increasing the opportunity to get promoted at work and/or obtain a more enjoyable job, learning more appropriate ways of expressing anger and frustration, increasing opportunities for friendships and social interactions, increasing community involvement in the company of others, and so on. In this case, the long-term beneficial outcomes are of two parallel kinds: enhanced social opportunities and continued progress in the vocational setting.

It is also possible, of course, that certain interventions would have negative consequences for a student. Negative consequences take a number of different forms. A major one

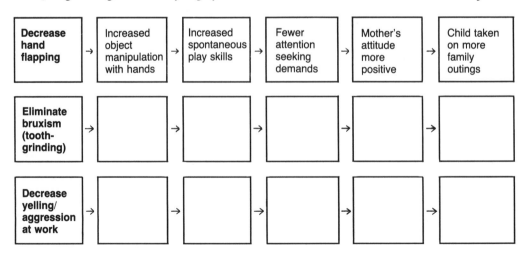

Decrease hand flapping	→	Increased object manipulation with hands	→	Increased spontaneous play skills	→	Fewer attention seeking demands	→	Mother's attitude more positive	→	Child taken on more family outings
Eliminate bruxism (tooth-grinding)	→		→		→		→		→	
Decrease yelling/ aggression at work	→		→		→		→		→	

FIGURE 1.1.   Setting events and ripple effects.

that we have often seen in classrooms occurs when the intervention takes time away from instruction, either because the method requires a great deal of the teacher's time, or because the child is placed in an artificial, nonlearning situation while the intervention is being carried out. Overcorrection procedures, for example, may require the use of 15 minutes to half an hour of a staff member's time (often the teacher's), as well as removing the student from scheduled activities during the intervention period. The intervention could also cost the child instructional time by using procedures that remove him or her from constructive social contexts. This often happens in various forms of timeout. Whether the student is required to sit on a chair in the corner with his or her back to the class, or sent to a timeout room, or studiously ignored by the teacher for a period of time, loss of learning opportunity is always involved.

It should be clear from these examples that deciding on an intervention strategy requires consideration of issues other than whether the intervention has been shown to be effective in a research study. Conventional behavior modification research rarely considers such criteria in evaluating a procedure for reducing excess behavior. Recent attempts to measure the acceptability of behavioral procedures (e.g., Norton, Austen, Allen, & Hilton, 1983) do not place the interventions in the context of a service delivery system, so the raters would not even be able to consider what other educational experiences the student was being denied. Part of the reason for this narrow perspective is a model of scientific research that focuses too strictly on immediate outcomes measured by single behavior changes. Another reason is the implicit "readiness" model assumed by many behavioral researchers. It is often argued that the goal of improving behaviors must precede the goal of skill development. This assumption is analyzed critically later in this chapter, but the immediate point is to emphasize that a decision making approach (as presented in Chapter 3) allows the teacher or clinician to consider such issues and thus focus on strat-egies that ensure that interventions do mesh with educational needs.

Another negative consequence or cost of intervening with one behavior is that it could increase the frequency of another excess behavior. (The exact mechanisms of why this is not uncommon are described in Chapter 2.) There are various circumstances in which such "side effects" might be judged acceptable. Singh, Manning, and Angell (1982) reported that when they successfully reduced rumination (regurgitating food that has been previously swallowed) in two profoundly handicapped 17-year-old twins, both persons showed a substantial increase in certain stereotyped behaviors. They asserted that the twins' caregivers found the stereotyped behavior "more manageable" and less aversive than rumination. Even more important than these caregiver concerns are the serious side effects (long-term consequences) of rumination, such as the risk of asphyxiation, dehydration, and damage, over time, to tooth enamel. These possible ripple effects make rumination a much more dangerous activity than other relatively innocuous stereotypic behaviors.

A further cost is when the removal of an excess behavior results in the decrease of a positive behavior. It is easy to imagine some ways that this could happen. Consider, for example, the following three students we know. Peter likes to play Lego, and can actually build some rather nice constructions. However, before he puts the pieces together he usually spends a few seconds waving them in front of his face in a repetitive way. What might be the consequences of devising a successful intervention for object flicking? William, who lives in a group home, is somewhat overweight and should be on a weight loss program. However, his major social activity is going to a pizza parlor after work with two of his friends. A dietary program involving food restriction would interfere more with this friendship than if he were encouraged to exercise more. Susan is beginning to acquire some independent toileting skills; however, she enjoys flushing the toilet over and over again—should her teacher worry about this repetitive behavior at this stage of training a new skill?

It seems to us that whenever one designs an intervention program, it is necessary for him or her to weigh the costs against the benefits. This is exactly like weighing pros and cons in decision making, except that in this particular context, it is limited to the specific costs **to the child** (*not* the financial costs) and the specific benefits to the child. Like the weighing of pros and cons, we think that clinicians will quickly be able to judge whether the costs of a particular behavior might outweigh the benefits. One simple rule should be that if the costs involve an increase in another behavior that is more serious than the one identified for intervention, then you would automatically rule out that choice. It is important to remember that at this stage of knowledge in our field, costs and benefits are only probabilities based on your guesses regarding outcomes, so you might proceed with your intervention as planned, but monitor very carefully the possible negative outcomes. Otherwise, if you do not monitor these other behaviors, it may not be quite so evident that a decrease in a positive skill (cost) has occurred along with the planned decrease in an excess behavior (benefit).

An interesting side issue is whether a gain of something undesirable is as negative as a loss of something good. In the formal research on human judgment, subjects do not give these two outcomes equal weight. Similarly, a loss of something bad is seen by most people as less positive than a gain of something good. We asked a group of experienced teachers to make judgments about how much better or worse off their pupils would be under various circumstances of this kind and found that there was no real preference expressed regarding such combinations of outcomes. Teachers tended to view the loss of a skill or the increase of an excess behavior as equally undesirable (Evans & Voeltz, 1982). This is encouraging, as we hope that by being sensitive to the range of possible outcomes when planning interventions, teachers and clinicians will be able to

devise innovative strategies that will be individually tailored to the long-term instructional needs of severely handicapped students.

PLANNING INSTRUCTIONAL PROGRAMS

One of the major decision making tasks confronting the teacher is to select, each year, priority instructional goals for a child's educational program. The development of a curriculum is not the primary focus of this book. But our principles for dealing with children's excess behaviors require, first, that any intervention program be planned and implemented within the context of the student's educational needs. Second, and more specifically, our approach requires that appropriate skills must be identified for instruction as alternatives to the excess behaviors. That is, remediating behavior problems is not an additive component, but is approached as an integral part of the child's educational plan. In this section, we discuss two approaches to program design that dominated intervention with severely handicapped learners until recently. Each of these approaches presents certain disadvantages, not only from a curricular perspective, but also with respect to the implementation of the decision model presented later in this book. Finally, we summarize the crucial components of a "criterion of ultimate functioning" approach to program design for severely handicapped learners, which we feel currently reflects promising educational practices and offers the framework best suited to incorporate the excess behavior change strategies that are the focus of this book.

The particular curricular approach that you implicitly follow also has crucial implications for how you would identify and conceptualize the educational and behavioral priorities in a student's total repertoire. The readiness approach—which we call the Getting Ready to Learn model—places the emphasis on reducing excess behavior prior to beginning skill instruction. The developmental model requires that the handicapped child receive instruction on skills according to the sequence of acquisition observed for nonhandicapped infants and young children. Finally, the model based upon the demands of adult life—which we refer to as the Criterion of Ultimate Functioning in accordance with the terminology used by Brown and his colleagues (Brown et al., 1976)—derives instructional content for a handicapped pupil based upon those functional skills that would be needed to participate, to the maximum extent possible, in integrated community environments after graduation. Each approach is described with particular attention paid to how it affects decisions and strategies for dealing with the excess behaviors in a student's repertoire.

Getting Ready to Learn

According to this model of intervention, children who exhibit severe behavior problems are less likely, and may even be unable, to function as efficient learners. Their behavior problems are seen as interfering with learning or, at the very least, interfering with teaching. This approach may include a recognition that the reason why a particular behavior problem will interfere with learning is that it reflects a serious difficulty for the child that must be remediated. Hence, a self-injurious behavior may indicate an underlying psychological deficit that must be remedied before that child would be physically capable of attending to an educational program. More often, however, the excess behaviors are simply viewed as interfering negative responses that are being emitted by the child at such high levels of frequency, intensity, and duration that no other sensory input and/or cognitive processing is possible for the child. At the very least, these excess behaviors must be temporarily interrupted for a long enough time interval for the teacher to present a stimulus (instructional cue) to the child, elicit a response, and deliver an effective reinforcer to motivate an increase in these adaptive responses. In addition, the excess behaviors are frequently regarded as being so child-intrusive that they must be reduced to near-zero levels prior to instruction, and maintained at those low levels for as long as neces-

sary in order for successful instructional performance to occur. As a consequence, a child's entire "educational program" might initially consist of numerous behavioral reduction goals and intervention plans designed to produce a compliant, attending learner—at which point, skill instruction would begin.

Problems with this approach should be readily apparent to those who work with severely handicapped children. First, these students often enter special education programs with multiple and serious behavior problems, many of which are likely to be judged by teachers, parents, and others as maladaptive, inappropriate, or interfering with learning. In actuality, we have very little empirical data to suggest that these various behaviors do in fact interfere with learning, though nearly all of them by definition are judged to be inappropriate and make it more difficult for parents and teachers to interact with the child. Such judgments are likely to be relatively arbitrary, and are not supported by information on later instructional progress. This is, of course, an unfortunate state of affairs that can be remedied fairly easily by simply exercising caution and ethical judgment in selecting those behaviors that might justifiably be decelerated prior to instruction.

There are other, more serious problems remaining. For one thing, there is evidence, examined in the next chapter, that many of these excess behaviors are "adaptive" for individual children. That is, these behaviors may be the child's only functional means of controlling his or her environment. Crying, tantrums, and running away may be the child's only available strategies for removing himself or herself from difficult situations. A child may not have learned the appropriate language and social behaviors to ask for a break from work, tell the teacher that she or he is tired, has a stomach-ache, and so on. In other cases, stereotyped motor movements may be the only "play" behaviors that the child has in his or her repertoire during free time. She or he may not have the skills to engage in more acceptable play and, oftentimes, even when the learner has the skills, the preferred play materials may not be accessible. The implications of this functional interpretation are not that excess behavior in these forms should be accepted; they clearly are inappropriate and both the learner and the environment will benefit from the acquisition of more appropriate strategies. What *is* indicated is that unless the child becomes fluent in acceptable, "positive" strategies to meet each particular need, the excess behavior is almost certain to reappear as soon as the specific management program is relaxed. Simply stated, the child *needs* the behavior to accomplish something. To really eliminate the behavior, the child must learn another functional skill to substitute in its place.

The Getting Ready to Learn approach is often used as a step in the placement process as well (i.e., the child must exhibit certain levels of acceptable behavior prior to placement in a community setting, etc.). According to this line of reasoning, the child's behavior will be shaped to acceptable levels that can be managed by the next environment: the targeted community setting. Such community settings are presumed to be unable and/or unwilling to accept severely handicapped individuals who display deviant and disturbing behavior. Therefore, the attempt has been to prepare the learner for those environments by eliminating these behaviors prior to placement. There are two rather fundamental problems with this perspective:

1. After considerable disappointment with programs to enhance maintenance and generalization, we are beginning to recognize that behavior in one environment may bear little relationship to behavior in a different environment. The more different that second environment is from the "controlling" or instructional environment, the more likely it is that the excess behaviors will reappear.
2. Research and program development efforts on integration suggest that the various community environments may actually be quite "forgiving" of the excess behaviors of severely handicapped learners (Voeltz, 1982). In fact, nonhandicapped peers and adults can do more than simply adjust to and accept the presence of these various excess behaviors. They can assist in delivering natural corrections to communicate to handicapped individuals the message that certain behaviors are not appropriate. This seems to be particularly true in peer interaction programs, where nonhandicapped children are surprisingly effective at modifying some of the more unusual behaviors displayed by their severely handicapped peers. Ironically, by removing severely handicapped learners from opportunities to interact with a variety of nonhandicapped persons other than teachers and caregivers, we may have actually removed opportunity for many natural "correction" procedures to take place.

Another, perhaps more fundamental, problem with requiring near-zero levels of excess behavior prior to community placements is, frankly, that some students may never make it. Autism, for example, is a diagnostic category partially defined by the presence of such excess behaviors. Nearly 20 years of concerted professional efforts in exemplary laboratory programs has failed to significantly alter the diagnostic status of most of these children. The classic follow-up study by Lovaas and his colleagues (Lovaas, Koegel, Simmons, & Long, 1973) essentially found that the autistic students who had maintained their various treatment gains were those students whose parents had been well trained and had continued to apply contingency management procedures to their children's behavior. This is quite different from anything like a permanent change in the child. Instead, it suggests a need to continue to control the child's behavior at all times using traditional behavior modification procedures. What this means is that some children are effectively limited in access to integrated community environments since their behavior seems to remain at an "unacceptable" level and changes only if a well trained intervention agent is present.

The Developmental Model

While the readiness model has dominated implicit decisions shaping behavioral interventions with handicapped children, the developmental approach to curriculum design has equally dominated special education, until recently. According to the developmental perspective, handicapped children are best characterized as learning less efficiently and at a slower rate than their nonhandicapped peers. As they increase in chronological age, their skill repertoires increasingly resemble those of younger nonhandicapped children. Within the developmental model, there may also be an emphasis upon establishing prerequisite *stages* of cognition, and so forth, so that particular skills are viewed as unattainable by the child until those prerequisites have been established. This has had considerable impact upon language intervention, for example, such that many severely handicapped children are described by clinicians as being "prelanguage" and consequently no serious efforts to teach a formal communication system are implemented until they are judged to have reached a certain stage of development (for a contrary perspective, see Reichle & Keogh, in press). Thus, we would argue that while such developmental information on a child and the related theories of development are valuable for designing teaching techniques and enhancing learner strategies, they are less useful as the source of curriculum goals.

The developmental standpoint has tended to have the effect of reducing the need for individualized decisions because educational programs have only to structure systematic movement of a handicapped child along the continuum of skill development in each of the traditional curricular domains. These continua have been mapped in considerable detail based upon the sequence of skills observed in "normal" babies and young children. Thus, by simply assessing the handicapped child in comparison to a skill sequence in, for example, the motor domain, the teacher can determine where the handicapped child has "left off," and would then proceed to target the next-appearing item as the instructional objective in that domain.

On the one hand, the positive features of the developmental approach no doubt explain its influence over the years in programs for handicapped children. First, there are well-researched sequences of development available in each of the curricular domains. The child development literature provides an extensive empirical base, and, thus, theoretical support, for the apparent necessity of this normative sequence of acquisition. There is also evidence that to at least some extent, handicapped children can be described as moving through these normative sequences of development albeit at a slower rate (Robinson & Robinson, 1983). Additionally, the extensive study of normally developing children has provided the content for numerous assessments and curricular packages based upon these normative skill sequences.

On the other hand, we can see several drawbacks in the application of this approach to the education of handicapped children. Some criticisms question the validity of the model's assumptions, and others relate primarily to the consequences of its use. First, not all developmental "milestones" (the behaviors included on any given skill sequence in a domain) are necessarily *prerequisites* to later development in that domain. In normally developing children, there is considerable evidence that certain of these milestones may never occur. A common example is the child who walks without ever crawling. In addition, many of the skills listed according to their normative appearance are not particularly important (e.g., hopping and skipping in the motor domain) and would not be selected as targeted objectives for severely handicapped students. It is also possible that even if crucial developmental milestones exist, they are not always noted in the available skill sequence. For example, the strategy used by a toddler to change position, unassisted, from sitting on the floor to standing (rolling over and pushing up his or her bottom from a "bear-walk" posture) is *not* included on published motor sequences.

An additional problem with basing educational objectives upon normative skill sequences is that many severely handicapped children exhibit multiple motor and sensory impairments that make it unlikely or impossible for them to acquire the "normal" form of the behavior. A child with severe cerebral palsy may be physically unable to proceed through the normal motor milestones of sitting, standing, and walking without support; a child who is deaf may be unable to acquire verbal language skills. A proposed solution to this problem has been to identify the *functions* of the particular behaviors, and to design an alternative *form* of each behavior that will enable the child to accomplish each function through either an alternative response mode (e.g., signing rather than talking) or with the help of a prosthesis or adaptive equipment (e.g., using a wheelchair rather than walking). If entire sequences of behavior can be replaced with alternative behaviors—successfully acquired and used by handicapped persons—then perhaps each behavior on such developmental sequences should be critically evaluated as to the *function* it has for the learner. If a particular behavior has no function, it could be omitted from the instructional program.

Because the skill sequences are listed for each separate area (motor, language, etc.), the developmental approach has often led to the teaching of isolated behaviors, one domain at a time, and by the various clinicians representing each discipline separately from one another. Thus, the speech therapist would define and teach language objectives, the occupational therapist might implement a self-feeding program, the physical therapist would outline a mobility program, and the special education teacher would assume responsibility for functional academics. Since these skills are then instructed by different professionals at scheduled times, the skills are not only taught in isolation from one another, they are most conveniently taught in massed-practice format. Typically, the skills would be "mastered" in the isolated or simulated instructional setting, but would not occur at other times throughout the day and in other situations and environments where they were actually intended for use. It seems ironic that the most severely handicapped individuals who are described as being least likely to generalize behavior from one situation to another are somehow expected to put these skills together for use in the activities of daily living.

If the behaviors being taught are essentially unrelated to current environmental needs, it is unlikely that they will be elicited by naturally occurring stimuli and maintained by natural consequences following performance. To some extent, we have compensated for this nonfunctionality and the absence of "intrinsic" motivations to perform the instructed behaviors by searching for increasingly powerful, individually relevant artificial contingencies. Unfortunately, it has proved extremely difficult to fade these artificial conditions while maintaining good performance, and even with an "ideal" instructional design, a significant percentage of severely handicapped students are noncompliant in these instructional programs (Haring & White, 1981). This noncompliance would be signaled by failure to attend or respond to instruction, unreliable performance of "acquired" skills, and the display of "avoidance" excess behaviors such as tantrums, aggression, self-stimulation, and so on. Instructional decisions may actually be responsible for some of the problem behaviors exhibited by students. If this is the case, simply adding on a behavioral program to consequate an excess behavior will not, ultimately, be successful as long as the student is required to conform to what she or he considers to be nonmeaningful activities. Thus, there are both behavioral and curricular reasons for critically evaluating the developmental approach to planning a program.

Finally, the most fundamental criticism of all is that even if we were to successfully motivate the acquisition of those developmentally sequenced skills that seemed most critical to later development, severely handicapped learners simply lack sufficient educational time, during the school years, to progress to the endpoint of adult functioning through this "bottom up" approach. By analogy to the ripple metaphor already described, the developmental perspective attempts to specify the means-ends steps that would take the learner to the desired endpoint skills at school-leaving age. But by starting at the beginning (even assuming the stages were correctly identified), only limited progress up the sequence seems likely. Even an outstanding public school program following this approach revealed just such disappointing results. The first "graduates" had behavioral repertoires similar to nonhandicapped young children, but almost none of the *adult* skills needed for the postschool world (VanDeventer et al., 1981).

The Criterion of Ultimate Functioning

The alternative approach to educational planning on behalf of severely handicapped students is to work from the "top down." Brown and his colleagues have articulated a curricular perspective that focuses upon the functional skills needed by adults in order to participate maximally in integrated community-based environments. Assessment would then constitute evaluating the child's current skills and capabilities in relationship to this "criterion of ultimate functioning" (Brown et al., 1976), and the measurement of progress is oriented toward how far one has to go rather than how far one has already come. Additional implications and components of this approach include:

1. The goals of instruction should not be focused upon the acquisition of isolated target behaviors, whether functional or nonfunctional. Instead, the instructional team must identify priority activities (Ford et al., 1984), natural "routines" (Neel et al., 1983), and skill clusters (Guess & Helmstetter, in press), which, if the learner could independently perform most or all of the component skills involved,

would be associated with the most meaningful participation in the next most desirable environment. Thus, the student in transition from preschool to elementary school might be taught the "survival skills" of social interaction, peer play, and compliance to the teacher demands that are characteristic of these more structured academic settings.

2. In order to achieve the goal of teaching chains and clusters of different behaviors, it would be worthwhile for the instructional team to plan IEPs in cooperation with one another and serve the learner according to an "integrated therapy model." The principle involved is that related professionals sharing responsibility for various components of an individual learner's treatment plan really work together, pooling information and blending intervention techniques so that the recommendations of each team member would be reflected in all programs. The professionals from each discipline might continue to provide direct therapy, but also consult with one another to integrate strategies and programs.

3. Assessment should not be exclusively focused upon the learner's repertoire, but contain all of the following steps:
   a. Ecological inventories of potential activities in four domains of living: domestic, school/vocational, leisure/recreation, and community integration
   b. The identification of priority activities in each domain for each individual learner
   c. A Nonhandicapped Person Inventory for each activity targeted for instruction, listing all the steps that are performed by a nonhandicapped peer engaging in the activity
   d. A Discrepancy Analysis, in which the handicapped person's repertoire is compared to the skills observed in the Nonhandicapped Person Inventory
   e. Training decisions based on whether the missing skills will be taught as is,

alternative forms will be taught (perhaps with the use of the "least restrictive" prosthesis), or skills will be performed by another person in the environment temporarily (see Meyer, McQuarter, & Kishi, 1984);

f. The identification of natural cues, correction procedures, and consequences for incorporation into the design of the instructional program (Falvey, Brown, Lyon, Baumgart, & Schroeder, 1980)

4. The focus of evaluation (and thus the location of instruction) shifts to peformance in criterion (natural) environments, situations, and in the presence of noninstructional persons who are found in those settings. You can see from this argument that it is not sufficient to consider a skill "mastered" just because your student performs the skill 80% of the time on 3 consecutive days for you. Instead, we would want to show that the student can perform the behavior independently, in the presence of those people not associated with the original instructional situation (e.g., peers, family members, store clerks, etc.), and in the community situation for which the behavior was originally intended.

Instructional methods influenced by the criterion of ultimate functioning model would, therefore, emphasize teaching those skills that are practical (or functional) for the student in actual, community environments. Since the activities themselves and the skills that have been taught are immediately useful in actual situations, we think that artificial motivation systems would be less important for acquisition and maintenance. Rather than teaching handicapped individuals in artificial and simulated situations, the approach stresses that the limited generalization skills of severely handicapped persons make it even more important that instruction take place in the locale where the skill is to be used, and in the context of the natural cues, correction procedures, and consequences of those settings. Hence, you would have to ask yourself if there were any reasons

for "getting ready" for a community environment in an often unrelated, instructional context. It seems preferable for instruction in skills and remediation of behavior problems to take place under circumstances closely related to the conditions characterizing the desired endpoint performance. The approach to excess behavior reflected throughout our book is consistent with this curricular orientation, and can be most easily incorporated into educational programs that are similarly focused upon the present and future functional needs of the individual.

A SUMMARY STATEMENT

Notice the term "criterion" in the criterion of ultimate functioning model just described. A criterion is essential for any form of judgment; it sets the standard against which a given instance can be evaluated. Thus, the curriculum model proposed by Brown and his colleagues (Brown et al., 1976) is really a *guide* to instructional decision making. It emphasizes the standard or criterion that should be used when weighing the pros and cons of one instructional program against another. One value of the model, therefore, is that it serves to focus attention on such considerations as the age-appropriateness of an activity, the relevance of an activity for living a quality existence in the least restrictive environment, and so forth. But the model is not prescriptive in the sense that it reveals details as to how to attain these outcomes; it places the emphasis at the end of the skill sequence—the outermost ring of the ripple pattern. That emphasis on the final outcomes we are all trying to achieve is having a salutary effect upon educational practices.

In our opinion, this decision emphasis is very positive because it highlights the role of the special educator as a professional. The ecological inventory, for example, is not something that can simply be looked up in a textbook from a methods class taken by the teacher in graduate school years earlier. The inventory must be carefully specified according to local conditions, the resources available in different neighborhoods, and the needs and expectations of the students' families. These individualized requirements resemble the philosophy behind the IEP. It is a very demanding task to really individualize an IEP. We all know how tempting it is just to follow standard guidelines or published models when developing the content of a student's IEP. The focus on the unique ecology of each student helps us to anticipate individual needs. And in the psychological assessment or consultation process, psychologists can use their knowledge of behavior/environment interactions to help specify critical skill needs far more effectively than they can suggest prescriptions based on the student's performance on a normatively referenced test like an IQ test.

Just as teachers and psychologists must make complex judgments regarding the progress of individual students and the curriculum goals most likely to promote the most successful educational outcomes, so formal studies of intervention methods must involve decisions regarding the efficacy of the techniques. Until recently the traditional evaluation model that was used implicitly in behavior modification research emphasized the careful measurement of dependent variables (target behaviors) that were often chosen according to their ease of being recorded rather than their clinical relevance. In the past few years, however, the field has become very aware that we must have greater concern for judgmental criteria such as the educational relevance of the outcome, the implications of the excess behavior change for skill acquisition, and the costs and benefits for the student's total repertoire. Another question that is increasingly being asked is whether the intervention method itself was in the best interests of the student.

As we have tried to show in this chapter, the intervention is not just an additional "treatment" imposed on the educational program. Strategies for reducing excess behaviors must be woven into the natural fabric of the instructional environment and the natural environment in general. Current "most promising practices" with respect to individualized curriculum design give us many indicators to new standards for evaluating intervention decisions, and in the final chapter we present several strategies that clinicians can apply to evaluate their own procedures and outcomes. For instance, we can expect behavior change to be most permanent if it is maintained by the reinforcing contingencies of the natural environment, or if the intervention is a component of the teaching strategy rather than a replacement of instruction geared toward the acquisition of functional skills. If intervention decisions are parts of the overall pattern of decisions regarding educational programming, then excess behaviors themselves must be seen as part of the total patterns of the child's behavioral repertoire. In the next chapter, we review some of the more prominent theories that have been proposed to explain excess behaviors. It is our theoretical assumptions about the causes and nature of excess behaviors such as self-injury, stereotyped mannerisms, and so on, that influence our decisions regarding these behaviors—their seriousness, their implication for the child's level of independence in integrated community settings, and their place in the complex patterns of the child's total behavioral system.

chapter 2

Analyzing Excess Behavior in the Classroom

Many different terms have been used to describe excess behavior in severely handicapped students. The most common labels, depending on the type of behavior, are "disruptive" (oppositional, coercive, aggressive), "self-injurious" (self-destructive, self-abusive), and "stereotypic" (manneristic, self-stimulating, ritualistic). There is also a large class of socially undesirable behaviors that seems to represent the lack or failure of usual regulatory skills; age-inappropriate responses such as drooling, bed wetting, and so on can be grouped into this category of undercontrolled behaviors. It might be a useful exercise to consider the following items of behavior and see whether you can fit them into these various categories: (1) raising his right arm, the child repeatedly extends and retracts his fingers toward his palm in a gripping/releasing type of motion, (2) a girl pushes her hand hard against her eye and then makes a fist and rubs her eye rapidly with her knuckles, (3) the teenage student stares off into the distance while smacking his lips together; with his right hand he pulls lightly but repeatedly at his clothes, as though picking hairs or lint from his shirt, (4) in the middle of an instructional task the student suddenly covers her ears with her hands, jumps

up, knocking over her chair, and runs crying to a corner of the classroom.

However you labelled these behaviors, we have attempted, as you perhaps suspected, to set you up! The four behaviors actually represent descriptions of the following events: (1) a nonhandicapped toddler waving goodbye; (2) a child with a severe allergy problem that causes her eyes to itch and water; (3) a student with a partial, psychomotor seizure disorder in which behavioral symptoms like lip smacking and lint picking are part of the seizure activity; (4) a 10-year-old autistic girl with an extreme sensitivity to high pitched sounds who heard a lawn mower outside the classroom window and ran to escape the noise. Of course, the way you labelled these behaviors could still have been quite accurate; for instance, it is certainly disruptive for a child to bolt from the teacher, or self-injurious to rub your eyes too hard. Yet the label clearly misses something of the content, causes, and purposes of the behavior. We are making two points with this exercise. One is that our set or expectancies toward particular students and their behaviors influences what we see and how we think about it. The other is that in order to evaluate and modify a behavior successfully, one must know certain critical details regarding its function. The purpose of this chapter is to examine these two issues in detail.

THINKING ABOUT BEHAVIOR

Expectancies Based on the Student Context

Expectancies about students influence judgments considerably. Gold (1972) asked highly experienced supervisors in a vocational training workshop to predict which of their moderately and severely retarded adolescent students would be able to learn to assemble a 24-piece bicycle gear. The supervisors were sure that none of their students were capable of this task; actually, all but one of the 64 teenagers learned the assembly task in the 55 trials allowed. In a classic study known as "Pygmalion in the Classroom," Rosenthal and Jacobson (1968) described how, by labelling children as "gifted," they were able to improve the evaluations and actual achievement scores of randomly selected children in a classroom. Although this study has been criticized and the effects not fully replicated, the fact remains that we are all somewhat influenced by the way children are labelled (Hobbs, 1975). The issues of labelling children are quite complex and more and more professionals are now aware of the biasing and potentially negative effect. We are most interested in the specifics of how one's preconceptions might influence judgment about excess behaviors.

A persuasive example of this comes from a study of teachers' responses to a videotape of a child in one-to-one instruction. After being given a little background information (e.g., a psychologist's report), the subjects observed the *same* child under different assumptions. In one, the child was labelled "severely delayed" and in another the child was identified as "moderately delayed." In addition to editing the videotapes to make such descriptions plausible, we chose scenes in which the child engaged in many or just a few excess behaviors. One scene, for example, depicted a 6-year-old autistic child being taught to sign "juice" and "cookie." During the instruction he ran from

the table and had to be retrieved by the teacher, had one minor tantrum (crying, kicking), and engaged in brief periods of hand flapping and body rocking. The teacher subjects were asked to design an IEP for this child, identifying four annual goals in any of the relevant need areas (e.g., cognitive, language, fine motor, self-help, socioemotional, etc.) and write one initial quarterly short-term objective with each goal. They were also asked to identify any behavioral or management needs that would affect programming for this child.

The most frequently mentioned annual goals dealt with language ("increase expressive language," "increase repertoire of signs") or adaptive behavior ("develop self-help skills," "toilet independently"). Only a very few of all goals and objectives reflected socioemotional concerns such as "increase independent play" and "develop adequate social skills." About 20% of the annual IEP goals were not concerned with skill development but with modifying excess behavior. We feel that the use of the IEP for deceleration objectives is inappropriate, as we will explain more fully later. The teachers were much more likely to focus on excess behaviors if the child was described as having several excess behaviors. The developmental level of the child did not influence the tendency to focus on excess behavior. This subtle inclination to focus on excess behavior could have considerable influence on how a child's IEP is developed and revised over the school years. For example, the rather positive objective of "increase ability to work independently" (although essentially a behavior management goal) was frequently suggested when the child was depicted as moderately delayed, but hardly ever mentioned when the child was depicted as severely delayed.

In the published behavior modification literature, it is our impression that the more limited the skill repertoire of the student, the less likely it is that interventions for seriously inappropriate behavior will focus on increasing alternative responses. Kazdin (1980) carried out a study in which he demonstrated that an aversive intervention was judged most acceptable when the target child was described as severely handicapped, or when the behavior itself seemed more severe. Fortunately, the judges did consider the reinforcement of incompatible behavior to be the most acceptable treatment regardless of the child's severity of delay. However, the judges in this study were undergraduate students, so we do not know whether these same attitudes would be found in representatives of those individuals in our educational system who actually make such decisions—teachers, psychologists, administrators, parents, and so on. Using student teachers as subjects, Witt, Elliott, and Marten (1984) found that severity of behavior problem was not a factor in making negative interventions more acceptable.

The Functional Analysis

Your feelings toward a student, what you have been told about him or her by the parent or former teacher, and your expectations based on age or developmental level all represent preconceptions that affect professional judgment. In order to appraise behavior as objectively as possible, one also needs to think carefully about one's prior assumptions regarding the *causes* of behavior. Behavioral psychology has encouraged us to avoid inferences about causes that come from "within the child." One of the most important contributions of applied behavior analysis is the concept of the *functional analysis*. The word "functional" is used repeatedly throughout this book because of the importance of always considering carefully the purpose, use, or function of any skill taught to a student (Chapter 1). However, in the context of the operant conditioning literature, the term has a slightly different connotation, the mathematical meaning. What Skinner originally meant by a functional analysis was an analysis that clearly revealed what manipulable environmental variables the behavior was a function of—in other words, what external events actually influence or determine the *present* occurrence of a given behavior. This rather simple idea proves to be very important for actually *changing* behavior. For example, a

child's reading disability might well have a genetic cause, but one can hardly alter a person's grandparents. If we say that a child is pulling another's hair because he or she is "jealous" of the other child, this explanation does not really tell you what to change to improve the situation. On the other hand, if you noticed that hair pulling incidents tend to occur after you have praised the other child, then an intervention becomes immediately obvious: you would devise a fairer way of distributing your social reinforcements, such as arranging group instructional activities that encourage interaction as opposed to parallel teaching.

The most straightforward way to do a functional analysis is to use your technical knowledge of behavior and your special knowledge of the individual student to formulate an idea—a hypothesis—regarding the factors that might be influencing the behavior of concern. You would then try to observe any systematic relationship between variation in these factors and variation in the student's behavior. When first exposed to principles of behavior modification, most teachers and other professionals are taught to do an "ABC" analysis of behavior—to record the Antecedent events that precede the Behavior and to note the Consequences. By systematically observing and recording these antecedents and consequences, it is possible to detect consistencies that suggest which variables are influencing the behavior. If the reinforcement is intrinsic to the behavior, as will be discussed later in this chapter, it is hard to observe. Similarly, the antecedents may be some contextual stimulus like the lighting or noise level in the classroom, not a discrete event. Even more difficult to detect are general conditions that are called *setting events* (Bijou & Baer, 1961)—prior experiences that alter the later probability of behavior (see Wahler & Fox, 1980). Krantz and Risley (1977) provided a nice example of this. In their study they showed that by arranging a quiet play period before a group activity, a kindergarten teacher was able to reduce substantially the disruptive and inattentive behavior of the children during a later reading activity.

At some stage it might become necessary to test your hypotheses about influential factors by arranging an informal experiment. If the hypothesis is that your student is cranky and irritable early in the school day because he or she arrives at school hungry after a long bus ride, then you could make a comparison between a typical week and a week when you give him or her a snack to eat on arrival at school. The experiment could be made slightly more formal by having someone else, such as your aide, provide you with a rating of the child's behavior each day, without telling the rater about your systematic variation in conditions.

This type of informal study uses what would be called an A-B design in single-subject research, since you are comparing one condition (A—the "baseline" condition) to another (B—the "treatment" condition). It is always pointed out that A-B designs do not provide totally convincing proof of a hypothesis because they do not control for the fact that some other event, perhaps the student's parents deciding to make his or her bedtime a little earlier, might have coincided with your intervention and thus actually been responsible for the improvement in mood. However, as you are only trying to test your hypothesis to your own satisfaction of what seems to work, it is not necessary to be rigid about such issues in practical situations. After all, you could always, in this example, ask the parent whether there was anything different about the second week, and perhaps learn about other environmental factors that influence the child's behavior; changes in routine seem to be significant setting events, as do clinical problems like depression in the parent. In some ways the functional analysis is like detective work—formulating hunches, gathering clues, and weighing the evidence as objectively as possible.

One of the most convincing demonstrations of a functional relationship is when repeated manipulations of a set of conditions influences the behavior in much the same way each time. Carr, Newsom, and Binkoff (1980) described a severely handicapped 9-year-old named Sam whose aggressive behaviors were pinching, pulling hair, and scratching. In some teaching sessions they presented Sam with a buttoning board and gave him verbal and physical prompts to practice buttoning. During these "demand" sessions the frequency of his aggressive responses was high. In low demand sessions he was simply handed the buttoning board task and during these sessions there was virtually no aggression exhibited. Some years ago, one of us was working with an autistic child in a preschool and was able to show that if she was brought into speech therapy from an activity she enjoyed (sitting with her favorite adult) she tended to be much more echolalic than if she came into the session from a situation she really disliked, which was being left in the playroom with the other children (Evans, 1971). If you have a careful and convincing test of your hypothesis, as in these two examples, you are entitled to speculate all you like about the possible causes of inappropriate behavior. The greatest danger is when we latch on to some fixed idea or belief about what the child needs and fail to look for objective evidence to support the notion.

Describing Behavior

Searching for the immediate causes of behavior—the functional analysis—involves, then, individual professional judgment, not following fixed rules. Another stage in the overall process of decision making is the definition or description of behavior. Because we describe behavior in everyday English, our choice of terms influences subsequent thoughts about the behavior. Earlier, we gave the example of the child covering her ears and leaving the work area. To label such behavior as "oppositional" would imply that we already knew about the motivation and purpose behind the behavior, and that might make us less likely to discover that the child was actually avoiding a high frequency, aversive noise. Behavioral labels carry surplus and sometimes misleading meaning. A teacher and an aide might not be able to agree on the rating of "crankiness" because the term means different things to different people. However, when trying to use the detailed physical descriptions of simple responses, it is often necessary to include criteria such as repetitiveness of context to prevent an observer from including "waving good-bye" in the counting of incidents of "hand flapping," to give one example. Sometimes the *intent* of a behavior, which must be inferred, must be considered in order to make any sense of what the child is doing. If a student reaches out toward a new toy, a description such as "child extended right arm across table" would be much less useful than saying "child tried to reach the electronic game." Here, by judging the intent and not just the physical observables, one is providing the most accurate description of the behavior.

This relates to another issue that will be important for the successful application of the ideas contained in this book. Our concern is with the way sequences and complex clusters of behavior are descriptively organized and separated into "chunks" by our definitions. Imagine a student who starts off by squirming in his or her chair, then making little whimpering sounds, then crying, and then screaming and lashing out with his or her arms in a major tantrum. For intervention purposes, it is a good idea to break down this behavior into its component chain of events because it would be better to intervene very early in the sequence rather than later after a major tantrum has developed. Often, the sequence of behaviors is less obvious than in this example, particularly if the behaviors seem to be unrelated to each other, such as a long period of finger flicking being reliably followed by a short burst of head banging. Regardless of why such a sequence occurs, the fact remains that if it does, it might be possible to modify the head banging by reducing the finger flicking. This is what is known as *indirect intervention* and its value is one of the major themes of this book.

Another organizational feature of behavior to consider is that of cluster, where the various

discriminable behaviors seem to occur together, such as when the student is rocking and finger flicking simultaneously. Should we think of this as one pattern of behavior, or is it more useful to think of them as two separate behaviors? If rocking, finger flicking, and tooth grinding all occur at the same time in a cluster, it certainly seems easier to design an intervention that interrupts finger flicking (e.g., brief physical restraint; see Chapter 5) than tooth grinding, a behavior that is relatively inaccessible. The problem becomes increasingly interesting when one realizes that positive behaviors are sometimes part of a cluster of excess behaviors. For example, we have observed a child whose only speech sounds co-occurred with incidents of running and flicking objects. Would we reduce this important language behavior by "successfully" intervening with running or flicking? If so, it would be an example of a negative side effect or cost, as discussed in Chapter 1. Finally, let us emphasize that *negative clusters* have been observed, such that when one behavior is occurring, some other excess is less likely to occur. Kathy, one of our students, would either grind her teeth and noisily blow with her lips pursed, *or* engage in another complex behavior involving twisting her fingers and banging her hands together. She never performed both patterns at the same time. Not unexpectedly, we discovered that when we reduced finger twisting, Kathy's other excess behaviors of blowing and mouth movements became more frequent (Evans & Voeltz, 1982).

A possible explanation for the existence of negative behavior clusters is the operant concept of *response class*. Response class refers to the observation that various topographically different responses can all achieve a given outcome. The physically disabled student who is learning to play with a toy like an electronic flute can get a pleasing sound out of the instrument by resting his or her hand on it, pushing a note with his or her index finger, or pressing down on it with his or her head or elbow. If the preferred response is not successful, then the child can try other members of the response class. Responses form a class when they are all controlled by the same reinforcing event. If Kathy was obtaining some sort of reinforcing sensory feedback from twisting and clapping her hands, then other responses producing distinctive sensory feedback, like the blowing and grinding, would be alternative members of that response class.

If responses can be thought of as organized according to their function or the purposes they achieve, one might imagine responses forming a cluster on the basis of some common, linking element. Think of a child lacking self-control skills. He or she might on one occasion reach out and grab another student's food in the cafeteria, on another occasion physically attack a peer who has taken his or her ball during a game on the playground, or repeatedly call out the teacher's name during academic instruction. These three very different behaviors can be thought of as related to the absence of one common "keystone" behavior, namely the self-control skill. "Keystone behavior" is a term used by Wahler (1975) for any response that seems critical for the performance of many others. If the other responses are desirable, we can think of the keystone behavior as much like a pivotal or prerequisite skill. One of the best published examples of this approach was reported by Russo, Cataldo, and Cushing (1981). Three mild to moderately delayed preschool children were in their study, each of whom exhibited a wide range of excess behaviors: tantrums, aggression (kicking, biting, and hair pulling), and self-injurious head banging. Intervention consisted in reinforcing compliance to adult requests. As their compliance increased, there was a dramatic and sustained decrease in their untreated negative behaviors. This suggests that noncompliance was a keystone behavior for the production of many inappropriate activities.

To summarize our discussion thus far, we have listed in Table 2.1 a glossary of terms that are necessary for the proper description and analysis of excess behaviors.

CLASSIFICATION AND MEASUREMENT OF EXCESS BEHAVIORS

Classification According to Function

As explained, the way in which we classify and describe excess behaviors will greatly influence the way we try to deal with them. Various authorities have proposed schemes for classifying and conceptualizing excess behaviors. We have not attempted an exhaustive review of these ideas in the following sections, but have selected those notions that have gained the greatest prominence and acceptance in the field. We do not, for example, discuss psychoanalytic theories of excess behavior, because, in our opinion, these no longer have any major currency for classroom teachers. However, it might be remembered, when dealing with professionals in other disciplines, that specialized knowledge and behavior can give alternative and possibly valuable perspectives on behavior we judge to be undesirable. Thus, pediatricians and psychiatrists are more likely to consider unusual behaviors as arising from organic causes: neurological processes, biochemical disturbances, or drug effects. Schuler (1980), whose field is communication disorders, is one of a growing number of people who have suggested that disruptive and other inappropriate behaviors often serve a communicative function for the child. Behavioral psychologists would probably be predisposed to look for the social attention or other rewarding consequences that follow the excess behavior. Physical therapists are skilled in recognizing that some movement disorders may be related to abnormal reflex development, or the ballistic consequences of reflexive actions, or undesirable positioning. A problem solving approach to the needs of individual students requires that various alternative hypotheses be formulated that in turn demand that our theoretical models and ideas about excess behavior be as broad as possible.

Forehand and Baumeister (1976) proposed categorizing excess behaviors into stereotyped acts, antisocial behavior, and classroom dis-

TABLE 2.1.   Glossary of terms used in the description and analysis of excess behavior

Cluster: Cluster refers to a number of separable responses that seem to typically occur simultaneously or closely together in time, such as drooling, mouthing hands, and vocalizing, or watching TV and eating popcorn.

Duration: Duration refers to how long a behavioral event continues. Many excess behaviors that are made up of a series of discrete movements (such as rocking back and forth) are best represented by recording their duration. As there is a finite period of time within which one can behave, a reduction in the duration of one behavior must inevitably result in the increase in duration of some others, assuming that they are incompatible.

Frequency: Frequency is the number of occurrences or repetition of a defined unit of behavior. In direct behavioral observation, it is useful to measure the frequency of discrete actions such as biting or urinating in pants. Many behaviors are considered excess behaviors only because of their high frequency.

Keystone behavior: When describing the organization among a number of responses in an individual child's repertoire, the keystone behavior is the one on which all the others appear to depend, rather like a pivotal or prerequisite skill.

Response class: Response class refers to a number of topographically different behaviors that are under one common source of environmental control, usually because they all fulfill the minimal criterion for a particular reinforcement. Thus, spitting, biting, and pushing might all form a response class (aggression) that serves to keep other children away. If one member of the response class is reinforced, all members of the class potentially increase in probability.

Sequence: Sequence refers to a succession of discrete responses in which it is likely that the presence of one response becomes a cue (discriminative stimulus) for the occurrence of the next; for example, the child has to first grab the book he or she is not allowed to have in order to be able to rip it. Thus, the second behavior is really dependent on the prior occurrence of the first.

Topography (form):   Topography refers to the physical form of the behavior. It is usually obtained by a careful and objective description of the precise motor movements involved. Thus, the response topography of pica (placing inedible objects in one's mouth) is very much like the response topography of eating french fries; banging an object on the desk has a topography similar to banging a drum.

For further details, see Voeltz and Evans (1982).

ruption. Another scheme, based on the message communicated by the different behaviors, was proposed by the Teaching Research group at the University of Oregon (V. Baldwin, personal communication, 1977):

1. *Self-indulgent, attention seeking* ("Me first"):   includes behaviors such as crying, whining, demands for teacher attention, and so on
2. *Noncompliant* ("I don't want to"):   refusals to perform a task, and so on
3. *Aggressive* ("I'll get you"):   purposeful hitting, pushing, biting, taking objects from others, and so on

4. *Self-stimulation* ("I'm doing my own thing"):   playing with sources of light, finger flicking, masturbating, rocking, and so on

A possible problem with this schema is the strong implication of intentionality in the behaviors, which could be unrealistic. Some behaviors fit functionally into more than one category, for example, self-injurious behavior can at various times be described as self-stimulatory or as attention seeking in different children or even in the same child in different situations. Some excess behaviors may have no identifiable function in terms of environmental events and emerge as components of neurological disturbances, such as seizure-induced behaviors. Another more neutral conceptualization of excess behavior would be within just two general categories: ritualisms and manipulatives, with a third category, self-injurious, located in either one depending on the major purpose that the behavior appears to serve (Evans & Voeltz, 1982).

Ritualistic behaviors are those that do not appear to be goal oriented but engage the child's attention during the time in which they occur. Many labels have been given to these, such as bizarre behaviors, stereotypes, perseveration, self-stimulation, and so on. It is often assumed that these behaviors are self-reinforcing, but in an excellent review, Baumeister (1978) has argued that a descriptor such as "self-stimulation" implies that the function is known. We wonder if terms like "ritualistic" do not also carry surplus meaning, creating the impression that we know for sure the behavior has no function, or has not acquired one. It would also be a mistake to refer to stereotyped or ritualistic behavior as "autistic behaviors" because although autistic children very often exhibit a number of these types of responses, so do many other handicapped children who do not fit the autistic syndrome. Another obvious feature of this type of response is that the behaviors occur in non-handicapped people with amazing frequency. It always caused some amusement among our research group to observe each other while we tried to devise a list of possible excess behaviors in our students—we were all chewing on pencils; twirling paper clips; tapping, shaking, or jiggling our legs; and so on! Of course, in severely handicapped persons, repetitive behaviors are more extreme in frequency or unusual in form, but one reason they seem so predominant in severely handicapped persons is because their range of other, more adaptive behaviors is rather limited. Another is that they are less likely to be able to access the environment successfully (make arrangements to go out, obtain leisure materials that are not im-

mediately visible, etc.), even to use the skills they do have.

Manipulative behaviors appear to be goal directed and under environmental control, usually occurring specifically in social contexts or serving to initiate or end a social interaction. In particular, such behaviors: (1) seemed intended to function as aversive consequences to others, thus reducing caregiver instructional efforts (e.g., temper tantrums, crying, etc.); or (2) occur whenever reinforcement for another behavior, previously reinforced, is not forthcoming (e.g., attention seeking, whining, pushing, shoving, etc.). Richard Neel (1983), at the University of Washington, suggests that all problem behaviors can be classified into three categories depending on *our* understanding of their intent. This useful distinction is as follows:

1. We know what the student wants, we consider it acceptable to do it, but the form is not correct (e.g., hugging a stranger to initiate a social interaction, or yelling loudly to indicate a want).
2. We know what the child wants but we prefer not to accede to the request (e.g., throwing materials off the table when no longer wishing to perform task).
3. We do not know what the behavior means and we do not know what its function might be (e.g., inappropriate laughing or shrieking).

No clear consensus exists as to whether self-injurious behaviors are predominantly self-stimulatory or manipulative in nature. As we will show later in this chapter, it is simply not possible to make general statements about individual children's inappropriate behaviors. Given this difficulty, and the overall problems of classification, there is a pressing need for a decision model that allows us to judge each child's behavior according to a unique set of circumstances. By the end of this chapter we will have summarized the most important dimensions that have been suggested for analyzing the variables that influence excess behavior. A major source for this information is the research on the incidence and etiology (origin) of excess behaviors.

Prevalence and Origin of Excess Behavior

One note of caution is in order. Much of the formal research on the prevalence of excess behavior in mentally retarded persons has been carried out with institutionalized individuals as subjects. It seems likely that these behaviors are, in fact, related to being institutionalized in large residential facilities (see Maisto, Baumeister, & Maisto, 1978). Relying on data derived from the AAMD *Adaptive Behavior Scale,* Borthwick, Meyers, and Eyman (1981) noted that institutionalized residents displayed much higher levels of disruptive, self-injurious, and stereotyped behaviors than the residents of any other type of facility; of course, one cannot really tell whether this was a cause or a consequence of their being placed in those environments. The direct negative effects of institutions are partly the lack of stimulation and enrichment, partly because of modeling and the lack of standards for "normal" appropriate behavior, and partly because of the presence (however occasional) of punitive or abusive methods of control by the staff. A convincing demonstration of this latter effect comes from an observational study of the self-injurious behavior of 20 autistic and mentally retarded children living in a state hospital in California (Edelson, Taubman, & Lovaas, 1983). In 19 of the children, self-injurious behavior showed substantial increases following staff behavior that was demanding, denying their own demands, or (verbally) punishing.

Institutionalization alone, however, is clearly not responsible for the presence of all excess behaviors. Our own data indicate that children in good quality public school programs and living in their natural homes or foster homes also displayed many excess behaviors, especially when left alone during periods of "down time" or free play. We surveyed all preschool and early elementary programs for severely and multiply handicapped children in the state of Hawaii over a 3-year period and found that behaviors such as finger flicking, mouthing body parts, finger posturing, and rocking were frequently observed. The mean percentage duration for such behaviors during unstructured free play was about 20% of the total available time, whereas during instructional situations the percentage durations were much lower, about 5%. Over 27 different responses were exhibited with at least some frequency by the group, but severely aggressive or self-injurious behaviors were not frequent in these young students. When found to be present, self-injurious behaviors were often persistent; for example, one child was observed to be engaged in tooth grinding for 48% of the time, even during instructional situations (Evans & Voeltz, 1982).

Fortunately, the incidence of severely self-injurious behavior is quite rare, although obviously when it does occur it has dramatically negative consequences both for the child and the caregivers. In a recent British survey (many of the children were institutionalized), 40% of the children under the age of 17 showed "stereotypic or repetitive motor activity"; 13% displayed less serious self-injurious behavior; and only one-tenth of 1% exhibited severely physically damaging behaviors such as head banging, eye gouging, and self-biting (Corbett & Cambell, 1981). A study by Baumeister (1978) demonstrates the limited effectiveness of attempting to improve behavior through behavioral management interventions in institutional environments: even when a special behavior modification program designed to control self-injurious behavior did result in improvement in some residents, the *overall* rate of self-injurious behavior (a prevalence of 10%) in the institution remained the same.

If our focus is on the prevention of future, more severe problem behavior, it could reasonably be expected that there would be good longitudinal data on the development of excess behaviors in severely handicapped children. Berkson (1983) has theorized that stereo-typed behaviors might be extensions of normal repetitive behaviors in infancy. We do not know whether maximizing severely handi-capped infants' opportunities to interact con-structively with the environment will lessen the chances of these repetitive behaviors being permanent. It is regrettable that there is so very little information on this topic, particularly to guide programming with young severely de-layed children. Our own 3-year investigation only scratches the surface of the needed infor-mation. One thing we did expect to find was that there would be incidents in which rela-tively minor self-stimulatory behavior grad-ually worsened into self-injurious behavior. Fortunately, we saw no such incidents, al-though there were certainly children who showed little or no improvement in excess behaviors over the period of observation. The consequences might well be different for chil-dren in areas that lack public preschool pro-grams. Clinically, in other experiences with individual children, we do know of cases where a minor face slapping behavior grad-ually evolved into serious chin pounding, and we know of another child who flicked his fingernails against his teeth, which developed into a severe banging of his finger tips against his front teeth. All in all, there is little or no hard evidence regarding the origins of different types of excess behavior, although there are a number of promising theories.

Before reviewing the major theories, it would be helpful to relate the discussion to the issues we presented in Chapter 1, in which we argued that special education teachers and other professionals involved in the educational process are consumers of research information. It was suggested that the research provides a rich source of hypotheses regarding those fac-tors that might be important for understanding the excess behaviors within an individual student.

So, before reading over the next section, try the following exercise. Pick one or two excess behaviors from any student with whom you have had direct experience. List them on a sheet of paper, and then write down all the factors that you think might relate to the fre-quency or duration of each behavior. You should have a list of variables that seem to control or regulate this behavior. Note that this is not a treatment plan—you need not think of new things that might influence the behavior but should concentrate on those that do so currently, that is, do a hypothetical functional analysis. Later, we shall consider how the formal theories might add to the possibilities considered in your functional analysis.

THEORETICAL MODELS OF EXCESS BEHAVIOR

Biological Factors

We do not intend to review the many biological principles that might contribute to the under-standing of excess behavior. This is a highly specialized area of knowledge and the reader must refer to the appropriate pediatric and general medical texts; a brief but excellent summary of some of the important issues is provided by Cataldo and Harris (1982). We feel that biological factors must at least be considered as part of a comprehensive decision model, especially as we advocate a stronger interdisciplinary role for all concerned with the development of severely handicapped persons. Thus, educators and psychologists should be aware of which characteristics of a student's behavior might require particular medical in-tervention. Also, medical treatments are often attempted without involving teachers and other professionals in the decision; many severely handicapped school children will be routinely under the care of a physician or be referred to specialized medical services throughout their school careers. Students may be placed on or taken off medication according to a schedule that is not carefully related to the educational program. Only some physicians, trained in developmentally or educationally oriented set-tings, will have the sophistication and knowl-edge to participate as an equal member of the professional team and try to interrelate the medical interventions with the needs and concerns of an educational program. Teachers and psychologists are sometimes too willing to defer to the knowledge of the medical profession when confronted with serious behavior problems. To use effectively the strategy of consultation (see Chapter 3), those involved with the child on a day-to-day basis must have some insight into those features of behavior for which a medical intervention seems critical. Teachers are also in a unique position to monitor the effects of medication by keeping objective data on cognitive performance, general behavior patterns, and physiological or behavioral side effects (such as excessive drowsiness, increased activity, poor balance or coordination, irritation and dryness of the mouth, and other possible consequences, including stereotyped motor behavior, of the various drugs used with behavior disordered children).

Just as there is no drug that has yet been shown to have a direct therapeutic effect on specific behaviors, so there are very few known neurological disturbances that produce excess behaviors *directly*. Where the stereotyped behavior is also very rhythmic, it is possible to imagine that the behavior is "driven" by neural oscillatory processes that are responsible for maintaining internal biorhythms in motor and autonomic responses (Berkson, 1983). Seizure activity can trigger automatic, repetitive behavior as well as more complex aggression, and some movement disorders such as tremors, spasms, tics, and so on, are related to known neurological conditions. In some severely handicapped students the usual regulatory functions of the central nervous system are interferred with, and, thus, secondary behaviors develop to try to establish better homeostatic control. We know of a teenage girl who would tantrum to be able to remove her shoes and socks and other items of warm clothing; it appeared, although we could not prove it conclusively, that her thermoregulatory processes were not adequate, thus causing her severe heat discomfort. One possible clue to behavior problems being related to

hormonal (such as premenstrual tension syndrome) or neural regulation is that the behavior is clearly cyclical, or occurs regularly at certain times of the year—when the pollen count is high, when the child is overtired, and so on. Food allergies have been reported in severely handicapped and autistic children and are often unrecognized. One child in our experience was allergic to the gluten in wheat products—it increased mucous secretion from his eyes and nose and caused him to rub his face vigorously, which looked like a stereotyped behavior. A child in our research project was found to have a testicular cyst that may have been causing him pain; it went undiagnosed for some time as his behavior of rubbing at his crotch did not seem very different from a number of mildly self-injurious behaviors he displayed.

The only syndrome of mental retardation that seems to be directly causal of self-injury is the Lesch-Nyhan syndrome (see Russo, Carr, & Lovaas, 1980, for a behavioral review). Thankfully a rare disorder, this genetic anomaly in males causes the nonmetabolism of purine due to an enzyme deficiency, resulting in an excess of uric acid in the blood. Behaviorally, the syndrome is associated with severe self-biting of fingers, tongue, and lips. It is tempting to suppose that any child behaving in such an extreme way must have a lowered sensitivity to pain, and there are rare medical disorders in which pain sensitivity is impaired. In general, however, there is no evidence that this can explain self-injurious behavior in severely handicapped children. In fact, the opposite hypothesis seems much more likely as an explanation. Self-injurious behavior may begin in response to pain. For example, head banging in normally developing infants is associated with teething and other pains like ear infections.

Is there any reason to suppose that the self-infliction of one painful experience could in some way reduce another, more severe pain? Actually, there has been considerable professional and lay interest in just such mechanisms. Neuropetides such as the endorphins have been discovered, which are produced in the nervous system in response to pain and are chemically similar to opiates. Thus, there may be some mechanism whereby the self-inducement of pain stimulates these endogenous opiates, which either attenuates other diffuse pain or stimulate those centers of the brain (the limbic system) that seem to mediate pleasurable experiences. Although drug treatments based on these hypotheses are being attempted (e.g., use of naloxone, an opiate antagonist) (Davidson, Kleene, Carroll, & Rockowitz, 1983), it should be pointed out that the direct relevance of these neurochemicals for explaining behavior disorders in mentally retarded children is highly speculative. The ready use of pharmacological interventions seems especially disturbing to us when the effectiveness of behavioral interventions has been so carefully and systematically documented.

Self-Regulatory and Developmental Factors

Within psychology there are various theories of homeostasis—the need for bodily systems to maintain equilibrium, or checks and balances—that are tied to physiological concepts and can thus be thought of as extensions of biological models. The most prominent of these conceptual models is that of arousal. Arousal is a major explanatory mechanism in studies of behavior, and the neurological pathways whereby sensory input serves to keep the cortex in a state of activity have been carefully mapped out. Organisms attempt to maintain optimal levels of arousal and will make efforts to increase stimulation in monotonous situations and will try to decrease sensory input in overstimulating situations. Theories relating disturbances in arousal level to infantile autism have been popular for some time (e.g., Ornitz & Ritvo, 1968; Rimland, 1964). The issue has proved rather confusing because some authorities have argued that autistic children are underaroused (Rimland, 1964), and others have argued that they are overaroused (Hutt & Hutt, 1968). Some resolution of this debate is possible if it is argued that it is the regulation of arousal that is faulty and a particular child might be over- or under-aroused at different

times (Zentall & Zentall, 1983). Thus, stereotyped behaviors can be thought of as modulating the optimal level of stimulus input. Some repetitive behaviors clearly decrease arousal— we gently rock the baby to sleep or sit dreamily in the swing chair on a hot afternoon. Other stereotypic responses induce arousal; for instance, children who stare at a light source and flick their fingers in front of their eyes produce a perceptual effect similar to the strobe lights of a disco. We know one child who engaged in these ''light-play'' hand mannerisms that appeared to induce major psychomotor seizures during which she attacked others; the seizures and the aggression were brought under control by interrupting the hand movements.

To complicate matters somewhat, excess behaviors may also be thought of as indicative of heightened arousal levels. Novel stimuli and strange surroundings tend to increase arousal, and Runco, Charlop, and Schreibman (in press) noted that the introduction of a new person such as a teacher or therapist served to increase excess behavior in some autistic children. Certain environments seem to increase sensory arousal and thus exacerbate excess behavior; for instance, neon rather than incandescent light produces greater amounts of stereotypic behavior (Colman, Frankel, Ritvo, & Freeman, 1976). Conversely, the presence of interesting activities and things to do have been shown to be powerful antagonists of self-stimulatory behavior. It is sometimes hard to separate the effects of the interesting task from the performance of an activity that is topographically incompatible with the excess behavior. In a study we carried out at the University of Hawaii (Meyer, Evans, Wuerch, & Brennan, in press), we observed that when a student was trained to play with certain leisure materials, there was an initial increase in the category of behavior designated ''self-stimulation with play materials'' during free time periods. This effect might be expected because the training brought the student into contact with the interesting play activities for the first time, and flicking them and tapping them and so on can be considered an indication that the student was interested in the materials. This interpretation was supported by a simultaneous decrease in previously high levels of self-stimulation that did not involve play materials.

Generally, there is good evidence that in certain circumstances, stimulating activities that do not require any particular response from the child can serve to reduce excess behavior. An interesting example of this is provided by Donnellan, Anderson, and Mesaros (in press), who carried out direct observation of seven autistic children in their family homes. They recorded the number of 10-second intervals in which ritualistic-stereotypic behavior was observed, such as flapping hands or objects, gazing at lights, jumping, and spinning self or objects. When the children were alone, these behaviors occurred twice as often as when they were with other members of the family, regardless of the actual family activity. However, in a thorough review of theories of excess behavior, Romanczyk, Kistner, and Plienis (1982) make an important observation. They cite earlier unpublished data of Romanczyk's in which seven autistic children were exposed to either a bare, simple environment, or a complex environment filled with interesting toys. When considering the total frequency of excess behavior, some of the children increased their stereotypic behaviors in the enriched situation and some decreased them. Even more importantly, the frequency of excess behaviors within the same child did not show a systematic change; some behaviors increased in frequency and some decreased. Romanczyk and his colleagues noted: ''These data strongly suggest that self-stimulation cannot be considered to represent a unitary response class for all subjects. Given that self-stimulatory behaviors may be independent of each other, multiple-response behavioral analysis is necessary'' (p. 198).

Intrinsic and Extrinsic Reinforcement Models

Another important set of theoretical concepts relates to the consequences of excess behavior. Note that a theory that argues that excess behavior serves to increase sensory input in monotonous situations is really very similar to one that says that the sensory consequences, or feedback, from the excess behavior are somehow reinforcing. The emphasis in the latter case, however, is more on the positive aspects of the sensory experience: young children will press their eyeballs with their fingers to experience the formless, changing patterns of light and color, or spin round and round until they are dizzy or enjoy the sensations of riding in a roller coaster.

One type of design that has attempted to show the intrisically reinforcing properties of the excess behavior is one in which the opportunity to engage in the excess behavior serves a rewarding function for performing some other activity. However, this is not a very convincing demonstration because the reinforcing power of any high frequency response (Premack's principle) is not taken into account. A representative example of this approach is a study by Hung (1978), showing that autistic children could be effectively reinforced by tokens if the backup for the tokens was the opportunity to engage in self-stimulatory behavior. This tactic has obvious implications for motivating children for whom it is very difficult to find effective reinforcers. But a more direct test of the intrinsic reinforcement theory has been provided by Rincover (1978) in an intervention technique he called *sensory extinction*. When the sensory consequences of the behavior were removed (for example the table surface was carpeted so that the reinforcing sound of the plate spinning was eliminated), the behavior itself showed considerable reduction in frequency. While this may be a useful way of thinking about the auditory, tactile, and visual sensory feedback, it is usually assumed that the feedback for stereotypic behaviors such as rocking, spinning, flapping, and so on, is proprioceptive and vestibular (Ornitz, 1971), which would be much harder to attenuate by any environmental change. Nevertheless, a very significant principle emerges: when choosing an alternative adaptive skill to replace the excess behavior, it would be sensible to find one that is not just stimulating (as would be required by the arousal hypothesis) but also produces a similar type of sensory feedback.

An example of implementing such a tactic has been provided by Favell, McGimsey, and Schell (1982), who reduced the self-injurious behavior of six older adolescent children by matching alternative responses in this fashion. For example, popcorn was made available to a couple of the children who had pica, and the incidents of eating inappropriate substances decreased. A very visually interesting toy—a prism that refracted light—was provided for one boy who repeatedly poked his eyes. Other toys that were less visual in function were not as effective, suggesting that the result was not simply due to the toys busying this student's hands. Overall, however, the design of this study did not allow for a vigorous test of the hypothesis that the precise stimulus feedback produced by the toys is critical. Also, unfortunately, age-inappropriate toys were selected for this demonstration study, such as a squeaky rubber toy for a 20-year-old.

One obvious difficulty with sensory extinction techniques is that they may require the use of particular devices that are neither natural nor appropriate, or require environmental modifications that could not be duplicated in everyday work, living, and recreational situations likely to be encountered by handicapped individuals. Some procedure for fading the environmental manipulations is therefore very important and will have important implications for the use of any kind of restraint, as is discussed in Chapter 5 in more detail. For instance, Rincover and Devany (1982) used a padded helmet with a child who frequently banged his head. They described a systematic procedure for removing the helmet—"fading" it out by removing it for short periods each day—and showed that the improvement in behavior continued despite the absence of the helmet. This particular study also lacked an important experimental control. At the same time as the helmet was introduced, the child was provided with an educational program that involved high levels of social reinforcement

(praise and physical contact) and edible rewards, so the beneficial results may have been related to the positive influence of these setting events. (Of course, if this had been a classroom demonstration by a teacher, it would have been a very acceptable documentation of an informal hypothesis.) Another child who banged his head was provided instruction in a part of the classroom that was covered with 1-inch thick foam mats on the walls and floor. Again, this is an environmental intervention that would be hard to replicate in other settings. It is also interesting to note that the teaching programs in this and other studies of behavior management in nonschool settings were chosen as though they were secondary, minor issues. Thus, one child in Rincover and Devany's study who was a 4-year-old described as having "virtually no self-help or play skills" was being taught a simultaneous two-choice discrimination with artificial stimuli. It is hard to see how such a task could be related to the needs of current and future natural environments.

One reason that the studies just mentioned do not provide very good tests of the theoretical explanations of excess behavior is that intervention studies are typically not very suitable for carrying out functional analyses of behavior (i.e., finding out what currently influences behavior). Because of the enormous variability in excess behavior over time, within situations, and within patterns of individual responding, multiple baseline recording across situations and over reasonably lengthy periods of time are required (see also Baumeister, MacLean, Kelly, & Kasari, 1980). The same problem exists in the very exciting studies that have attempted to demonstrate the external, socially reinforcing consequences for excess behavior. This hypothesis asserts that excess behavior is maintained either because it produces a great deal of adult attention, or because it serves to remove the child from the demands of a social or instructional situation that is aversive (negative reinforcement).

The evidence for the first of these processes (caregiver attention) comes from numerous early behavior modification studies showing that the removal of social reinforcement—by selectively ignoring inappropriate behavior—does reduce the frequency of many excess behaviors. The evidence for the second process (removes the student from an aversive experience) has been around for some time but has recently become more prominent as an explanation for disruptive and other excess behaviors. Some of this increased interest was triggered by an article written by Plummer, Baer, and LeBlanc (1977) that emphasized the idea that inappropriate behaviors serve the function of avoidance of failure or escape from demands. They showed that timeout did not produce response decrement in two preschool autistic children, but instead appeared to be a negative reinforcer and exacerbated behaviors such as grabbing materials, hoarding toys, tantrumming, and so on. What was effective was a procedure in which the teacher gave "paced instructions" irrespective of the children's behavior, instead of the more usual procedure in which disruptive behavior results in an interruption in the instructional requirements.

In a valuable series of studies, Carr and his associates (Carr, Newsom, & Binkoff, 1976, 1980) revealed that self-injurious behavior decreases during nondemand situations, free play, and general enrichment activities. Weeks and Gaylord-Ross (1981) replicated these findings with an interesting demonstration that problem behavior occurred at higher rates in demand or aversive conditions than in no-demand conditions, and on difficult as opposed to easy tasks. Weeks and Gaylord-Ross are careful to point out, however, that the students in their study were selected on the grounds that it appeared that their disruptive behavior was maintained by negative reinforcement. They suggest the need for developing clear criteria for "determining whether aberrant behavior is maintained by positive reinforcement, negative reinforcement, or intrinsic reinforcement" (p. 461). Carr (in press) has also recently made a strong case for considering the communicative intent of excess behavior. It is worth remembering that if an excess behavior is maintained by negative reinforcement—that is, it allows the student to escape an aversive situation—it would first have to have begun in response to an aversive situation. A common example is the use of tantrums by a child to get his or her teacher to stop requiring that he or she work on an instructional task that he or she dislikes. If a tantrum successfully convinces a teacher to stop the session, the child has been negatively reinforced for tantrum behaviors and is likely to use this effective "leave-taking" strategy whenever he or she wants a demand situation to end. Baumeister and Forehand (1971) showed that some excess behaviors can be considered emotional responses such as anger or frustration. In their studies, the discontinuation of reinforcement or the removal of some positive event such as food produced considerable increases in rocking in institutionalized individuals.

Absence of Alternative Skills

The final theoretical perspective considered briefly here is related to the idea introduced in Chapter 1 that an individual's behavioral repertoire constitutes a system. We have already pointed out that the reduction in one inappropriate behavior might well result in the increase in some other response. An individual will exhibit behaviors that appear to us maladaptive and undesirable at least partly because there are no other more acceptable or effective responses available. Baumeister et al. (1980) expressed this position rather nicely:

> the extent to which a particular setting elicits specific types of activities has a great deal to do with naturally occurring variations in the expression of stereotypy. . . . We suggest that stereotypic responding is directly related to the repertoire of appropriate behavior the child has in any situation. Given a context in which the socially defined appropriate behavior is either not available or not demanded, then we can expect to observe high rates of aberrant responding. (pp. 510–511)

A related concept is that of *substitutability* of behaviors. If our behaviors constitute a closed system, then changing one behavior will always influence the presence of others. Rachlin (1980) comments:

> If a given behavior was occurring, however dysfunctional in the long run, it must have been serving some function in the short run. If the dysfunctional behavior is reduced, the behavior that substitutes for it may also be dysfunctional (as when eating candy substitutes for tobacco smoking) . . . When one behavior is eliminated, another must take its place because organisms are always behaving . . . But whether the new behavior will be as harmful as the old depends on the situation. (pp. 156–158)

Multiple Influences

We can now return to the exercise that you were asked to consider on page 34. How has this discussion of possible "causal" variables influenced your thinking since you developed your list of possible influences? In order to summarize the factors that you might have considered, we have listed in Table 2.2 a series of questions that should be asked about any excess behavior. We pose them as questions because a sine qua non of decision making is to formulate questions, possibilities, or hypotheses about behavior before attempting a functional analysis.

Perhaps you can think of other questions that could reasonably be asked; in a decision making approach there are always many considerations that might have a bearing on the modification of excess behavior. The questions in Table 2.2 should guide you in conducting a functional analysis. But when it comes to selecting priorities and designing interventions related to the ongoing skill development programs for the student, there are other important considerations to weigh. These are discussed in Chapter 3.

A SUMMARY STATEMENT

Inappropriate behavior in severely handicapped individuals is what we call "multiply determined." Many factors influence the appearance of excess behavior. Some of these are general, related to pathological and traumatic influences on brain development and physi-

TABLE 2.2.   Checklist of questions to ask about excess behaviors

Is the behavior very rhythmic or cyclical? _____

Are there any physiological symptoms closely associated with the behavior? _____

What related elements seem to go along with this behavior, such as signs of pain, discomfort, changes in mood, and so forth? _____

What are the general effects of the behavior on arousal? _____

What are the exact sensory consequences of the behavior? _____

In what settings is the behavior most prevalent? _____

What discriminative cues seem to elicit (set off, trigger) the behavior? _____

What general setting events seem to precede the behavior? _____

Are there simple environmental modifications (change in position, etc.) that influence this behavior? _____

What general instructional factors elicit the behavior (e.g., demands, frustrating situations, adult or peer interactions, etc.)? _____

Does this behavior result in social reinforcement (attention, etc.)? _____

Does this excess behavior serve to reduce social or instructional demands either immediately or in general? _____

What appropriate behaviors are topographically incompatible with the behavior? _____

What are the deficits in other behaviors that serve the same function as the excess behavior? _____

What other excess behaviors precede or accompany the behavior? _____

ological processes. These factors often do not have much current relevance for intervention unless specific organic problems can be identified and redressed. Even behaviors that start out from organic causes soon acquire environmental and social components: the child whose excess behavior began in response to an allergy might well continue such behavior in order to gain social attention. While we agree with the point made by Weeks and Gaylord-Ross (1981) regarding the importance of considering different controlling variables, we believe that one excess behavior within a child might serve multiple functions; the explanation of a self-stimulatory behavior might be related to its sensory feedback properties, *and* the fact that there are few other alternative behaviors available to the child, *and* the social attention the behavior elicits from peers, family members, and so on. Furthermore, we believe, severely handicapped individuals exhibit *many* excess behaviors, each having different sources of environmental control. As no one theory is correct for all types of excess behavior, either in general or in the case of the individual student, we feel the task of the professional is to consider as many hypotheses for the individual as possible.

chapter 3

An Overview of the Decision Model

with Kristine Reneé Derer and Rae Y. Hanashiro

One of the most important points made in the preceding chapter is that each child's individual behaviors are part of a system, a network of interrelated responses. The importance of these behavioral interrelationships is becoming increasingly recognized in child behavior therapy (see Voeltz & Evans, 1982). Two implications are particularly notable. One is methodological: in order to evaluate the effects of a behavioral intervention, a number of outcome variables should be monitored. Altering the frequency of an excess behavior will almost certainly have extensive repercussions, both good (positive collateral effects) and bad (negative collateral effects, or side effects). The other implication is more pragmatic and clinical: the identification of the most critical "target" response is not as obvious as was once assumed. Severely handicapped students rarely show just one inappropriate behavior. Of the many excess behaviors the child may perform, some will obviously stand out as being more serious and in greater need of intervention. But if behaviors are part of an interconnected system, the behavior that seems the most serious is not necessarily the best one to target for an intervention. If a complex choice is involved, then it seems clear to us that the clinician or teacher must have made a complex decision when planning an intervention; as Hawkins (1975) expressed it so clearly, we must pose the question, "Who decided *that* was the problem?" Designing interventions, therefore, involves formalizing some of the decision making processes that teachers already follow in response to undesirable behavior (see Chapter 1).

In this chapter, we introduce a decision model, beginning with a summary of the important issues that have determined each of the components involved. These are stated as basic assumptions, and are supported by current thinking regarding the function of educational programs and the rights of handicapped persons to a normalized pattern of life. Next, we provide tested guidelines that have been utilized to determine the seriousness or importance of different behavior problems: teachers and other clinicians have used these guidelines to decide which behaviors need to be changed and which skills need to be taught. In this section, we mention certain variables that seem to influence how clinicians make these decisions and report work that supports the three levels of seriousness in our decision model. How serious a behavior is will affect the priorities assigned to the modifications of each of the behaviors in different circumstances. The final section of the chapter is an overview of the decision model, with a detailed explanation of the three levels of intervention decisions and how decisions can be made regarding which level of programming applies to any given excess behavior. This section also includes information on other processes that are components of the decision model and occur in existing services, such as how consultation fits into the intervention plan. Thus, this chapter is intended to provide background on the use of the model. The specific application is then illustrated in Chapter 4 with a detailed example of how each step would be addressed for a severely handicapped student with multiple behavior problems.

UNDERLYING ASSUMPTIONS

The decision model presented in this book is based upon the implications generated by four basic assumptions: (1) the IEP is an educational plan; (2) not all excess behaviors are equal priority targets; (3) to decrease a behavior, increase a skill; and (4) interventions for handicapped persons must be normalized. These are implicitly discussed throughout the book, but are summarized below in order to make explicit and to highlight the issues raised by each assumption.

The IEP Is an Educational Plan

The purpose of the IEP is to provide a plan for education. This means that educational programming should reflect goals and priorities designed to establish new skills in children who have severe handicapping conditions and many behavioral deficits. The intent of Public Law 94-142 and the Individualized Education Program that is mandated by that legislation is that handicapped children will be provided with an

appropriate education. This is best interpreted as a habilitative program to provide the child with the various skills necessary for optimal functioning in current and future integrated environments. It is not a "behavior management plan" with an emphasis on decreasing or eliminating behavior. This does not mean that there would never be an occasion in which the teacher would be attempting to decrease a negative behavior. There will be many situations when it is desirable to decrease an excess behavior and the school will be a suitable place to implement that effort. As teachers and other clinicians already know, many of these excess behaviors will make it difficult for a handicapped person to function effectively in an integrated community environment, as would the absence of a needed skill. But the important point to remember is that behavioral reduction programs are appropriate only as supplements to a comprehensive, educational plan—a program that can be held accountable each school year for the teaching of meaningful new skills. The IEP must stand alone as an educational plan, and should not be compromised by substituting goals to decrease behavior for goals that would establish critical skills.

Interestingly enough, the recent empirical evidence regarding negative behaviors provides us with an additional justification for approaching excess behaviors in the context of an educational plan. Recognizing the function performed by an excess behavior and the deficit implied by the student's use of that behavior rather than a more positive one should provide educators with immediate suggestions as to what instructional goals should be priorities for the IEP (see the discussion on assumption #3 under the heading "To Decrease a Behavior, Increase a Skill," below).

Not All Excess Behaviors Are Equal Priority Targets

Although the IEP identifies priorities, it does not define the total context of a child's educational experience. During the typical classroom day, a host of learning opportunities exists that are compatible with but not formally a component of planned learning and skill building activities. And, as we have already seen, teachers often implement informal intervention decisions although they are not clearly articulated treatment plans. Even these informal plans may be written, or sometimes posted as classroom rules or procedures to be followed with regard to certain children, and they are generally implemented by all adults responsible for any part of the child's program. Thus, even informal intervention plans can potentially occupy valuable learning time, particularly if the procedure involves restricted response opportunities such as timeout, restraint, or overcorrection. There are, of course, also occasions where an excess behavior is so serious that it must be stopped and permanently modified as soon as possible. In such cases, the decision to decrease that behavior in the child's already minimal repertoire may well result in postponing the teaching of a needed skill that otherwise might have been added to an instructional program.

Our proposed model recognizes that there are situations in which modifying an excess behavior would be high priority. There are some very crucial instances in which an excess behavior must be modified if the child is to have any opportunity whatsoever to participate effectively in the community. However, because severely handicapped children have little educational programming time in proportion to their learning needs, so few positive skills, and because most excess behaviors will in fact be most effectively decreased by meeting educational needs rather than by applying behavioral reduction techniques, direct programming to modify a behavior should be considered a priority *only when unavoidable.*

Under what circumstances would a teacher replace a skill development goal with a behavioral management goal on a child's IEP? What rationale would ethically support the use of precious instructional time to decrease rather than increase behaviors? Life- or health-threatening behaviors represent such priorities, and obviously those excess behaviors that threaten the life or the health of a child and may

cause irreversible physical harm must be modified at once. Behaviors that interfere with the performance of a needed skill might be justified as targets for intervention, although they would not *replace* an instructional goal on the IEP, as would behaviors that prevent a child from functioning in the community and at home. However, reasons such as social pressure, expediency, or the personal preference of caregivers lack clear ethical justification to target a behavior for change. Each of these indicates that the needs of others are given more weight than the best interests of the child. Behaviors identified for reasons that fail to consider the child's total repertoire and potential outcomes should be dealt with by means other than the child's educational program. After all, the provision of a free and appropriate public school program does not preclude the development of additional services for handicapped children that might be needed outside the context of the school program, in the community, and so on. Just as nonhandicapped children may require the assistance of psychological counseling, for example, to deal with a personal crisis, severely handicapped children should have access to additional professional ''treatments'' when needed. These treatments may and should be coordinated with the child's school program. But they would not supplant that program any more than a therapy or group counseling program for an adolescent having problems should imply that he or she is removed from his or her junior year in high school.

To Decrease a Behavior, Increase a Skill

In our view, the most lasting approach to decreasing a behavior is to provide a positive alternative that accomplishes the same function for the child. This perspective that the acquisition of acceptable alternatives to undesirable behavior is the most advantageous procedure for producing long-lasting reductions in excess behaviors has been articulated for some time in current texts in behavior modification (e.g., Sulzer-Azaroff & Mayer, 1977). The theoretical support for this procedure derives from the critical functions that the excess behaviors perform for children (outlined in Chapter 2). To the extent that a new skill can be taught that is incompatible with the excess behavior and/or performs the same functions for the child's need to control his or her environment, an "indirect reduction" in the excess behavior should occur. That is, the excess behavior should be modified indirectly by the substitution of a positive and possibly incompatible skill without a prior (or even simultaneous) program to reduce the excess behavior itself. This position is being increasingly argued by clinicians from the various disciplines (Carr, 1983; Durand, 1982) and can be supported by evidence from intervention research reports (Horner & Budd, 1983; Whitman, Sciback, & Reid, 1983).

The principle of reducing excess behavior by increasing appropriate skills should be the major emphasis, even in those cases where the behavior is so serious that it demands immediate attention. This approach to children's problems from an educational perspective assumes, of course, that one reason children exhibit a behavior is to accomplish a purpose—a critical function. One task of effective programming is to identify and teach the most powerful alternative positive behavior, which can replace the negative one precisely because it addresses this function for the child. This approach is of particular relevance for severely handicapped children whose existing behavior repertoires are the most limited. Yet, these are the very students for whom it has been argued that clinicians should focus initially upon the reduction of behaviors as a *prerequisite* to teaching new skills (see, for example, Lovaas, 1981). The decision model presented here requires, instead, that clinicians must identify alternative positive behaviors and assign instructional priority to such goals whenever an excess behavior has been judged serious enough to require modification.

Interventions for Handicapped Persons Must Be Normalized

There is no justification for deliberately imposing painful, psychologically humiliating, or physically harmful aversive consequences on children whose quality of life may already be precarious and who have few skills that allow them to structure compensating positive experiences from the environment and from caregivers. We strongly support the *Resolution on Intrusive Interventions* passed by The Association for Persons with Severe Handicaps (TASH), which is printed here as Table 3.1 (The Association for Persons with Severe Handicaps, 1981). It is based upon the results of a relatively long history of remediating severe behavior problems with intrusive and aversive procedures. In many instances, these procedures are not effective even in short-term use. They must be judged even less "effective" if the long-term use is considered as well: even where behavioral control during a treatment phase can be demonstrated, generalization and maintenance of those "improvements" has not typically occurred. This resolution challenges the professional community to develop educative options in the area of behavior management. Perhaps the reason for our limited success in this area is that for the most part, severely handicapped learners continue to be subjected to deviant, noneducative environments that do not support the establishment or maintenance of adaptive behavior. It may be that if severely handicapped students were to remain in supportive, educative environments in integrated community settings, these individuals would present behavioral repertoires quite different from those typically described in this population. The extremes of behavior and the extremes of behavior management strategies developed to deal with such behavior in a "patchwork" fashion might become rare if not obsolete occurrences. We shall never know, of course, unless alternative placements and services and the conditions necessary for a proper, empirical evaluation of such issues becomes a reality. Thus, this book represents a systematic approach to dealing with student's behavioral needs through the type of alternative educative approach advocated in this resolution.

The TASH resolution and this fourth assumption that interventions must be normalized clearly conflict with traditional ap-

TABLE 3.1. Resolution on intrusive interventions adopted by The Association for Persons with Severe Handicaps

---

Resolution on Intrusive Interventions
(Passed, October 1981)

WHEREAS, in order to realize the goals and objectives of The Association for Persons with Severe Handicaps, including the right of each severely handicapped person to grow, develop, and enjoy life in integrated and normalized community environments, the following resolution is adopted:

WHEREAS, educational and other habilitative services must employ instructional and management strategies which are consistent with the right of each individual with severe handicaps to an effective treatment which does not compromise the equal important right to freedom from harm. This requires educational and habilitative procedures free from indiscriminant use of drugs, aversive stimuli, environmental deprivation, or exclusion from services; and

WHEREAS, TASH supports a cessation of the use of any treatment option which exhibits some or all of the following characteristics: (1) obvious signs of physical pain experienced by the individual; (2) potential or actual physical side effects, including tissue damage, physical illness, severe stress, and/or death, that would properly require the involvement of medical personnel; (3) dehumanization of persons with severe handicaps because the procedures are normally unacceptable for nonhandicapped persons in community environment; (4) extreme ambivalence and discomfort by family, staff, and/or caregivers regarding the necessity of such extreme strategies or their own involvement in such interventions; and (5) obvious repulsion and/or stress felt by nonhandicapped peers and community members who cannot reconcile extreme procedures with acceptable standard practice;

RESOLVED, that The Association for Persons with Severe Handicaps' resources and expertise be dedicated to the development, implementation, evaluation, dissemination, and advocacy of educational and management practices which are appropriate for use in integrated environments and which are consistent with the commitment to a high quality of life for individuals with severe handicaps.

---

proaches in behavior modification intervention research. This literature continues to reveal a surprisingly high use of intrusive and aversive methods to decrease the occurrence of excess behavior. Most readers are well aware that the most obvious way to decelerate a response is to introduce an extinction paradigm in which the reinforcement that once followed the response is either removed altogether or made non-contingent. (This latter point is worth mentioning because we would never *remove* social approval, praise, and rewards when interacting with children but would try to make certain that these are delivered contingent on other, more appropriate responses.) The second most obvious way is to arrange that the response one wishes to decelerate is followed immediately by an aversive consequence—known techni-

cally as punishment. Remember that behavior followed by *both* positive (reinforcement) and aversive (punishment) events rarely decreases unless clear, alternative ways of obtaining the positive events exist for the individual. Punishment contingencies, therefore, require that extinction (removal of positive consequences) is in effect as well. As we saw in Chapter 2, many excess behaviors seem to have some sort of intrinsic feedback or sensorily reinforcing properties that are difficult to remove. Excess behaviors may also serve some goal directed or functional purpose for which the child has no alternative strategy. When an individual has only a limited repertoire of skills to begin with, therefore, reducing one response without teaching an alternative is likely to be ineffective in the long run.

These are good reasons for not simply decelerating behaviors. But, equally important
are the reasons for not deliberately causing a
child pain or discomfort as part of education,
treatment, or rehabilitation. Not all aversive
events used in punishment contingencies actually cause physical pain, but most cause distress to the recipient: being shouted at, having
one's head and face covered with a bag or
sprayed with water, being forced to run up and
down stairs over and over, and so on. These
aversive situations can largely be defined as
such by the kinds of behaviors they elicit:
struggling to escape from the source of the
stimulus, avoidance of people, crying, and
becoming angry and aggressive are such signs
(see, e.g., Mayhew & Harris, 1978). Aversive
events can also be defined by virtue of their *not*
being commonly used with nonhandicapped
student peers. Many complex arguments have
been presented for and against the use of such
aversive procedures with handicapped persons
(see LaVigna & Donnellan, in press). The
general professional consensus seems to be that
such interventions are to be avoided and, if
they are to be used at all, their use should be
carefully guided by ethical safeguards. Treatment procedures are to be reviewed by responsible committees (and outside experts in extreme cases), the intervention plans carefully
formulated, written permissions from guard-
ians obtained, and the results critically evaluated based upon data. The most authoritative
review of these standards is provided by the
task force of the Association for the Advancement of Behavior Therapy (Favell et al.,
1982), which recommended a strategy for the
systematic intervention with self-injurious behavior and guidelines for any use of aversives:

> In cases where the behavior is dangerous, inter-
> feres excessively with habilitative or humanizing
> activities, or has failed to improve when treated
> with the less intrusive procedures outlined above,
> a punishing consequence such as overcorrection,
> or in extremely severe cases, shock for self-injury
> may also be necessary (p. 545).

While these standards do represent a valuable advance in decision making, we disagree

that the failure of other methods should be part
of the judgment, as one cannot determine
whether such failure reflects an incorrect functional analysis, poor treatment planning, or a
history of repeated failure to provide a comprehensive, state-of-the-art remedial educational
program and habilitative living environment.
In contrast, this text supports the TASH resolution in asserting the general principle that
handicapped individuals have a right to effective interventions that do not inflict pain, tissue
damage, humiliation, discomfort, and stigma
as expected side effects accompanying behavior change. This commitment to developing
and validating alternative, educative approaches
to children's behavior problems requires a parallel commitment to providing appropriate,
integrated, community-based education (and
other habilitative) services. Thus, our procedures depart from the recommendations of
the AABT guidelines. We *do* agree that non-
punishment interventions should be systematically implemented prior to the use of any negative consequence as part of a clinical intervention
plan. Thus, teachers should first design ecological and curricular interventions before they
attempt contingent negative consequences for
the excess behavior. In Chapter 5, we provide
more explicit intervention guidelines on this
issue. We use the term *negative consequences*
rather than punishment (see page 135) to signal
our exclusion of intrusive interventions from
clinical application: unlike the AABT guidelines, we do not recognize the necessity of
using intrusive interventions to modify even
severe excess behaviors. At the same time, we
should emphasize that our learners should not
be separated and thus "protected" from the
various natural negative consequences that do
occur (and can be quite effective) in criterion
community environments. Nonhandicapped
peers, for example, should obviously not tease
or ridicule a severely handicapped child who is
finger flicking, but disapproving looks and
firm verbal or other behavioral consequences
from these peers *should* occur (see Chapter 5,
pp. 136–137 for a more explicit discussion of
this issue).

CRITERIA FOR
SELECTING PRIORITY GOALS

In addition to the four general principles described above that we would like you to consider when designing behavioral interventions, other aspects of the students' behaviors must be included in the judgment process. Whenever teachers and parents identify goals as instructional objectives for children's educational programs, they use—not always consciously—certain criteria. Decisions to intervene with any aspect of a child's repertoire usually involve at least three types of considerations: seriousness of the behavior, potential outcomes (the "ripple" effect), and legal-ethical concerns. Thus, when selecting a skill for instruction, teachers might typically consider such issues as degree of deficit of the skill (seriousness), other skills that could be more readily taught if this skill were present (outcome), and the significance of the skill for transition to a less restrictive environment (legal-ethical). In Chapter 6, we present evaluation criteria that can be applied to the selection of skill acquisition goals. When selecting *excess* behaviors as the targets for intervention, however, such considerations are not generally explicitly stated. There has been a tendency to intervene with excess behaviors without considering their relationships to other problem behaviors, the child's skills, and the environmental context (Voeltz & Evans, 1983). Most journal articles describing successful interventions with particular excess behaviors in handicapped children fail to provide information regarding these other factors, and provide only a superficial rationale for the selection of the target behavior in the study. Sometimes it is obvious why a behavior was selected for intervention, as in the case of severe, self-injurious behavior, but even when this is true, it is highly likely that the child exhibited various other problem behaviors as well as extreme skill deficits. This issue is not a new one (Hawkins, 1975), so perhaps we should be surprised that it has taken us so long to actually develop systematic selection criteria.

Think for a moment about the reasons you might give for changing the following behaviors:

Doug is 14 and is severely mentally retarded. An adult visitor comes into the classroom, and Doug goes up to him or her with a lovely wide grin and gives him or her a big hug.

Mary is sitting quietly in her chair in a corner of the classroom. She is staring off into space and rocking slowly back and forth. She has one hand inside her jeans and appears to be masturbating.

Ed is living in a group home. At meal times, he lunges across the table and grabs the closest glass of water belonging to another resident, spilling the water on the table and the floor.

Chris, an autistic child, sits at home for long periods, paging through the yellow pages of the telephone directory. He is looking for pictures of wheels, bicycles, cars, and so forth. Whenever he finds a picture he likes, he tears it out of the phone book.

The reasons you might give for wanting to change these behaviors involve logistical and pragmatic considerations in addition to trying to decide whether they are appropriate or not. Consider Doug's behavior. Physical affection such as this would be desirable behavior if it involved a close family member or even a good friend whom he hadn't seen for some time; it is not socially appropriate behavior in the example given. Persons may tolerate Doug's display of affection, excusing him "because he is handicapped," but his adolescent peers might be less willing to accept it. Consequently, not changing the behavior might result in social isolation from nonhandicapped peers who would avoid him. Mary's dignity as an individual conforming to social propriety would be preserved by a program that taught her to masturbate only in private. Ed's behavior is disruptive in a number of ways: it interferes with the serving of the meal, it could result in one of the other residents becoming angry and retaliating in some way, and it might be used as a justification by group home staff for not taking him along on community outings.

Chris's ripping pictures out of the phone book happened to be a particular irritant to the other members of his family, for obvious reasons. Another feature of this behavior that was of concern to his family was that it seemed to be "generalizing"; Chris was becoming increasingly likely to tear up other things and was leaving shredded paper scattered throughout the house.

How does one decide that changing such behaviors might be a priority? Each of the students in the examples undoubtedly has a complex of educational needs in addition to more than one excess behavior that might be the focus of an intervention. Criteria that have been recommended in order to assign priorities include the effect of the child's excess behavior on the environment (Gaylord-Ross, 1980; Renzaglia & Bates, 1983), the degree of expected cooperation from parents or family members (Tharp & Wetzel, 1969), and the likelihood of being successful in changing the behavior (Sulzer-Azaroff & Reese, 1982). As noted earlier in this chapter, some clinicians have emphasized the need to reduce certain types of excess behavior such as self-stimulation and noncompliance before instruction can begin (Koegel, Egel, & Dunlap, 1980). Heads (1978) suggested five formal criteria that could be applied to goal selection, that is, that a goal must be: (1) stated behaviorally, (2) include a quantitative criterion to measure attainment, (3) realistic for the child, (4) realizable with available resources, and (5) maintainable by naturally occurring contingencies following treatment.

There are, then, various selection criteria that have been recommended, all of which have merit. We developed a comprehensive list of 17 reasons including all those criteria cited in the published literature and based upon our own experiences as those reasons that were clearly nontrivial in nature. The list is presented here to allow you to rate the importance of each as a reason for assigning priority to change a student's behavior. Some of the reasons apply to selecting curriculum objectives, while others clearly refer to modifying excess behavior. Take a few moments to go through the list and assign a rating to each item based upon how important you feel that particular criterion is. A high rating of 20 should indicate a "very important consideration," a rating of 15 for an "important consideration," 10 for "undecided," 5 for "not very important," and a low of 0 for "not a consideration at all." You may use any rating assigning any number from 0 to 20 based upon how seriously you would consider that individual reason:

1. The behavior would be immediately functional for the child.
   Rating: ____
2. The behavior is damaging to materials, and so on, in the child's environment.
   Rating: ____
3. The behavior is markedly deficient in comparison to the child's level in other areas (i.e., it is a weakness).
   Rating: ____
4. Given an otherwise equal need, this behavior will probably be easier to modify than another.
   Rating: ____
5. The behavior is a major concern for the child's parents/caregivers.
   Rating: ____
6. The behavior may interfere with learning unless it is modified.
   Rating: ____
7. The behavior is an appropriate activity that the child would probably enjoy being able to do.
   Rating: ____
8. The behavior would replace existing negative behaviors with a positive alternative.
   Rating: ____
9. Attainment of the behavior would increase the child's independence.
   Rating: ____
10. The currently available staff (and/or parent) time, materials, and physical facilities are adequate to conduct the necessary intervention.
    Rating: ____

11. The behavior would increase acceptance of the child by parents, teachers, and peers.
Rating: ____
12. The behavior is dangerous to others in the child's environment.
Rating: ____
13. The behavior is age-appropriate and thus consistent with normalization concerns.
Rating: ____
14. The behavior is dangerous to the child.
Rating: ____
15. The behavior is one that would broadly affect the child's repertoire, that is, positive collateral or side effects are likely to occur in more than one area after intervention.
Rating: ____
16. The behavior is developmentally appropriate given the child's functioning level.
Rating: ____
17. The behavior is a prerequisite to learning other adaptive behaviors.

Now go back and look at the number ratings you have given each item, and rank order the items in importance for you by noting which item was given the highest rating, and so forth. Table 3.2 provides information on the relative importance assigned to these items by a group of experienced special education teachers, educational assistants, and a sample of doctoral students working on their Ph.D. in clinical psychology at the University of Hawaii (Evans & Voeltz, 1982; Voeltz et al., 1982).

As you might expect, the different professions had slightly different perspectives. The psychologists considered the positive side effects to be an important consideration and were less concerned with normalization; they were also more concerned with issues of ease of implementation and likelihood of success. Educational assistants and the undergraduates (who were included in the study to see how the average lay person would rate the criteria) also rated some of the items differently from the two professional groups. Clearly there are no right or wrong answers, and the most interesting feature of the results is that the special education teachers rated virtually all the items as at least somewhat important considerations! But if all of these considerations are nearly equally important and should be taken into account, how should they weigh in our decision making? The formal model described at the end of this chapter is designed to make certain broad distinctions to ensure that the most meaningful criteria are considered in relation to the student's needs, as opposed to the convenience of those in his or her environment (e.g., the teacher or caregiver).

Through a factor analysis of the responses, we were able to categorize all the criteria on our list into six major groups. These are listed below and illustrated with quotes from an interview study we conducted with a smaller group of teachers who were working with severely handicapped children in public school programs in Hawaii.

CATEGORY 1: The behavior represents an *urgent child need* (Items 1, 3, 7, and 14).

I.E.: What makes problems pressing?
Teacher: My most important consideration is things that cause bodily harm, that are dangerous to their own well-being.

CATEGORY 2: The behavior represents a *concern for others* (Items 2, 12).

I.E.: What kinds of things do you consider real behavior problems?
Teacher: Disruptiveness to all the others in the room. Or if harm will come to her, or to one of the other kids—or myself! Our other boy, Tom, injured me this year. In fact I had a broken thumb from him. It was an accident, but it was caused by his jumping behavior.

I.E.: Hazardous life being a teacher!
Teacher: Beginning of this year it was!

CATEGORY 3: The behavior affects the *child's adjustment* (Items 5-9, 11, and 13).

I.E.: What if the parents say, "Look, I don't like my child mouthing things. It doesn't look right when I take him out in public." What would you do then?

TABLE 3.2.   Summary of ratings of importance of criteria for selecting target behaviors

Decision criteria item	Teachers' mean rating ($N = 36$)	Teachers' rank order ($N = 36$)	Educational assistants' rank order ($N = 101$)	Psychologists' rank order ($N = 21$)
14. Dangerous to child	19.86	1	5	1
12. Dangerous to others	19.42	2	3	2
6. Interferes with learning	18.50	3	2	7
8. Replaces negative behaviors	17.97	4	7	4
9. Increases independence	17.92	5	4	9
1. Immediately functional	17.58	6	9	8
17. Prerequisite to other behaviors	17.42	7	8	5
11. Increases acceptance	17.31	8	1	6
15. Multiple effects	16.50	9	10	3
5. Parent concern	16.19	10	6	10
7. Enjoyable activity	15.81	11	12	14
10. Adequate resources	14.53	12	11	12
2. Damages materials	14.36	13	13	13
13. Age-appropriate	12.81	14	15	17
3. Weakness compared to other behaviors	12.60	15	17	16
16. Developmentally appropriate	12.56	16	14	15
4. Easy to modify	11.06	17	16	11

Teacher: I'd try to first explain the stage that the child is going through so that they could accept it more, then maybe find objects or time that would be conducive to the parent allowing it to happen. So I'm trying to work out with the parent what is convenient for them, what is feasible for them.

I.E.: Do you think these issues of social acceptance should be important in deciding which behaviors to work on?

Teacher: Oh yes, especially with a lot of the regular students coming into the class and our kids going out on the playground at recess time.

CATEGORY 4: The behavior would provide the child with a *positive repertoire* (Items 13-15 and 17).

I.E.: Let's take the self-stimulation, what are the various negative factors about that?

Teacher: The only thing I can see with it is that it prevents her from doing many other things, so she doesn't learn.

CATEGORY 5: The behavior change would be *functional for the child* and would meet more than one need (Items 1, 4, and 15).

I.E.: Let's take the toileting accidents as an example. What are the negative consequences of that behavior? Why is that of importance?

Teacher: Really, it's health reasons. She has this tendency to get, like, rashes and I refuse to put her in a diaper. The whole purpose is to try to make her as independent as possible. And social ostracism!

CATEGORY 6: The behavior change has *instructional utility* (Items 2, 10, and 16).

I.E.: And why are you concerned about the self-stimming?

Teacher: While she is self-stimming, it could be very frustrating for the teacher to have this child constantly doing hand wringing rather than touching the object.

As you no doubt already realized, whenever intervention plans are constructed—whether these are informal classroom procedures or are a part of a student's educational program and IEP—a large number of factors must be simultaneously considered. The flowchart summarized below and detailed in the next chapter allows the teacher to systematize this complex judgment task.

THE FLOW CHART

By using the flowchart, teachers can arrive at decisions that take into account the child's skill needs, differences in the severity of certain excess behaviors, potential longer term outcomes for the child, recommendations regarding which types of procedures are best to implement once an intervention decision has been made, and legal-ethical criteria that are relevant to the decision process.

The flowchart is organized into three levels, with all decisons regarding excess behavior beginning on Level I (see Figure 3.1). The chart is designed to require systematic movement through a sequence of considerations reflecting the seriousness of consequences for either changing or choosing not to change the behaviors identified during assessment. Level I decisions involve excess behaviors that pose a threat to the life of the child or are likely to result in irreversible physical harm. These behaviors are rare and will be clearly evident to persons who know the child well. Level II decisions focus on behaviors that have direct serious consequences for the child. Often these behaviors will be dangerous to others or have the potential for becoming more health threatening to the child in the future. Level III decisions involve behaviors whose negative effects tend to reside in the child's social environment. These behaviors have consequences that are indirect (e.g., lack of community acceptance, damage to the environment) and may not require that major revisions to the instructional program must be made.

Two additional points are important to keep in mind when using the flowchart. First, all excess behaviors are considered at each level of the decision process. That is, a given excess behavior is not automatically assumed to be one that should be addressed at a particular level. Instead, one considers all of the behaviors beginning at Level I and concludes the process through Level III. A Level II decision would mean, then, that Level I had already

been considered, and similarly, a Level III decison means that a behavior was already considered for possible intervention at both Levels I and II but was of such a nature that it is more appropriately dealt with at Level III. Secondly, although the three levels are depicted separately, no one level can be used in isolation. The process is interconnected, always beginning with the general assessment of the pupil's skill needs, planning the educational program and incorporating strategies to remediate high-priority excess behaviors, and concluding with plans to resolve or accommodate and monitor the more secondary concerns.

Level I: Urgent Behaviors
Requiring Immediate Attention

The first level of the flowchart deals with relatively rare instances in which the excess behavior threatens the child's life or health, or may cause irreversible physical harm. If such behaviors occur with sufficient intensity, examples of excess targets to be considered at this level might include eye poking and head banging. Another example might be chronic vomiting with concomitant weight loss. The collateral weight loss would qualify this excess behavior as life threatening, as would other physical side effects such as dehydration. Any remaining excess behaviors that do not meet these criteria would be ruled out as priorities on Level I. The teacher, related professionals, and parents would then design the IEP goals and plan and prioritize curriculum objectives based on the criteria discussed in Chapter 1. If a behavior had been identified as a priority at Level I, the IEP would be affected, and a major goal would be to replace this excess behavior with positive alternatives. Thus, if a life- or health-threatening excess behavior were identified, the next task would be to select an equal power incompatible skill. This skill would have two major characteristics:

1.   The skill would be topographically incompatible with the excess behavior such that the skill and the excess cannot be performed simultaneously.

54

FIGURE 3.1. The flowchart for decisions regarding excess behavior. (Reprinted with permission, with some revisions, from Voeltz, Evans, Derer, & Hanashiro, 1983.)

LEVEL I START

Assessment: conduct discrepancy analysis for child with multiple needs/excess.

Is any discrepancy life-threatening?

YES — Can I identify an "equal power" incompatible skill?

YES — Can I prevent excess while teaching skill to child?

YES — IMPLEMENT ECOLOGICAL/CURRICULAR COMPONENT.

Incorporate skills into IEP planning of curriculum objectives.

Teach skills and prevent excess.

After skill mastery, fade prevention.

GO TO LEVEL II.

NO — Can I conduct skill training simultaneously with effort to decrease excess?

YES — IMPLEMENT CURRICULAR/NEGATIVE CONSEQUENCES COMPONENT.

Incorporate skills into IEP planning of curriculum objectives.

Teach skills and consequate excess.

After skill mastery, fade negative consequences.

GO TO LEVEL II.

NO

Can I eliminate excess by reinforcing its absence?

YES — Implement DRO procedure.

NO — Can I eliminate excess through negative consequences?

YES — Implement DRO + negative consequences procedure.

Fade negative consequences and maintain DRO procedure.

Can I identify an "equal power" alternative skill?

YES — Plan curriculum objective and implement DRI.

NO — STOP. MAINTAIN DRO AND GO TO LEVEL II.

NO — STOP. REEVALUATE DECISIONS/CONSULTATION. GO TO LEVEL II.

NO — Rule out identifying excess behaviors as priorities.

Plan and prioritize curriculum objectives (IEP).

GO TO LEVEL II.

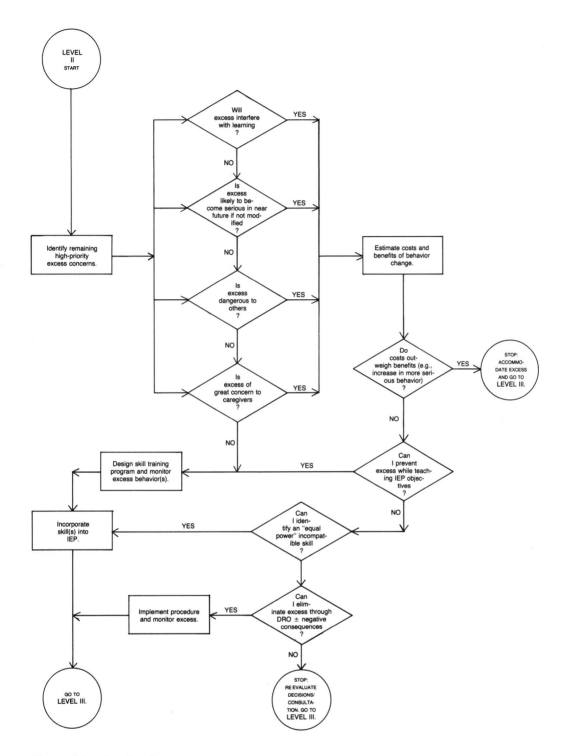

FIGURE 3.1. (*continued*)

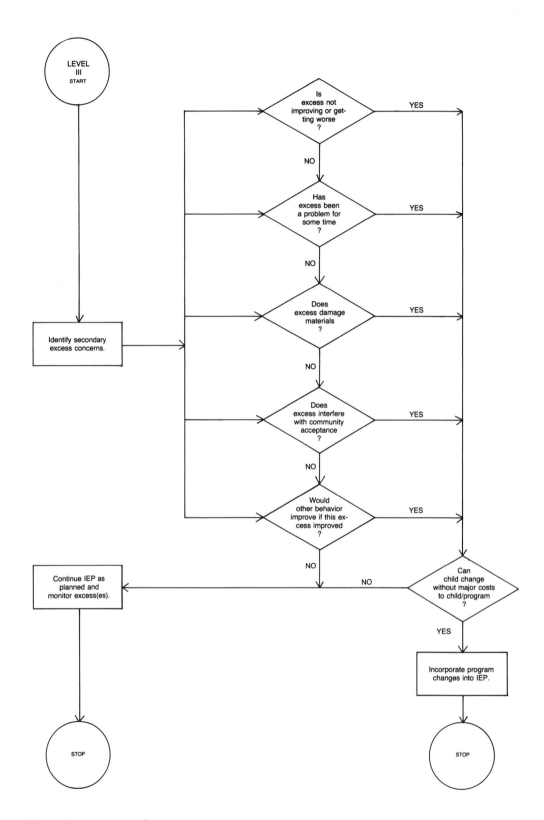

FIGURE 3.1. (continued)

2. The skill would generate sufficient opportunities for reinforcement, thereby allowing it to compete with the excess behavior.

It should also be taken into consideration that the reinforcement for the skill is at least somewhat similar to the reinforcement obtained through the excess behavior.

For example, with a behavior such as chronic vomiting, social interactions in the form of negative attention or the opportunity to play with the vomit may function to maintain the behavior. A possible curricular intervention would be the training of a leisure skill requiring object manipulation with both hands. The physical redirection of the child's hands away from the face would be incompatible with at least some components of the excess behavioral chain. The social praise and the intrinsically reinforcing properties of the activity serve to provide alternative reinforcing opportunities. Obviously, however, the early part of the response would have to be prevented, and if it cannot be, then a curricular/negative consequences component would be conducted simultaneously. An example would be teaching feeding skills and momentarily removing the food paired with a verbal ''No'' when the child begins the response chain that appears to lead to vomiting.

If skill training cannot be conducted simultaneously with efforts to decrease the excess, the next decision point examines the possibility of eliminating the excess behavior through the reinforcement of its absence (differential reinforcement of other behaviors, or DRO). A major consideration in using DRO is whether the excess behavior occurs at a low enough frequency or duration to allow the reinforcement of other behaviors. Only if the excess cannot be eliminated through the use of DRO alone could a negative consequence procedure then be added to the program. If the negative consequences procedure does not produce a rapid reduction in the excess behavior, then a complete reevaluation of the decisons and procedures should be conducted. This would be a very legitimate time for you to

seek outside consultation. If the negative consequences procedure is successful in establishing control over the behavior and reducing its frequency, then the procedure is faded while continuing the DRO. Following that, an alternative skill is identified and a program is implemented to teach the skill: differential reinforcement of incompatible behavior (DRI).

Before proceeding to a discussion of Level II decisions, we would like to suggest a perspective on outside consultation whenever you are confronted with instructional and behavioral problems that seem to require additional advice and assistance. Consultation is an important process that is often misused. In some cases, the consultant has an unrealistic view of the kinds of assistance she or he is being asked to provide and the kinds of change possibilities that are feasible. In other cases, the clinician who requests help from a consultant anticipates that the ''outside expert'' will enter the classroom with all the information needed to immediately solve the problem. For many teachers, a request for consultation often produces further psychological testing or a medical evaluation that seems to bear little relationship to the specific problems experienced in the classroom. In contrast, consultation should involve the addition of an outside and at least equally experienced clinician who can contribute fresh insight into the situation *based upon the information generally already known to the teacher*.

The decision making orientation adopted in this manual provides a possible useful strategy for interdisciplinary cooperation. We recommend that you do not seek consultation in the spirit of passing responsibility on to someone else of higher authority who has unique knowledge and will therefore be able to provide answers that have eluded the instructional team thus far. Consultation should instead be an opportunity to solve a problem by obtaining another view of the issue that is of concern to you. Representatives of the different disciplines work best when each respects the other's specialized professional knowledge but problem solving is a shared activity. Thus, in seeking consultation, it is most helpful if you can pose specific questions and encourage your support personnel from physical therapy, occupational therapy, speech pathology, psychology, social work, medicine, and so forth to join you in conjoint discussion and decison making. Consultation can also be quite informative: often simply discussing issues with fellow teachers will generate new ideas and helpful alternative ways of thinking about problem behaviors before their effects on you, the child, or the parents and the wider community become too unpleasant.

Level II: Serious Behaviors Requiring Formal Consideration

It is possible that you have identified and planned for a life-threatening excess behavior at Level I, or you may have ruled out addressing any of a student's excess behaviors at that level. In either case, the next step is to consider all remaining excess behaviors (i.e., those not considered at Level I) at Level II. Prior to addressing behaviors at Level II, as noted above, the IEP has been formulated and priority instructional goals and objectives have been established. In addition, however, the student exhibits a number of behaviors that are sufficiently serious to warrant consideration at Level II and corresponding modifications in the instructional program.

On Level II, decisions are made for serious behaviors that do not threaten the life or health of the child. These high, but not urgent, priority concerns are delineated by the immediate and direct consequences of the excess behavior. The decision process at this level begins with a series of questions to assist in determining how serious a particular behavior is for a child. Some of the questions can be answered by examining the best available factual information (e.g., is the behavior dangerous to others?). For other questions, you will need to rely on your own best judgment in attempting to answer the question. For example, the issue of which excess behaviors interfere with learning has not been resolved in existing intervention studies, nor is it always

easy to distinguish between interfering with learning per se and interfering with teaching. Let us look at some of the ways excess behavior disrupts the educational process.

Some behaviors interfere with teaching because of arbitrary rules or idiosyncratic standards we all adopt as educators. For instance, it might be difficult to integrate a particular severely handicapped child into regular third grade for music—even though he or she may have the basic skills—if the music teacher insists that children sit still with hands folded while she or he instructs. In this case, arm flapping interferes with teaching and not with learning. It is often recommended that we analyze the demands of such environments and use these standards for goal setting in order to aid integration. However, it is also possible to modify the expectations of those environments: it might be much easier to change a teacher's attitude than to completely reduce a child's arm flapping at a particular point in time. This is then a problem of providing support or consultation to those who are hesitant about their ability to tolerate deviant behavior.

A rather more fundamental type of disruption can be seen in behaviors like bolting, tantrumming, and noncompliance that would be difficult to accommodate in most instructional situations, although many of these can be worked around or obviated by creative changes in classroom design or routines. Some excess behaviors interfere only with the specifics of the learning task, so that flicking objects is not compatible with playing a wind instrument, but pounding objects would not be so disruptive to learning percussion instruments. This type of interference often involves topographical incompatibility between a dominant motor response (or abnormal reflexive movement in children with cerebral palsy, etc.) and the execution of a skill sequence.

The most fundamental type of interference is revealed in behaviors that disrupt the *process* of learning. For example, some self-stimulatory behaviors may serve actually to restrict stimulus input; seizure-like behaviors may also interfere with cue reception and appropriate attention; excess behaviors may modulate arousal and interfere with optimal cortical functioning. While many of these hypothesized relationships are controversial and beyond the scope of the present model, a teacher who is sensitive to expected rates of behavior change or acquisition can identify such interference with basic learning processes by keeping appropriate data on acquisition rates for each new task. One example of specific decision rules for deciding when to alter task requirements and instruction based upon insufficient pupil progress is provided by White and Haring (1980). If the teacher uses such a system to develop estimates regarding the amount of time a student might need to learn a new skill and then notices a marked decrease in learning while the student is finger flicking, this evidence would be used to justify addressing finger flicking at Level II of the flowchart.

To reiterate, one crucial reason for addressing an excess behavior at Level II is that the behavior interferes with learning. Other questions that are addressed at this level are: Is the excess likely to become more serious in the near future unless modified? Is the behavior dangerous to others? Is the excess of great concern to caregivers? If the answer to one or more of these questions is "yes" for a particular excess behavior, the next step would be to conduct a cost-benefit analysis. Even though the behavior is serious enough to warrant an affirmative answer for one or more of these questions at Level II, it is possible that the costs of intervening would outweigh the benefits. This cost-benefit analysis is described in detail in the next chapter. But if either the costs are too great to intervene at this time or if none of the behaviors in the student's repertoire were answered with a "yes" at Level II, you would then proceed to Level III.

Level III: Excess Behavior Reflecting "Normal Deviance"

Having completed the decision process for those behaviors that are of major concern (e.g., life/health-threatening, interfering with learn-

ing, etc.), we must now decide whether any of the remaining excess behaviors warrant consideration for intervention. At Level III, we examine behaviors whose negative effects tend to reside more in the child's social environment and whose presence does not directly threaten others or interfere with learning. Even though they may be considered "deviant," behaviors at Level III do not necessarily interfere with a child's ability to function in the environment.

It may be helpful to provide an analogy, since most (if not all) nonhandicapped people also exhibit "Level III decision" excess behaviors such as nail biting, picking, and so forth. Sometimes, we choose to change such behavior, but often we do not. We may choose not to do so because the behavior is difficult to change (that is, it is a habit), and we may "depend on it" for some reason. For example, a person who attempts to give up nail biting may experience an increase in generalized anxiety such that she or he finds it more difficult to deal with everyday situations. Such behavior (e.g., leg swinging, chewing on pencils) may serve a self-mediating function in that they allow the individual to reduce outside distractions or stress while concentrating on a difficult task. Thus, we may choose not to change nail biting because of the increase in generalized anxiety and not to change pencil chewing because the behavior allows us to better concentrate on difficult tasks.

A Level III decision to change a behavior takes into consideration the behavior itself, the effect of the behavior on the environment, the function the behavior serves, and the amount of effort that would be required to change the behavior. In some cases, the behavior itself is not as difficult to tolerate as would be an intervention program to change it! Thus, the final question to be addressed at Level III is whether or not changing a behavior would be of major "cost" to either the child or the program. If the behavior itself is in this category of relatively minor deviance, it is difficult to justify using considerable programming time (the child's and the program's) and resources to modify it.

FLOWCHART COMPONENTS

The flowchart uses symbols to indicate the type of action to be performed at each step. Circles indicate that a decision has been reached, resulting in movement to a different section of the flowchart and, finally, the end of the decision process. Some of these circles will require moving to specific curricular components, to a different level of the flowchart, or to a reevaluation of a previous decision or procedure. For example, the *ecological/curricular component* presents a sequence for teaching skills while preventing excess behavior. Prevention can occur through restructuring the environment or through response interruption. The *curricular/negative consequences component* presents a sequence for teaching skills simultaneously with efforts to decrease an excess. *Reevaluation/consultation* requires a thorough examination of all factors leading to the decision to intervene with a particular behavior and the possibility of seeking outside consultation. An *accommodation* decision allows that the behavior may continue as is, with changes in the environment or in the attitudes/behaviors of significant others to adjust to the presence of the behavior (which may or may not be modified at some future date).

Within the rectangles, you will find tasks that must be performed and temporary procedures to implement. Some of these tasks include assessment procedures, prediction of potential outcomes resulting from decisions to change a behavior, and monitoring of frequency/intensity/duration of specific excess behaviors. The diamonds contain the questions one needs to ask. These questions aid in analyzing the seriousness of the problem, the legal-ethical concerns involved, and the potential solutions and outcomes for the child. Each question is a decision point and requires either a *yes* or *no* answer. The direction of the arrow at each decision point indicates the next step in the process based on the answer given. Figure 3.2 summarizes these actions required by each symbol, and you might want to return to Figure 3.1 (see pages 54–56) and briefly glance at the kinds of questions and statements found within each symbol in the flowchart itself.

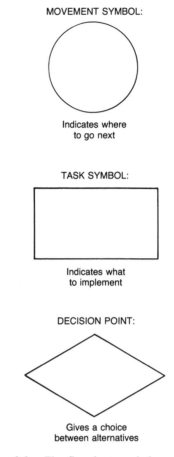

FIGURE 3.2. The flowchart symbols and actions required.

A SUMMARY STATEMENT

The flowchart described in this chapter is designed to require a systematic movement through a sequence of considerations reflecting the seriousness of consequences for either changing or choosing not to change the behaviors identified during assessment. What we have called Level I decisions focus on excess behaviors that pose a threat to the life of the child or are likely to result in irreversible physical harm or endanger the child's health. These behaviors are relatively rare and will be clearly evident to persons who know the child well. Level II decisions focus on behaviors that have direct, serious consequences for the child. Often these behaviors will be dangerous to others or have the potential for becoming dangerous to the child in the future. Level III decisions focus upon behaviors whose negative effects tend to reside in the child's social environment. These behaviors have consequences that are indirect. For example, they may interfere with community acceptance, cause physical damage to the child's surroundings, and so on. Dealing with Level III behaviors usually does not require major IEP and program revisions.

Each decision point in the flowchart requires skilled judgments for which data are not always available either with respect to your particular student or for the particular behavior problem across children. Despite many years of research in behavior modification, there are really no behavior problems seen in severely handicapped children for which there are clear prescriptions for the most effective type of intervention. This does not really concern us. Children, to use a common truism, are all very different and the unique features of individual behavior can be very idiosyncratic. This leads us to believe that it is particularly necessary for teachers to approach problem behavior from the perspective of making decisions, not from following procedures in a rigid fashion. On one hand, the published literature is certainly a convenient *source* of ideas for types of interventions that have been attempted in the past. On the other hand, there has been a great deal of use of aversive procedures relative to the teaching of alternatives. And there often is little information given on: (a) the decision process used, or (b) the child, to allow accurate generalizations of a given procedure to a specific child.

For these reasons we feel this guide to decision making is a useful one to follow, but not in a rigid fashion. We have discussed many issues related to the judgment of behavior in this chapter and we feel that now you should select a few behaviors from your own students or clients and see whether these ideas can be implemented. To assist you to do this, we will go over the model itself in step-by-step detail using an example. This is the purpose of the next chapter. Then, in Appendix A, we provide some blank protocols for using the decision flowchart that we would encourage you to use.

chapter 4

The Decision Model
A Sample Program Design

*with Kristine Reneé Derer
and Rae Y. Hanashiro*

This chapter introduces the flowchart decision model by illustrating its general principles and applying the model to a hypothetical student who has multiple educational and behavioral needs. Step-by-step explanations of the tasks that would be performed when using the flowchart in order to make decisions about excess behavior in conjunction with a child's education program are followed by appropriate modifications to that child's IEP. The format to guide and document these decisions and accompanying program modifications is thus filled in for our sample child throughout this chapter; however, we have provided a blank task book in Appendix A that teachers and other clinicians can reproduce for use in program planning for students in their programs.

For example, while reading the following initial description of Jerry, it would be useful to think about the decisions you would make if you were his teacher on the first day of class. This description of a sample student is based on a combination of characteristics we have seen in a number of our students in recent years. We think the description, therefore, is quite realistic but recognize that the students you work with may be very different. They may be older, or more severely handicapped, or have physical impairments. However, the example is designed to illustrate the model, not the child. As you read through the example, try to keep the judgment process in mind.

Jerry

Jerry is an 8-year-old boy enrolled with four other children in a self-contained classroom for children with developmental delays and autistic-like behavior. His classroom is located on an elementary school campus that enrolls a larger number of nonhandicapped children. He has made good progress in self-help skills, uses bathroom facilities when prompted, can dress himself except for buttons and snaps, and uses a spoon and fork (but not a knife) to eat independently. He is helped with bathing (his parents run his bath for him) and requires help with hair care and tooth brushing. He has some receptive language, can identify some objects in his environment when they are labeled by someone else, and can respond to simple two-action commands. He does not understand polar adjectives (big/little) or elements in time (yesterday/tomorrow).

Jerry is nonvocal, but has a repertoire of about 20 signs and can use verb-object combinations. He attempts to imitate speech sounds and will pair *ba* and *mm* with the sign for words beginning with the same sound. He can identify the colors red, green, and yellow, and the shapes circle, square, and triangle, but only in relatively artificial, table-top tasks; for example, he does not seem to understand street crossing signals. Also, as a result of his previous instructional program emphasis, he has good matching skills and is beginning to use scissors, crayons, and paste. On the playground, Jerry will use all of the play equipment but must be pushed on the swing. He catches a ball and will play with it, but will not throw it back to another person. During free time, he will play alone with a push toy or a puzzle for 2 to 3 minutes, but does not use any other, more age-appropriate toys. He does not initiate interactions with other children but will parallel play (play next to another child) and he will play chase games if another child initiates the activity. He likes music, listening to the radio, and watching TV.

In both one-to-one and small group situations and instruction, Jerry has displayed a high level of self-abusive behavior. In a severe tantrum, he will stiffen his arms and back, suck both thumbs, and then make crying sounds and bite down on both thumbs. Next he starts screaming and begins pounding the sides of his head with his palms. Each incident may last as long as 1 hour. He will also begin these tantrums by head slapping, and the frequency of head slapping has been as high as 40 times per school day. He sometimes pokes his fingers gently into his ears during free play and one-to-one instruction. He has been observed to smell, throw, flick, rub, and pound objects during free play and instruction. During individual and small group instruction, he will often flap his arms, cover his ears with his hands, mouth his thumbs, pull and twist his clothing, tap his fingers on objects or against his body, cry, scream, and kick. His parents have reported that many of these behaviors also occur at home, and they are particularly concerned about the tantrum-like behaviors that include self-injurious and disruptive behaviors. Last year, a restraint procedure was used to attempt to reduce head slapping. Jerry started to bite the teacher during the restraining procedure, and it became increasingly difficult to control him. Recently, he has begun to hit and bite other children during free play.

Jerry rides to school on the regular school bus and is escorted to class by the educational assistant. He eats lunch in the classroom and goes on field trips with his classmates. Jerry attends whole-school assemblies in the cafeteria and plays on the K–3 playground at recess accompanied by the regular education students.

What do you see as Jerry's major needs? Do these needs include behavior changes? If they do, what behaviors would you change and why would you change them? Which changes would be reflected in Jerry's IEP objectives? How would you feel if, after an entire year of trying to improve Jerry's behavior, nothing got better? What if one of his behaviors got worse? These and similar questions are all issues teachers must consider. They are usually asked (and answered) intuitively—until perhaps a crisis situation develops, such as another child getting hurt, or the parents requesting a meeting because the situation at home has become unmanageable in their eyes.

To answer these questions in a way that systematically applies the principles and practices introduced in the previous chapters, Jerry's situation and needs will be addressed by using the flowchart and the accompanying task book. (For your reference, a blank version of this task book is included in Appendix A.)

DEFINITION OF TERMS

Although this book is specifically designed to assist teachers in making judgments about excess behavior, one of our major assumptions, as we have seen, is that changes in inappropriate behaviors are best accomplished through a curricular approach, that is, by teaching new skills. Throughout the book, there is an emphasis on skills that are incompatible with or provide an alternative to the excess behavior. In some instances, this requires the identification of an *"equal power" incompatible skill.* An equal power incompatible skill has two major characteristics:

1. The skill is topographically incompatible with the excess behavior in that the skill and the excess behavior cannot be performed simultaneously.
2. The skill generates sufficient opportunities for reinforcement, thereby allowing it to compete with the excess behavior.

In other instances, one might need to identify an *"equal power" alternative skill.* An equal power alternative skill need not be incompatible topographically with the excess behavior, but it must generate high levels of reinforcement. An equal power alternative skill would thus provide the child with a skill that she or he can perform in place of the excess behavior without losing access to positive consequences.

Because of the emphasis placed on developing skills as a means to reduce excess behavior,

DRI and the modified DRO procedures are recommended throughout all levels of the flowchart. The *differential reinforcement of incompatible (or alternative) response (DRI)* procedure emphasizes the direct reinforcement of a specific skill or behavior. Throughout the decision model, DRI is the procedure of choice. In the absence of readily identifiable incompatible skills, *differential reinforcement of other behavior (DRO)* is recommended, until such time that specific skills can be identified. In DRO, the child is directly reinforced for not engaging in the problem behavior. In traditional use, DRO would allow for reinforcement to occur if the child is engaging in any behavior other than the target excess behavior, thus potentially allowing the reinforcement of other excess behaviors. However, in the modified version of DRO recommended here, clinicians would tighten the requirements for reinforcement so that the child would be rewarded for the absence of the target *and* the absence of any other excess behavior as well.

To develop a clear understanding of the way in which the various factors influence decisions about excess behavior, each level of the flowchart is discussed separately in the next section. Decision points throughout the flowchart are illustrated with reference to Jerry, the child described in the vignette. The actual steps involved in the decision process are indicated on the right side of each page. On the left side are general considerations involved in performing each step and specific thoughts on how the question or task applies to the child in the vignette. More detailed explanations of certain procedures appear as notes. The process is interconnected, always beginning with general assessment and ending with plans for resolving or accommodating and monitoring the more secondary concerns.

LEVEL I: URGENT BEHAVIORS REQUIRING IMMEDIATE ATTENTION

Before attempting to decide which behaviors require intervention, we need to analyze systematically the child's performance level in each behavioral and curricular area and determine which skills would be most useful for the child to learn. The vignette describing Jerry contains much of the summary information that is likely to be available from the more traditional assessment procedures and an examination of the child's past attainments in school programs. Our task is to integrate that information so that we can determine to what extent Jerry's excess behaviors prevent his participation in chronologically age-appropriate activities. Ecological inventories and discrepancy analysis procedures allow us to consider simultaneously his skills and his behaviors within the appropriate context: criterion situations and environments.

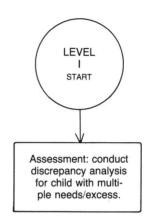

CONSIDERATIONS

Ecological inventory strategies are designed to assist teachers in identifying the skills needed by severely handicapped students to function in a variety of environments. (For additional information, see Brown, Branston-McClean, Baumgart, Vincent, Falvey, & Schroeder, 1979.)

Procedures can begin by identifying the more global environments such as leisure, vocational, domestic, community, and so on. Then, we need to identify specific subenvironments for the student, which is what we have done for Jerry. These subenvironments are listed in STEP 1.

Future environments may include the environments the child will be functioning in next year, or when she or he enters junior high school or high school, or when she or he becomes an adult. The idea is to project realistic possibilities for the child.

For Jerry, the future environments we are considering are 7th grade and activities that will be appropriate about 4 years hence when he will be 12 years old.

STEP 1.   LIST SOME LEAST RESTRICTIVE ENVIRONMENTS IN WHICH THE CHILD CAN FUNCTION.

(domestic)   parent's home
(educational)   self-contained classroom for severely handicapped students, public school elementary campus, lunch, recess
(community)   shopping center with parent, neighborhood
(leisure)   school playground, friend's house

STEP 2.   LIST SOME FUTURE LEAST RESTRICTIVE ENVIRONMENTS IN WHICH THE CHILD COULD FUNCTION.

(domestic)   friend's home
(educational)   self-contained classroom for moderately handicapped students on public school intermediate campus, transitions and social interactions with nonhandicapped peers
(community)   public transportation, fast food restaurant
(leisure)   neighborhood park, video arcade, swimming pool

STEP 3. FOR EACH ENVIRONMENT LISTED IN STEP 1, IDENTIFY THE SKILLS THAT THE CHILD HAS THAT ALLOW HIM OR HER TO PARTICIPATE.

The skills listed in this step are those that the child has already acquired. STEP 3 should include as many skills as can be identified for as many environments as possible.

Here we list under the appropriate environments some of Jerry's skills that were described in the vignette.

(domestic)   eats independently; listens to radio; signs "food," "drink," "rest" with cue; plays with magazine and balls; watches TV

(educational)   follows directions; signs "food," "drink," "rest," "ball," and "toilet" with cue; places circle, square, and triangle in shape box or form board

(community)   walks from store to store with escort; eats in restaurant when accompanied; signs "eat" and "drink" with cue

(leisure)   uses playground equipment; engages in other-initiated play; signs "rest" and "drink" with cue

STEP 4. FOR EACH ENVIRONMENT LISTED IN STEP 2, IDENTIFY THE SKILLS THAT WOULD ALLOW THE CHILD TO PARTICIPATE.

Here we list some of the skills that Jerry will need in order to function in the future environments. STEP 4 should include as many skills as can be identified for as many environments as possible.

(domestic)   dress/toilet independently, engage in age-appropriate leisure activity, play cooperatively, sign needs/wants/feelings spontaneously

(educational)   work 20 minutes independently, interact with peers, go to and from class alone, have functional math/reading skills

(community)   ride bus independently, select appropriate bus to school and home, select correct fare

(leisure)   use bathroom facilities, play on basketball court, go to and from park independently, interact with peers

* * *Note* * *

DISCREPANCY ANALYSIS: By comparing the skills listed for the current environments (STEP 3) with those listed for future environments (STEP 4), we can determine the specific areas to emphasize in order to prepare Jerry to participate as fully as possible in the activities available to him at age 12. From this comparison we can identify which skills we will attempt to teach Jerry during the coming school year. For each skill that we decide to teach, we need to conduct a discrepancy analysis. In a discrepancy analysis, we identify the sequence of steps in the performance of the skill, the steps Jerry already has in his repertoire, and the steps Jerry will need to learn.

* * * * * * * *

STEP 5.   FOR EACH SKILL FROM STEP 4 THAT
          HAD BEEN SELECTED FOR INSTRUC-
          TION, CONDUCT A DISCREPANCY
          ANALYSIS.

Although we have delineated steps for only one skill, the discrepancy analysis is performed for each skill selected for instruction (Brown et al., 1979). At times there will be some overlapping of these skills (e.g., language), and at other times these skills will be unique to the particular environment (e.g., bus riding).

The steps identified for each task will form the curriculum during the coming school year. In some cases, we will be able to teach Jerry the specific steps involved. In other cases, task or environmental adaptations or, perhaps, prosthetic devices might be appropriate. Every effort to ensure as full participation as possible should be made.

For Jerry, skills like walking unassisted to and from locations and turn-taking are subskills that will be required across environments. Other skills, like recognizing time to leave, might best be dealt with through an adaptive aid (a prosthetic) like a wrist watch with an alarm.

Environment _neighborhood park_   Skill _play on basketball court_

In Column A, list what a nonhandicapped similar age peer does.

In Column B, place a $+$ if the handicapped child can perform the step and a $-$ if the child cannot perform it.

In Column C, write what the handicapped child does if she or he cannot perform the step.

A	B	C
walks to and from park independently	$-$	walks with assistance to and from park
carries ball while walking	$-$	drops ball to put fingers in ears while walking
locates basketball court	$-$	wanders around, flicks object
asks to play; plays alone	$-$	bites or hits others; pounds on ball
takes turns with others	$-$	has mild/severe tantrums
throws/retrieves ball	$+$	
recognizes time to go	$-$	does not recognize time, lies down, tantrums
says good-bye to others	$-$	ignores others

STEP 6. LIST THE EXCESS BEHAVIORS DISPLAYED BY THE CHILD THAT CREATE A DISCREPANCY IN THE PERFORMANCE OF THE SKILLS IDENTIFIED IN STEP 5.

In STEP 6, we list the excess behaviors that the child displays in lieu of the correct step performance for each skill needed for each environment. These excess behaviors are identified by reviewing Column C of the discrepancy analysis for each skill and selecting those behaviors judged to be excesses.

slaps head	*bites self*	*pokes ears*
cries	*screams*	*kicks*
mouths thumbs	*flaps arms*	*hits others*
bites others	*smells objects*	*throws objects*
flicks objects	*rubs objects*	*pounds objects*
pulls/twists clothes		

STEP 6 includes every behavior that Jerry has displayed while attempting to perform the skills we intend to teach. Although there are certain behaviors that could be listed under a general grouping (e.g., aggression, self-abuse, tantrum), it is important at this point in the decision process to list each behavior individually.

* * Note * *

Jerry's excess behaviors have now been identified in relation to his total skill repertoire and the environments in which he does or will function. Having identified those behaviors that create performance discrepancies, we now must begin to determine which behaviors will be given priority consideration. We would all agree that improvement in all 16 of Jerry's behaviors would be great, but we probably cannot intervene on all 16 and we may not all agree on which of those 16 behaviors should be targeted for intervention. Decisions made on Level I of the flowchart specifically concern the relatively rare instances of life- or health-threatening excess behaviors that cause or could cause irreversible physical harm. All other behaviors identified during the assessment stage sift down to Level II of the flowchart.

* * * * * * * *

This question is asked of each behavior listed in STEP 6 of the ecological inventory/discrepancy analysis. Factors that may indicate irreversible physical harm include the actual physical side effects of the behavior or high frequency/duration/intensity of a self-injurious behavior.

Of course, this is not the situation in Jerry's case. He does have one life/health-threatening behavior. Such behavior is rare, however. In most cases, the child does not exhibit a life/health-threatening behavior, and priorities would not be established for any behavior at Level I.

For children without life/health-threatening behaviors, goals can be selected from the skills identified during STEP 5 of the assessment procedure.

If no behaviors involve a threat to life or health, all excess behaviors would then be considered on Level II of the flowchart.

Here we list the life/health-threatening behavior and the reasons why we feel it poses a threat. These reasons are based on what would occur if the behavior continued at its present level or deteriorated. Jerry has one such behavior that will be considered on Level I. As we shall discuss later, it is appropriate to consider the remaining 15 behaviors on Level II.

IF THE ANSWER IS "NO, DISCREPANCIES ARE NOT LIFE/HEALTH-THREATENING," THEN

Rule out identifying excess behaviors as priorities.

NEXT, GO ON AND

Plan and prioritize curriculum objectives (IEP).

NOW,

GO TO LEVEL II.

See page 90.

IF THE ANSWER IS "YES, A LIFE/HEALTH-THREATENING DISCREPANCY DOES EXIST," THEN LIST THE BEHAVIOR(S) AND THE POSSIBLE RESULTS.

head slapping	*potential hearing loss, since it occurs on and around the ears*

It is important to identify a skill that is both topographically incompatible with the excess behavior and likely to generate high levels of reinforcement.

For Jerry, the skill must be one that requires him to use both hands. With the proper reinforcement, a signing program for expressing feelings might meet this need.

If it were not possible to identify a skill that is both incompatible and highly reinforcing, then we would need to focus our attention on direct efforts to reduce the behavior.

When considering whether a response can be prevented, we need to examine possible environmental restructuring (e.g., if noise triggers response, eliminate noise) and whether any behaviors occur immediately prior to the target behavior. These preceding behaviors could serve as a signal that the target behavior is about to occur.

Since screaming and biting behaviors always precede Jerry's head slapping, these behaviors can serve as a signal that he is about to start slapping his head. With this type of warning, it may be possible to effectively prevent the response from occurring. Thus, we implement the ecological/curricular component.

FOR EACH BEHAVIOR IDENTIFIED AS LIFE/HEALTH-THREATENING, ASK:

IF THE ANSWER IS "NO, AN 'EQUAL POWER' INCOMPATIBLE SKILL CANNOT BE IDENTI-FIED," THEN GO TO THE DRO QUESTION ON PAGE 73.

IF THE ANSWER IS "YES, AN 'EQUAL POWER' INCOMPATIBLE SKILL CAN BE IDENTIFIED," THEN ASK:

IF THE ANSWER IS "YES, THE EXCESS CAN BE PREVENTED WHILE TEACHING THE SKILL," THEN

IMPLEMENT ECOLOGICAL/CURRICULAR COMPONENT.

See page 76.

With a child who is stronger than Jerry, interrupting the hand-to-head movement might not be feasible. It might be necessary to consider adding to the curriculum a procedure to decrease the excess (i.e., negative consequences). Thus, the preferred procedure would be a consequence of brief duration that does not disrupt programming but is nevertheless effective.

If Jerry's head slapping were being maintained by teacher attention, then a brief 30-second timeout from teacher attention might be effective. Other more intrusive punishment procedures might not allow us to conduct skill training while punishing the excess (e.g., isolation timeout, some overcorrection procedures).

IF THE ANSWER IS "NO, THE EXCESS BE-HAVIOR CANNOT BE PREVENTED," THEN ASK:

IF THE ANSWER IS "YES, SKILL TRAINING CAN BE CONDUCTED SIMULTANEOUSLY WITH EFFORTS TO DECREASE EXCESS," THEN

> IMPLEMENT CURRICULAR/ NEGATIVE CONSEQUENCES COMPONENT.

See page 83.

* * *Note* * *

Up to this point, we have been emphasizing skill instruction (in conjunction with direct efforts to reduce excess behavior) as the best strategy for permanently influencing the occurrence of such behaviors. There may be instances in which prevention or punishment of a response while teaching a skill is not feasible. In these rare cases, the focus will shift to the life/health-threatening behavior itself. Skill programming does not get suspended but may need to be interrrupted while we are implementing procedures to decrease the life/health-threatening excess behavior. Thus, in answering the question "Can I conduct skill training simultaneously with effort to decrease the excess?", if we were to decide that simultaneous efforts were not possible, we would need to examine the possibility of using DRO or DRO plus negative consequences.

* * * * * * * *

When it is not possible to prevent or punish the behavior while teaching the skill, differential reinforcement of other behavior (DRO) should be attempted. A major consideration in using DRO is whether the behavior occurs at a low enough frequency or duration to allow the reinforcement of other behaviors. There must be periods of time during which the excess is not being displayed.

When implementing DRO, be consistent. Children need to know what they are being reinforced for doing. Be sure that the reinforcement used is a preferred one—there are consequences we perceive as punishments that can be functionally reinforcing, and consequences we perceive as rewards that can be functionally aversive to some children.

Had we determined that we could neither prevent nor consequate Jerry's head slapping while conducting skill training, we would then begin reinforcing Jerry for periods of time during which no head slapping occurs.

If DRO alone were not feasible due to the high frequency/duration of the excess, we would then consider adding a negative consequences procedure. The consequence procedure selected should be the least intrusive and most humane method as possible. It should be consistent, with the consequences delivered in an objective, nonemotional manner. The excess should be carefully monitored. Unless the procedure is extinction, increases in the excess behavior indicate that the program is not working.

IF THE ANSWER IS "NO, SKILL TRAINING CANNOT BE CONDUCTED SIMULTANEOUSLY WITH EFFORTS TO DECREASE EXCESS," THEN ASK:

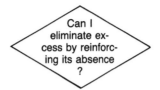

IF THE ANSWER IS "YES, THE EXCESS CAN BE ELIMINATED BY REINFORCING ITS ABSENCE," THEN

Implement DRO procedure.

NEXT, GO TO ALTERNATIVE SKILL QUESTION ON PAGE 75.

IF THE ANSWER IS "NO, THE EXCESS CANNOT BE ELIMINATED BY REINFORCING ITS ABSENCE," THEN ASK:

Failure to reduce the excess behavior through skill training, DRO, or negative consequences requires a careful review of all decisions and all procedures implemented by the team. We need to reexamine possible consequences maintaining the behavior, actual opportunities for reinforcement, appropriateness of the skills selected for training, and the reliability of our trainers in implementing the procedure (treatment integrity). By returning to the first decision point of Level I—Can I identify an equal power incompatible skill?—we can approach these issues in a systematic manner. If a reevaluation does not produce results, outside consultation should be considered. While reevaluation/consultation procedures are being conducted, we should proceed to Level II to consider the remaining excess behaviors in the child's repertoire.

Creating opportunities for re-inforcement is a necessary component of any program that uses punishment. By implementing DRO concurrently with efforts to decrease the excess, we can begin to strengthen alternative behaviors.

Had we decided to implement a DRO plus a negative consequences procedure for Jerry's head banging, we could perhaps have selected overcorrection combined with positive reinforcement for not banging his head.

Here we must begin to fade the negative consequences procedure. For example, when using overcorrection, we could pair the overcorrection technique with a verbal warning. We could then reduce the duration of overcorrection (subject to the behavior remaining at a low rate). Then we could begin to increase the interval between the verbal warning and the overcorrection procedure.

IF THE ANSWER IS "NO, THE EXCESS CANNOT BE ELIMINATED WITH A NEGATIVE CONSEQUENCES PROCEDURE," THEN

STOP REEVALUATE DECISIONS/ CONSULTATION. GO TO **LEVEL II.**

See page 90.

IF THE ANSWER IS "YES, THE EXCESS CAN BE ELIMINATED WITH A NEGATIVE CONSEQUENCES PROCEDURE," THEN

Implement DRO + negative consequences procedure.

See negative consequences considerations, page 86, STEP 5.

NEXT,

Fade negative consequences and maintain DRO procedure.

* * * * * * *

Once the life/health-threatening excess behavior has been brought under control, we can return to our original focus—skill building.

* * * * * * *

An "equal power" alternative skill is one that the child can do instead of the excess behavior. It may be incompatible, but it doesn't have to be. It must be one that will generate enough reinforcement for the child so that she or he will eventually be more motivated to perform the skill instead of the excess behavior. Typically, this skill should be one that accomplishes the same function accomplished by the excess, but in a positive, socially acceptable way.

At this point, we would continue DRO for the life/health-threatening behavior, and we would proceed to Level II of the flowchart to consider the remaining excess behaviors.

FOLLOWING THE IMPLEMENTATION OF DRO OR DRO + NEGATIVE CONSEQUENCES, ASK:

IF THE ANSWER IS "NO, AN 'EQUAL POWER' ALTERNATIVE SKILL CANNOT BE IDENTIFIED," THEN

See page 90.

IF THE ANSWER IS "YES, AN 'EQUAL POWER' ALTERNATIVE SKILL CAN BE IDENTIFIED," THEN

If we had decided to implement a DRO or DRO plus negative consequences procedure and we were able to identify an alternative skill, we would now design a skill program for implementation. Since Jerry enjoys music, we could select a musical toy for training and provide reinforcement for playing with the toy (differential reinforcement of an incompatible or alternative response, which we will refer to as DRI).

Plan curriculum objective and implement DRI.

NEXT,

We would then add our musical toy
program to the skills selected during
the assessment procedure (p. 67) for
inclusion in the IEP.

Plan and prioritize curriculum objectives (IEP).

NOW,

Now we proceed to Level II of the
flowchart to consider the remaining
excess behaviors.

See page 90.

The Ecological/Curricular Component

CONSIDERATIONS

Table 4.1 depicts the goals and
objectives identified for Jerry
following the needs assessment. Since
we did identify a life/health-
threatening behavior that could be
prevented, we need to modify the IEP
to include the program for skill
development while preventing excess
behavior.

IMPLEMENT ECOLOGICAL/ CURRICULAR COMPONENT.

Incorporate skills into IEP planning of curriculum objectives.

STEP 1. IN COLUMN A, LIST THE LIFE/
HEALTH-THREATENING BE-
HAVIOR(S). IN COLUMN B, LIST THE
BEHAVIOR(S) OR STIMULUS EVENT(S)
THAT SIGNAL(S) THE ONSET OF THE
TARGET EXCESS BEHAVIOR.

Here we list Jerry's head slapping and
the accompanying behaviors that serve
as a signal that head slapping is about
to occur (from p. 71). Had the
behavior been signaled by a stimulus
event (e.g., a loud noise), we would
describe that event in Column B.

A	B
head slapping	*crying and screaming followed by biting down on both thumbs*

TABLE 4.1.   IEP prior to Level I decisions

Prioritized annual goals and short-term objectives

Annual goal no. 1:   Increase communication skills

Short-term objective(s):
1.   Jerry will increase his signing repertoire from the present level of 20 signs to 30 signs.
2.   Jerry will respond to questions with a three-word sentence 75% of the time.
3.   Jerry will increase vocalization 50% over baseline rates by: (a) verbalizing initial sound of words in signing repertoire, and (b) vocalizing while signing words in signing repertoire.
4.   Given a naturally occurring stimulus, Jerry will indicate needs and wants without prompting by signing a two-word sentence.

Annual goal no. 2:   Increase functional reading and math skills

Short-term objective(s):
1.   Given the cue "Give the cashier a (denomination)," Jerry will select the correct coin 75% of the time.
2.   When presented the word and two distracters, Jerry will correctly identify the following words 75% of the time: walk, wait, stop, men, women, keep out, boys, girls, water, exit, in, out, push, pull, enter, milk, bus.
3.   When shown the following words, Jerry will indicate appropriate meaning by matching, demonstrating, or signing: walk, wait, stop, men, women, keep out, boys, girls, water, danger, exit, in, out, push, pull, enter, milk, bus.

Annual goal no. 3:   Increase community living skills

Short-term objective(s)
1.   When accompanied by a same-age peer, Jerry will locate the bus stop, board the bus, pay the fare, and select an appropriate seat without verbal cue.
2.   When arriving at school, Jerry will exit the bus with his school bag, walk to his classroom and put his things away independently.
3.   During snack and lunch periods, Jerry will prepare the table, eat/drink using appropriate utensils, clear the table, and return all items to their appropriate places (e.g., tray to cafeteria drop-off station) with verbal cueing.

Annual goal no. 4:   Increase adaptive/social skills

Short-term objective(s):
1.   Jerry will increase duration of independent interaction with materials: (a) from 3 minutes to 10 minutes with preferred items, (b) from 30 seconds to 5 minutes with nonpreferred items.
2.   Jerry will appropriately greet/say good-bye to visitors, teachers, and peers without a verbal cue from the instructor.
3.   Given a naturally occurring free time situation, Jerry will appropriately manipulate materials for lego, music stick, and electronic beanbag for three out of four sessions attempted.

STEP 2. DESCRIBE IN DETAIL THE SKILL TO
         BE TAUGHT AND THE PROCEDURE
         TO BE USED.

In STEP 2, we outline the exact
procedure and skill program we wish
to implement. The incompatible skill
selected for training is signing the
phrase "Help me."

This cue reflects what occurs in the
natural environment eliciting the
particular response.

This cue reflects the task demand—
the specific instructional cue for the
task the child is to do.

Here we describe in behavioral terms
exactly what task we expect the child
to do.

Here we describe in detail what the
trainer must do to ensure successful
task performance.

Natural cue	*Present in nonreinforcing/punishing environment*
Verbal cue	*"Sign for me to help you."*
Task description	*Child holds left hand palm up, 2–3 inches from body at midline, holds right hand on top of left, curved as if holding a cup. Child then abruptly moves both hands to touch body, then out, then touching body again to sign "Help me."*
Prompting procedure	*1) Full physical assist—give firm manual guidance for both hands; 2) Partial physical assist—while touching wrists, guide child's hands in direction of sign; 3) Gesture—model the sign*

STEP 3. IN Part A, DESCRIBE THE EVENTS THAT APPEAR TO BE MAINTAINING THE EXCESS BEHAVIOR. IN Part B, DESCRIBE THE REINFORCING EVENTS TO BE USED THAT MIGHT SUCCESSFULLY COMPETE WITH THE EVENTS DESCRIBED IN Part A.

The assumption here is that all behavior serves a purpose. In Part A, we attempt to identify the purpose. In Part B, we attempt to identify other events (reinforcers) that could serve the same function.

An examination of the data indicates that head slapping results in the termination of ongoing events regardless of the precipitating stimulus (e.g., other child's tantrum, repetitive task, low preference activity). Thus, it would appear that head slapping is being maintained by the opportunity to escape an aversive situation.

Part A *Head slapping results in stopping the ongoing activity, or at least temporarily interrupting the ongoing activity.*

Our hypothesis is that head slapping is being maintained by the opportunity to escape from an aversive situation. Now, our task is to identify other events that would serve as an appropriate means of escape. The opportunity to select activities would allow Jerry to exert control over his environment and more adaptively fulfills the same function. We will use opportunities to choose activities to directly reinforce the incompatible skill—signing "Help me"—thus rendering the skill "equal power."

Part B *Contingent upon signing "Help me," Jerry can obtain teacher assistance and is occasionally then allowed to take a break or to select something else to do from a group of preferred activities.*

STEP 4.   DESCRIBE IN DETAIL THE PREVEN-
          TION TECHNIQUE TO BE EMPLOYED.

Here we describe exactly how we intend to prevent Jerry from slapping his head.

As Jerry removes his thumbs from his mouth and begins to move his hands toward his head, the trainer places his or her hands on Jerry's forearms and delivers the skill cue.

STEP 5.   DESCRIBE ANY CHANGES TO THE
          ENVIRONMENT THAT WOULD BE
          NEEDED.

At times, a program may require some environmental restructuring (e.g., change in seating, activities, illumination, etc.). For example, if a particular activity were highly correlated with the presence of excess behavior, we would want to examine the skill level of the activity in relation to the abilities of the child. It is possible that the activity might be too easy or too difficult for the child.

The trainer needs to have access to a variety of activities and programs that can be conducted in the immediate area. The trainer should ensure that several of the activities are highly preferred by the child.

Jerry's program requires an increased number of activities available for training.

STEP 6.   DESCRIBE ANY CHANGES NOT
          INCLUDED IN STEPS 1–5 THAT
          WOULD BE NEEDED FOR PROGRAM
          SUCCESS.

In Jerry's case, our program requires that Jerry be able to make choices from among various activities. Making choices is a skill that needs to be directly taught and should be incorporated into a variety of activities throughout the day. Wuerch and Voeltz (1982) offer specific strategies for teaching children to make choices.

In order for the reinforcement to be effective, Jerry needs to learn how to make choices from the activities presented to him. Since he does not have this skill, he will need a program to teach the skill.

TABLE 4.2.   Changes to IEP following ecological/curricular component

Prioritized annual goals and short-term objectives[a]

Annual goal. no. 1:   Increase communication skills

Short-term objective(s):

1. Jerry will increase his signing repertoire from the present level of 20 signs to 30 signs.
2. Jerry will respond to questions with a three-word sentence 75% of the time.
3. Jerry will increase vocalization 50% over baseline rates by: (a) verbalizing initial sound of words in signing repertoire, and (b) vocalizing while signing words in signing repertoire.
4. Given a naturally occurring stimulus, Jerry will indicate needs and wants without prompting by signing a two-word sentence.
5. Following an attempt to bite his thumbs, Jerry will sign "Help me" 100% of the time.

Annual goal no. 4:   Increase adaptive/social skills

Short-term objective(s):

1. Jerry will increase duration of independent interaction with materials: (a) from 3 minutes to 10 minutes with preferred items, (b) from 30 seconds to 5 minutes with nonpreferred items.
2. Jerry will appropriately greet/say good-bye to visitors, teachers, and peers without a verbal cue from the instructor 80% of the time.
3. Given a naturally occurring free time situation, Jerry will appropriately manipulate materials for lego, music stick, and electronic beanbag for three out of four sessions attempted.
4. When presented with two or more activities and a verbal cue, Jerry will select an activity to work on or play with by pointing to/signing his preference.

[a]All other goals and objectives would remain as listed in Table 4.1; for subsequent modifications to the IEP based upon additional decisions, see also Tables 4.3 and 4.4.

STEP 7.   IN THE SPACE PROVIDED, WRITE THE NEW CURRICULUM OBJECTIVE; THEN, INCORPORATE OBJECTIVE INTO IEP.

Here we list objectives as they would appear in the child's IEP.

For this program, we will add two objectives to Jerry's IEP, one for signing "Help me" and one for making choices. Table 4.2 depicts Jerry's revised IEP.

Following an attempt to bite his thumbs, Jerry will sign "Help me" (Goal #1, Objective #5). When presented with two or more activities and the verbal cue "Jerry, which do you want to do?", Jerry will select an activity by pointing or signing 80% of the time (Goal #4, Objective #4).

NEXT,

The trainers begin instruction
according to the program outlined in
STEPS 1–6 of the Ecological/
Curricular Component.

> Teach skills
> and prevent excess.

THEN,

Once the skill has been mastered,
trainers begin to fade the prevention
procedure.

> After skill mastery,
> fade prevention.

IN THE SPACE PROVIDED, INDICATE THE PROCEDURE FOR FADING THE PREVENTION COMPONENT.

Level	Procedure
1.	*As child begins hand-to-head motion, trainer places hands firmly on child's forearms and delivers skill cue.*
2.	*As child begins hand-to-head motion, trainer touches child's forearms and delivers skill cue.*
3.	*As child begins hand-to-head motion, trainer delivers skill cue, waits: a) 2 seconds, b) 4 seconds, c) 6 seconds, d) 8 seconds, e) 10 seconds, then touches child's arms.*
4.	*As child begins hand-to-head motion, trainer delivers skill cue.*

In Jerry's case, we would fade the
prevention on a graduated pressure
basis. Then we would substitute the
skill cue for the prevention.

NOW,

Now that the life/health-threatening
excess behavior is under control, we
can begin to consider whether any of
the other 15 excess behaviors in
Jerry's repertoire should be modified
at Level II.

GO TO
LEVEL II.

See page 90.

Curricular/Negative Consequences Component

The Curricular/Negative Consequences Component is designed for implementation with a behavior that CANNOT BE PREVENTED while teaching an incompatible skill. Within this decision manual, a negative consequence is defined as *any event* that, when presented, reduces the future occurrence of the target response that it previously followed. It need not be limited to stimuli thought to be negative (e.g., a verbal reprimand). It may involve contingent removal of positive reinforcement (response cost), contingent ignoring (extinction), manipulation of reinforcement schedules (DRO, DRI), and so forth. A critical factor in the successful implementation of the Curricular/Negative Consequences Component is that the procedure selected not detract from instructional time. For example, a 15-second activity timeout allows instruction to be ongoing. A 15-minute isolation timeout prevents instruction from continuing. In addition to the brevity of the negative consequences procedure, legal-ethical issues must be addressed. The Curricular/Negative Consequences Component contains questions designed to address these issues. In addition, we discuss the issues involved in the use of nonintrusive intervention procedures in more detail in Chapter 5, paying particular attention to how such strategies may or may not be appropriate for use in educational and community training environments, including the child's home.

CONSIDERATIONS

Table 4.1 depicts the goals and objectives identified for Jerry following needs assessment. Had a nonpreventable, life/health-threatening behavior been identified, we would need to modify the IEP to include the program for skill development while consequating the excess behavior.

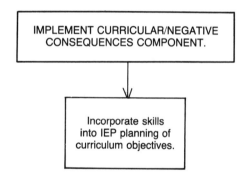

Here we would enter the non-preventable, life/health-threatening behavior. If we had been unable to prevent Jerry's head slapping, we would enter it in the space provided.

STEP 1.   ENTER THE LIFE/HEALTH-THREATENING BEHAVIOR(S) IN THE SPACE PROVIDED.

head slapping

STEP 2.   DESCRIBE IN DETAIL THE SKILL TO
BE TAUGHT AND THE PROCEDURE
TO BE USED.

In STEP 2, we outline the exact
procedure and skill program we wish
to implement. The incompatible skill
selected for training is signing "Help
me."

This cue reflects what occurs in the
natural environment that elicits the
particular response.

Natural cue

*Present in nonreinforcing/punishing
environment*

Verbal cue

This cue reflects the task demand—
the specific instructional cue for the
task the child is to do.

*Following negative consequence, turn
toward child; say "Sign for me to help
you."*

Task description

Here we describe in behavioral terms
exactly what task we expect the child
to do.

*Child holds left hand palm up, 2–3
inches from waist at midline, holds right
hand on top of left, curved as if holding
a cup. Child then abruptly moves both
hands to touch body, then out, then
touching body again to sign "Help me."*

Prompting procedure

Here we describe in detail what the
trainer must do to ensure successful
task performance.

*1) Full physical assist—give firm manual
guidance for both hands; 2) Partial
physical assist—while touching wrists,
guide child's hands in direction of sign;
3) Gesture—model the sign*

STEP 3. IN Part A, DESCRIBE THE EVENTS THAT APPEAR TO MAINTAIN THE EXCESS BEHAVIOR; IN Part B, DESCRIBE THE REINFORCING EVENTS TO BE USED THAT MIGHT SUCCESSFULLY COMPETE WITH THE EVENTS DESCRIBED IN Part A.

The assumption here is that all behavior serves a purpose. In Part A, we attempt to define the purpose. In Part B, we attempt to identify other events (reinforcers) that could serve the same function.

Had we determined that head slapping was being maintained (reinforced) by teacher attention (or any other reinforcing event), we would describe it in detail here. The description should include the contingent event, the duration of the event, the frequency of the event (i.e., schedule of reinforcement), and any other details pertinent to maintaining the target behavior.

Part A *Head slapping results in immediate attention from teacher. Teacher-student contact is negative, involves physical contact (holding hands), and occurs over a prolonged period of time (10–60 minutes), resulting in negative attention approximately once every 9 minutes.*

Our hypothesis is that head slapping is being maintained by teacher attention. In Part B, we attempt to control the quality, duration, and frequency of teacher attention to directly reinforce our incompatible skill, thus rendering the skill "equal power."

Part B *Contingent upon signing "Help me," teacher will offer assistance and then engage in 2 minutes of positive interaction including back/shoulder patting, talking with enthusiasm about how good it is that Jerry was trying hard but that it is ok to take a break, and so on.*

STEP 4. DESCRIBE IN DETAIL THE NEGATIVE CONSEQUENCES PROCEDURE TO BE USED.

Contingent upon student's hands moving toward head, trainer says "No" and immediately leaves the area for 30 seconds.

Here we describe how we intend to decrease the behavior. In this case, there are two components: 1) verbal reprimand, and 2) timeout—withdrawal of a stimulus (teacher) previously associated with reinforcement (attention). The inclusion of the paired verbal component allows us to later fade the more intrusive timeout negative consequences procedure.

Critical to the use of any negative consequence is compliance with the ethical, legal, and professional standards that serve to protect the rights of the handicapped child. Any negative consequences procedure used must conform to these standards.

STEP 5.   FOR THE NEGATIVE CONSEQUENCES TECHNIQUE IN STEP 4, ANSWER THE FOLLOWING QUESTIONS:

Since the technique does not involve any physical contact, we answer "Yes."

Question 1:   Does the technique avoid the use of physical pain?   YES   NO

Since our timeout period is brief and it has been determined that attention reinforces head slapping, a third party would probably view it as humane. Thus, we answer, "Yes."

Question 2:   Would a "third party" consider the technique humane?   YES   NO

It is critical that any procedure selected conform to state regulations regarding the use of punishment in the schools. Since our timeout procedure does conform, we answer "Yes."

Question 3:   Is the technique one that can be legally used within the community?   YES   NO

Consent regulations of the state and local educational agency should be consulted. In addition, Figure 4.1 presents an adaptation of the levels of consent suggested by Heads (1978). Our procedure requires permission from parents, which we have obtained. Thus we answer "Yes."

Question 4:   Have the proper consent forms been obtained from parents/guardians?   YES   NO

Our procedure requires 30 seconds per incident. At the maximum, it would require 20 minutes per day. In addition, it is directly tied to the instructional program. Thus, we answer "Yes."

Question 5:   Is the technique sufficiently brief to be implemented without interfering with programming?   YES   NO

A "NO" ANSWER TO *ANY* OF THESE QUESTIONS REQUIRES THE SELECTION OF AN ALTERNATIVE NEGATIVE CONSEQUENCES TECHNIQUE.

IF ALL OF THESE QUESTIONS RECEIVED A "YES" ANSWER, THEN BEGIN STEP 6.

FIGURE 4.1.

Behavioral Techniques Consent and Review Procedures: Checklist

Child's name _____ Teacher's name _____

School setting _____ Date begun _____ Review date _____

Directions: *For each of the intervention techniques listed below under each group, check those that are in use for this child. For Groups B through D, an individual procedure entry is required for each technique, with a copy of the intervention program attached.*

	Technique[a]	Check if used	Consent and review procedure followed
GROUP A	Positive reinforcement Social disapproval Token economy (positive S^R only) Timeout I (within view) Extinction of non-health-threatening behaviors Graduated guidance Redirection Response cost I (removal of toy, etc.) Modeling		
GROUP B	Timeout II (removed from view or room) Response cost II (restriction from activity) Overcorrection Restitution Positive practice Token economy (with response cost)		
GROUP C	Required relaxation Response cost III (removal of food tray) Timeout III (timeout room)		
GROUP D	Contingent use of physical restraint Extinction of health-threatening behavior Application of noxious behavior Satiation Contingent physically intrusive stimuli		

[a]For Group A, consent may be obtained through standard consent forms at school entry. For Groups B through D, approval of client, parent or guardian, and agency's human rights committee is required. Heads includes a last group of intrusive and highly aversive procedures (e.g., slapping, shock, food deprivation, contingent extremely cold room temperatures) that require approval of an agency administrator, a behavior analysis expert consultant, state agency director, and the state human rights committee. As these are generally illegal and clearly inappropriate for use in habilitative programs with children, we have not included them in the checklist.

STEP 6. DESCRIBE ANY CHANGES NOT INCLUDED IN STEPS 1–5 THAT WOULD BE NEEDED FOR PROGRAM SUCCESS.

Here we would include changes in staffing, resources, environment, materials, and so on, that would ensure program success. In the case we have outlined, no additional changes would be needed.

none

STEP 7. IN THE SPACE PROVIDED, WRITE THE NEW CURRICULUM OBJECTIVE; THEN, INCORPORATE OBJECTIVE INTO IEP.

Here we list the objectives as they would appear in the child's IEP.

For this program, we will add two objectives, reflecting a gradual movement toward a natural environmental cue. Table 4.3 depicts the revised IEP.

Following a head slapping incident and timeout, Jerry will sign "Help me."

Following an attempt to bite his thumbs and the verbal cue "Sign for me to help you," Jerry will sign "Help me."

TABLE 4.3. Changes to IEP following curricular/negative consequences component

Prioritized annual goals and short-term objectives[a]

Annual goal no. 1: Increase communication skills

Short-term objective(s):
1. Jerry will increase his signing repertoire from the present level of 20 signs to 30 signs.
2. Jerry will respond to questions with a three-word sentence 75% of the time.
3. Jerry will increase vocalization 50% over baseline rates by: (a) verbalizing initial sound of words in signing repertoire, and (b) vocalizing while signing words in signing repertoire.
4. Given a naturally occurring stimulus, Jerry will indicate needs and wants without prompting by signing a two-word sentence.
5. Jerry will sign "Help me" when prompted by the teacher following an attempt to bite his thumbs and following timeout for a head-slapping incident.

[a]All other goals and objectives would remain as listed in Table 4.1; for subsequent modifications to the IEP based upon additional decisions, see also Table 4.4.

NEXT,

The trainers begin instruction according to the program outlined in STEPS 1–6 of the Curricular/Negative Consequences Component.

> Teach skills and consequate excess.

THEN,

Once the skill has been mastered, trainers begin to fade the negative consequences procedure.

> After skill mastery, fade negative consequences.

IN THE SPACE PROVIDED, INDICATE THE PROCEDURE FOR FADING THE NEGATIVE CONSEQUENCES COMPONENT.

Level	Procedure
1.	*Verbal ''No'' followed by 30-second timeout. Then, deliver skill cue.*
2.	*Verbal ''No'' followed by timeout (decreased by 5-second intervals to 15 seconds). Then, deliver skill cue.*
3.	*Verbal ''No'' followed by timeout (decreased by 5-second intervals to 5 seconds). Then, deliver skill cue.*
4.	*Verbal ''No'' followed by skill cue.*
5.	*On hand-to-head movement, skill cue is given.*

In the case outlined, timeout could be gradually reduced from 30 seconds to 5 seconds. Then we could begin to rely on the verbal aspect and finally fade to the skill cue alone.

NOW,

With the life/health-threatening excess behavior under control, we can proceed to Level II to consider the remaining excess behaviors.

GO TO LEVEL II.

See page 90.

LEVEL II: SERIOUS BEHAVIORS REQUIRING FORMAL CONSIDERATION

Once we have completed the decision process for the life/health-threatening behaviors, we can turn our attention to the remaining excess behaviors in a child's repertoire. On Level II, decisions are made for serious behaviors that do not threaten the life or health of the child. These high, but not urgent, priority concerns are delineated by the immediate and direct consequences of the excess behavior.

CONSIDERATIONS

At this point, we refer to STEP 6 of the assessment section (p. 69) to find those behaviors not considered on Level I.

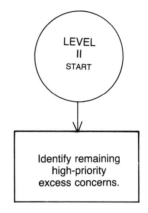

LIST ALL EXCESS BEHAVIORS NOT CON-
SIDERED ON LEVEL I.

Through the discrepancy analysis, we determined that Jerry has 16 behaviors that interfere with his performance of various skills. One behavior, head slapping, we considered on Level I. We list the remaining 15 behaviors here.

bites self	*pokes ears*	*cries*
screams	*kicks*	*mouths thumbs*
flaps hands	*hits others*	*bites others*
smells objects	*throws objects*	*flicks objects*
		pulls/twists
rubs objects	*pounds objects*	*clothing*

Of concern here is whether the behavior actually prevents the child from acquiring the skills needed to do the activity. For example, the child's attention may be absorbed by the excess behavior so that she or he does not discriminate any learning stimuli.

THEN, FOR EACH EXCESS BEHAVIOR LISTED, ASK:

IF THE ANSWER IS "YES, THE EXCESS DOES INTERFERE WITH LEARNING," THEN ENTER THE BEHAVIOR UNDER STEP 1 OF THE COST-BENEFIT ANALYSIS ON PAGE 94.

Suppose we believe that, although many of Jerry's behaviors make it difficult to teach an activity, no single behavior actually interferes with learning. However, when crying, screaming, and kicking (tantrum behaviors) occur in combination, they prevent Jerry from doing his work and may interfere with learning. Thus, we answer "yes" for the tantrum behaviors and enter *cries, screams,* and *kicks* on p. 94. For the remaining behaviors, we go on to the next question.

IF THE ANSWER IS "NO, THE EXCESS DOES NOT INTERFERE WITH LEARNING," THEN ASK:

This question considers potential changes in frequency, intensity, duration, or topography of the excess behavior. Our concern is whether the excess may pose a major threat to the child's life or health in the future.

IF THE ANSWER IS "YES, THE EXCESS IS LIKELY TO BECOME SERIOUS," THEN ENTER THE BEHAVIOR UNDER STEP 1 OF THE COST-BENEFIT ANALYSIS ON PAGE 94.

We are concerned that Jerry's self-biting may become more serious. His thumbs show some callousing and his parents reported that he recently drew blood during a biting episode. Thus, we answer "yes" and enter *bites self* on p. 94. None of the other behaviors seem to be getting worse, so we go on to the next question.

This question considers whether the child's behavior is likely to result in physical harm to others in the child's environment. The target behavior should be analyzed in terms of its direct effect on others (throwing objects versus throwing objects at people) and its intensity (tapping with palm of hand versus hitting with palm of hand).

IF THE ANSWER IS "NO, THE EXCESS IS NOT LIKELY TO BECOME SERIOUS," THEN ASK:

IF THE ANSWER IS "YES, THE EXCESS IS DANGEROUS TO OTHERS," THEN ENTER THE BEHAVIOR UNDER STEP 1 OF THE COST-BENEFIT ANALYSIS ON PAGE 94.

Jerry hits other children hard enough to cause bruising and bites hard enough to break the skin. Thus, we answer "yes" and enter *hits others* and *bites others* on p. 94. Jerry does not throw objects at people and no other behavior is particularly dangerous, so we go on to the next question.

Of concern here are the parents' emotional distress over the behavior, whether the parents will limit the child's environment exposure in order to preclude the child's displaying the excess behavior in public, and so on. Regardless of success in modifying behavior, these concerns indicate that the parents are probably in need of additional support and reassurance.

IF THE ANSWER IS "NO, THE EXCESS IS NOT DANGEROUS," THEN ASK:

IF THE ANSWER IS "YES, THE EXCESS IS OF GREAT CONCERN TO CAREGIVERS," THEN ENTER THE BEHAVIOR UNDER STEP 1 OF THE COST-BENEFIT ANALYSIS ON PAGE 94.

Jerry's parents have indicated that they want to stop taking him to stores and beaches because of his tantrumming (crying, screaming, kicking), which has already been entered for consideration in the cost-benefit analysis. They have not indicated distress over any of the remaining behaviors.

Behaviors that receive "no" as an answer to all of the questions on Level II are monitored but not identified for intervention at this point. Such behaviors will receive consideration on Level III.

IF THE ANSWER IS "NO, THE EXCESS IS NOT OF GREAT CONCERN TO CAREGIVERS," THEN GO TO SKILL TRAINING PROGRAM ON PAGE 98.

IF THE ANSWER TO ANY OF THE PREVIOUS QUESTIONS WAS "YES," THEN CONDUCT A COST-BENEFIT ANALYSIS FOR THAT EXCESS BEHAVIOR.

* * *Note* * *

As we discussed in Chapter 1, the *cost-benefit analysis* for Level II examines the impact that decreasing an excess behavior may have on the child's skills and other excess behaviors. Several of Jerry's behaviors seem to be interrelated. First, behaviors seem to form sequences where one response tends to elicit another: the sequence of behaviors leading to a full-scale temper tantrum in Jerry has already been described. Perhaps by modifying an early response in the chain, it might be possible to also reduce a later behavior that is more serious. Second, some of Jerry's behaviors seem to co-vary—they form a cluster of behaviors. This may be because they are actually related to one another, or it may be because each of these behaviors has similar functional relationships with the environment. Finally, some behaviors may appear to co-vary simply because of some general causal factor: for example, a general incident may affect a child's mood so that on a certain day (sometimes called a "bad day"), an entire cluster of negative behaviors occurs together—hitting others, crying, tantrumming, and so on. Unfortunately, we do not yet know how behaviors do co-vary except in accordance with the general principles just outlined. But by careful observation and by recognizing that such clusters may exist, teachers can hypothesize what such response relationships might be for individual children. They may be able to list behaviors that seem to occur just before an extremely negative behavior, and intuitively use these signs to interrupt extremely negative chains before the more serious behavior has a chance to take place. By making best possible estimates of potential and probable collateral effects as outlined in the next section, we believe that better decisions can be made regarding what target behaviors to select and which potential problems might need to be monitored.

* * * * * * * *

COST-BENEFIT ANALYSIS:

An estimation of costs and benefits of changing behavior needs to be done for all six behaviors identified as serious concerns on Level II.

> Estimate costs and benefits of behavior change.

STEP 1. IN COLUMN A, LIST THE EXCESS BEHAVIORS THAT RECEIVED A "YES" ANSWER TO ANY OF THE FIRST FOUR QUESTIONS OF LEVEL II:

Behaviors A	Positive effects B	Negative effects C
cries		thumb biting↑, head slapping↑
screams		thumb biting↑, head slapping↑
kicks		hitting↑, head slapping↑, thumb biting↑
bites thumbs	head slapping↓	relaxing (thumb sucking)↓
hits others	social skills↑, parallel play↑	smiling↓, vocalizing↓, kicking↑
bites others	social skills↑, parallel play↑	smiling↓, vocalizing↓, kicking↑

Here we list Jerry's six excess behaviors, which we have previously identified for Level II, in Column A. (Columns B and C will be explained and filled in at later steps.)

Here we are concerned with behaviors that occur in sequence, or within the same time frame, or as a general mood indicator, and so on.

STEP 2. FOR EACH BEHAVIOR LISTED IN STEP 1, ARE THERE ANY OTHER BEHAVIORS OR SKILLS THAT OCCUR WITH IT? IF "YES," THEN DESCRIBE THE BEHAVIORS THAT GO TOGETHER. THESE BEHAVIORS MAY INCLUDE OTHER EXCESSES OR POSITIVE SKILLS AND NEED NOT BE LIMITED TO THOSE LISTED IN STEP 1.

Jerry hits or bites other children in the context of a social situation (parallel play), but positive behaviors such as smiling and vocalizing also occur during this time.

Group 1—hitting and biting others occurs with smiling, vocalizing, and parallel play.

Jerry has two types of tantrums. In the mild tantrum, crying accompanies screaming and kicking and is followed by thumb sucking and calming himself.

Group 2—crying occurs with screaming and kicking and is followed by mouthing thumbs and relaxing.

In the severe tantrum, crying is accompanied by screaming, kicking, and thumb sucking followed by thumb biting and then head slapping.

Group 3—crying occurs with screaming, kicking, and mouthing thumbs, followed by thumb biting and head slapping.

STEP 3. FOR EACH EXCESS BEHAVIOR LISTED IN STEP 1, ASK:

Question 1: Would a decrease in this behavior result in a significant decrease in another excess behavior? If yes, then enter the excess that would decrease in Column B of Step 1. Include an arrow to indicate direction of change.

Observations suggest that Jerry almost always bites his thumbs before slapping his head. It is possible that a decrease in thumb biting would result in a decrease in head slapping. We answer "yes" and enter *head slapping* under Column B for bites thumbs.

Question 2: Would a decrease in this behavior result in a significant increase in a positive behavior/skill? If yes, then enter the behavior/skill that would increase in Column B of STEP 1. Include an arrow to indicate direction of change.

We do not anticipate any direct increase in positive behaviors/skills as a result of decreases in any of the listed behaviors. We do expect an indirect increase in parallel play resulting from decreases in aggressive hitting and biting. We answer "yes" and enter *parallel play* under Column B for hits others and bites others.

If hitting and biting others during free play were to decrease, it is possible that kicking would replace them. We answer "yes" and enter *kicking* under Column C for hits others and for bites others. A decrease in the kicking portion of Jerry's tantrum behavior might result in an alternative such as hitting. We answer "yes" and enter *hitting* under Column C for kicks others.

Since biting and hitting others occur within a social context, it is possible that decreases in smiling and vocalizing may accompany decreases in aggressive biting and hitting. We answer "yes" and enter *smiling* and *vocalizing* under Column C for hits others and for bites others. When Jerry mouths his thumbs, the action appears to relax him. Decreases in thumb biting may result in decreases in his ability to relax himself. We answer "yes" and enter *relaxing (thumb sucking)* under Column C for bites thumbs.

For aggressive hitting and biting, a cooperative play program may result in increases in social skills. We answer "yes," and enter *social skills* under Column B for hits others and for bites others.

For tantrums (cries, screams, kicks), a timeout program may result in increases in biting thumbs and head slapping. We answer "yes," and enter *thumb biting* and *head slapping* under Column C for kicks, screams, and cries.

For thumb biting, response interruption plus signing "help me" may result in a decrease in self-calming (thumb sucking). We answer "yes" and enter *relaxing (thumb sucking)* under Column C for bites thumbs.

Question 3: Would a decrease in this behavior result in an unacceptable increase in another excess behavior? If yes, then enter the excess that would increase in Column C of STEP 1. Include an arrow to indicate direction of change.

Question 4: Would a decrease in this behavior result in an unacceptable decrease in a positive behavior/skill? If yes, then enter the behavior/skill that would decrease in Column C of STEP 1. Include an arrow to indicate direction of change.

Question 5: Would the intervention I plan to use have any effect on the child's behavior other than changing this behavior? If yes, list positive effects in Column B and negative effects in Column C of STEP 1. Include an arrow to indicate direction of change.

NOW ASK:

For each behavior listed in STEP 1, we compare the positive and negative side effects. We are then in a position to predict whether or not the total impact resulting from a change in one behavior would be acceptable.

IF THE ANSWER IS "YES, THE COSTS OUT-WEIGH THE BENEFITS," THEN

For aggressive hitting and biting, we feel that the benefits outweigh the costs, provided that the social skills issue is resolved. For biting thumbs, the benefits are higher provided that the self-relaxation (thumb sucking) issue is resolved. Hitting others, biting others, and biting thumbs all receive a qualified "no" and will be considered in the next question. The possibility of increased thumb biting and head slapping as a result of decreases in kicking, screaming, and crying is not acceptable. We answer "yes" for the mild tantrum behavior. We will accommodate these excess behaviors and provide Jerry's parents with consultation to help them deal with his tantrumming in public. In Chapter 5, we propose several ecological modifications that the parents might use.

See page 101.

IF THE ANSWER IS "NO, THE COSTS DO NOT OUTWEIGH THE BENEFITS," THEN ASK:

When considering prevention as a solution, we must determine what would actually be required to prevent the response from occurring and whether the environment could be effectively rearranged to allow prevention to occur consistently.

IF THE ANSWER IS "YES, THE EXCESS CAN BE PREVENTED," THEN

Jerry's thumb biting is a preventable response. A highly desirable benefit of eliminating thumb biting is the potential decrease in head slapping, but mouthing thumbs (relaxing) may also decrease. We will prevent biting by interrupting the hand-to-mouth motion and having Jerry sign what he wants. We will also add a procedure that allows Jerry a way to relax himself as an alternative to thumb sucking. Since Jerry likes music, we will teach him how to calm himself by listening to cassette music with headphones.

> Design skill training program and monitor excess behavior(s).

NEXT,

We will add a target objective for the music program to the IEP and make the necessary changes to the signing program (see Table 4.4).

> Incorporate skill(s) into IEP.

TABLE 4.4.   Changes to IEP following Level II decisions

Prioritized annual goals and short-term objectives[a]

Annual goal no. 1:   Increase communication skills

Short-term objective(s):

5.   Jerry will sign "Help me" when prompted by the teacher: (a) following an attempt to bite his thumbs, (b) following timeout for a head slapping incident, and (c) following crying/screaming and prior to putting his thumbs in his mouth.

Annual goal no. 4:   Increase adaptive/social skills

Short-term objective(s):

5.   Given the verbal cue "Jerry, listen to your music," Jerry will go to the music area, put on the headphones, and turn on the cassette player until the teacher says, "Music time is over, Jerry." (approximately 5 minutes)

6.   During recess and prior to school, Jerry will engage in cooperative play by: (a) asking peer to play, (b) sharing game with peer, and (c) taking turns on playground equipment with peer.

[a]All other goals and objectives would remain as listed in Tables 4.1 and 4.2.

NOW,

If there were no other behaviors to
consider on Level II, we would then
proceed to Level III.

GO TO
LEVEL III.

See page 101.

IF THE ANSWER IS "NO, THE EXCESS CANNOT
BE PREVENTED WHILE TEACHING IEP OBJEC-
TIVES," THEN ASK:

Aggressive hitting and biting are not
easily prevented since they only occur
during free time where adult supervision is limited. Also, the antecedent
events are the naturally occurring
behaviors of peers, and these cannot
be directed the way we can program
changes in caregiver behavior. In
selecting an incompatible skill, our
cost-benefit concern for potential
decreases in smiling and vocalizing
must be taken into consideration.
Other considerations for selecting an
equal power incompatible skill are
discussed on page 64.

Can
I iden-
tify an "equal
power" incompat-
ible skill
?

IF THE ANSWER IS "YES, AN 'EQUAL POWER'
INCOMPATIBLE SKILL CAN BE IDENTIFIED,"
THEN

We determine that teaching cooperative play skills would be incompatible with hitting and biting others
and would offset our cost-benefit
concern for decreases in social skills.
We add the cooperative play program
to the IEP. (See Table 4.4.)

Incorporate
skill(s) into
IEP.

NOW,

Since we have resolved all issues
regarding Jerry's six behaviors chosen
for consideration on Level II, we
proceed to Level III to consider the
remaining nine behaviors.

GO TO
LEVEL III.

See page 101.

DRO and negative consequences are discussed on page 74.

If we had been unable to identify an incompatible skill for Jerry, our next option would have been the use of DRO, then DRO plus negative consequences. For example, had we chosen to intervene with Jerry's screaming, we would have concluded that screaming is not preventable and silence as an incompatible skill is not a reasonable option. We would then have attempted to implement DRO or DRO plus negative consequences.

If it were not possible to eliminate the excess through DRO ± negative consequences, we would review the entire decision process at Level II. (See p. 74 for considerations.) If the reevaluation does not produce satisfactory results, outside consultation might be considered. (See p. 74 for considerations.)

Had we chosen to intervene with screaming, we would implement a DRO (reinforcement for not screaming) or a DRO plus negative consequences (reinforcement for not screaming, contingent activity timeout for screaming) procedure and monitor the behavior. The IEP would remain as is; it would not be modified to include the program. Prior to implementing a program that includes a negative consequence, questions regarding the particular technique to be used must be answered. (See p. 86.)

We would then proceed to Level III to consider the remaining behaviors.

IF THE ANSWER IS "NO, AN 'EQUAL POWER' INCOMPATIBLE SKILL CANNOT BE IDENTIFIED," THEN ASK:

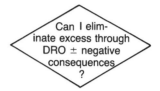

IF THE ANSWER IS "NO, THE EXCESS CANNOT BE ELIMINATED THROUGH DRO ± NEGATIVE CONSEQUENCES," THEN

See page 101.

IF THE ANSWER IS "YES, THE EXCESS CAN BE ELIMINATED THROUGH DRO ± NEGATIVE CONSEQUENCES," THEN

Implement procedure and monitor excess.

(Answer negative consequences questions on p. 86.)

NOW,

See page 101.

LEVEL III: BEHAVIORS REFLECTING "NORMAL DEVIANCE"

Having completed the decision process for those behaviors that are of major concern (i.e., life/health-threatening or otherwise serious), we now must decide whether any of the remaining excess behaviors warrant consideration for intervention. At Level III, we examine behaviors with negative effects that tend to reside more in the child's social environment and that do not directly threaten others or interfere with learning. Even though they may be considered "deviant," behaviors at Level III do not necessarily interfere with a child's ability to function in the environment.

A Level III decision to change a behavior takes into consideration the behavior itself, the effect of the behavior on the environment, the function the behavior serves, and the amount of effort required to change the behavior. Level III decisions—unlike behaviors dealt with on Levels I and II—may be affected by considerations relating to staff and program resources. Thus, the cost-benefit analysis at Level III relates more to the costs to the program (e.g., staff time, resources, etc.) in order to change the behavior in comparison to the costs of not changing the behavior and simply continuing to monitor its occurrence.

CONSIDERATIONS

At this point, we refer to STEP 6 of the assessment section (p. 69) to find those behaviors not considered on Level I and II.

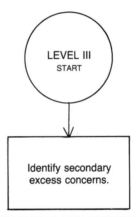

LIST ALL BEHAVIORS THAT WERE IDENTIFIED IN STEP 1 OF THE ASSESSMENT SECTION THAT HAVE NOT BEEN CONSIDERED ON LEVELS I AND II.

Through the discrepancy analysis, we determined that Jerry has 16 behaviors that interfere with his performance of various skills. One behavior—head slapping—was dealt with on Level I. Six behaviors—hitting others, biting others, biting thumbs, crying, screaming, and kicking—were dealt with on Level II. The remaining nine behaviors are listed here.

smells objects	*throws objects*	*flicks objects*
rubs objects	*pounds objects*	*mouths objects*
		pulls/twists
flaps hands	*pokes ears*	*clothing*

FOR EACH BEHAVIOR LISTED, ASK:

In order to answer this question, we must carefully analyze the data for as long a period of time as possible because many excess behaviors undergo short-term variability.

Is excess not improving or getting worse ?

IF THE ANSWER IS "YES, THE EXCESS IS NOT IMPROVING OR IS GETTING WORSE," THEN ENTER THE BEHAVIOR UNDER STEP 1 OF THE COST-BENEFIT ANALYSIS ON PAGE 106.

After consulting Jerry's records from last year, we discovered that pulling/twisting clothing is a new behavior that has been gradually increasing. Thus, we answer "yes" and enter *pulls/twists clothes* on page 106.

IF THE ANSWER IS "NO, THE EXCESS IS IMPROVING OR GETTING BETTER," THEN ASK:

At issue here is how long the excess behavior has been of concern to us or to the child's parents. Check with the parents and the child's records to determine whether it was considered a problem in the past. The mere presence of a behavior for long periods of time does not necessarily make it a concern. It must be seen as a problem to teachers and/or the child's parents.

Has excess been a problem for some time ?

IF THE ANSWER IS "YES, THE EXCESS HAS BEEN A PROBLEM FOR SOME TIME," THEN ENTER THE BEHAVIOR UNDER STEP 1 OF THE COST-BENEFIT ANALYSIS ON PAGE 106.

Although Jerry has displayed most of his excess behaviors throughout his life, we would consider only ear poking a real problem. Ancillary personnel, classroom staff, and his records from last year have all indicated that his ear poking concerns them. Thus we answer "yes," and enter *pokes ears* on page 106.

IF THE ANSWER IS "NO, THE EXCESS HAS NOT
BEEN A PROBLEM OVER TIME," THEN ASK:

This question is concerned with
irreversible damage to the materials
with which a child comes into
contact. It should not be confused
with damage resulting from normal
wear and tear or single-incident
accidents.

IF THE ANSWER IS "YES, THE EXCESS DOES
DAMAGE MATERIALS," THEN ENTER THE
BEHAVIOR UNDER STEP 1 OF THE COST-
BENEFIT ANALYSIS ON PAGE 106.

No behavior has resulted in irreversible damage to materials.
Although Jerry throws objects, no
glass is used in the classroom, so no
breakage has occurred. His parents
have reported that Jerry does not
throw glass objects at home. We
conclude no behavior is particularly
damaging to the environment.

IF THE ANSWER IS "NO, THE EXCESS DOES
NOT DAMAGE THE MATERIALS," THEN ASK:

This question considers only those
behaviors in which the child engages
regardless of environments. Behaviors
that occur only during instructional
time or in private are not of concern.
One issue is whether or not the child
is being or might be excluded from
public activities because of the excess
behavior. The behavior of store and
restaurant employees, summer play
program managers, game arcade
workers and the people who frequent
these places will provide us with a
measure of "deviance" for the child.

IF THE ANSWER IS "YES, THE EXCESS DOES INTERFERE WITH COMMUNITY ACCEPTANCE, THEN ENTER THE BEHAVIOR UNDER STEP 1 OF THE COST-BENEFIT ANALYSIS ON PAGE 106.

Jerry's throwing behavior has created some problems with the cafeteria staff at school. His parents have reported that he throws items from the shelf in stores and throws food and utensils in restaurants. This has created some problems with the managers of the establishments. Thus, we answer "yes" and enter *throws objects* on page 106.

IF THE ANSWER IS "NO, THE EXCESS DOES NOT INTERFERE WITH COMMUNITY ACCEPT-ANCE," THEN ASK:

It is important to consider the effect of changing this excess behavior on other behaviors in the child's repertoire. Would the child engage in more appropriate activities if the excess were eliminated? Does the excess behavior trigger another excess behavior? When answering these questions, we must be specific and identify the direct effects.

IF THE ANSWER IS "YES, OTHER BEHAVIOR WOULD IMPROVE IF THIS EXCESS IM-PROVED," THEN ENTER THE BEHAVIOR UNDER STEP 1 OF THE COST-BENEFIT ANALY-SIS ON PAGE 106.

We believe that Jerry's ability to complete fine motor tasks would probably improve if he did not spend as much time as he now does flicking and rubbing objects with which he is working. Since he always flicks an object before he throws it, throwing might even decrease. Thus, we answer "yes" and enter *flicks objects* and *rubs objects* on page 106.

IF THE ANSWER IS "NO, AN IMPROVEMENT IN
THIS BEHAVIOR WOULD NOT RESULT IN
IMPROVEMENT IN OTHER BEHAVIORS," THEN

The behaviors that receive a "no"
answer to all of the questions on
Level III are monitored. No changes
in the IEP are made, and no interventions need to be designed for these
behaviors.

In Jerry's case, four behaviors
received a "no" answer: smelling
objects, pounding objects, hand
flapping, and mouthing thumbs.
Although we still monitor these
behaviors, no plans will be made for
changing any of them. However,
should our data show an increase in
any of the behaviors, we will ask the
same questions again. At that time, a
decision to intervene may result.

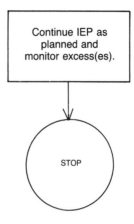

IF THE ANSWER TO ANY OF THE PREVIOUS
QUESTIONS WAS "YES," THEN CONDUCT A
COST-BENEFIT ANALYSIS FOR THAT EXCESS
BEHAVIOR.

** *Note* **

The cost-benefit analysis for Level III examines the seriousness of the behavior, the potential
increases in other equally serious behaviors, and the impact that a decision to change the behavior
would have on the child's educational program. Since the more serious behaviors have already been
dealt with on Levels I and II, Level III behaviors would be considered relatively minor concerns,
and major program changes often will not be appropriate. The Level III cost-benefit analysis is
designed to predict potential outcomes for both the child's repertoire and the child's educational
program and also involves decisions regarding costs in staff time and resource utilization. At Level
II, the behaviors were serious enough that intervention was needed regardless of whether a
substantial amount of time and resources would be required to change the behavior. But at Level
III, since the excess is not so serious, it is appropriate to ask questions such as whether too much
staff time would be used for intervention.

* * * * * * * *

COST-BENEFIT ANALYSIS

STEP 1. IN COLUMN A, LIST THE BEHAVIORS THAT RECEIVED A "YES" ANSWER FOR ANY OF THE FIRST FIVE QUESTIONS OF LEVEL III.

An estimation of costs and benefits of changing behavior needs to be done for all five behaviors identified as secondary concerns on Level III.

Here we list Jerry's five excess behaviors, which we have previously identified for Level III, in Column A. (Columns B, C, and D will be explained and filled in in later steps.)

Behaviors A	Positive effects B	Negative effects C	Program effects D
pulls/twists clothes		*matching↓, biting thumbs↑, tantrums↑, head slapping↑*	*STOP-1*
pokes ears			
throws objects		*tantrums↑, ball throwing↓*	*STOP-3*
rubs objects	*toy use↑, fine motor↑, independence↑*		
flicks objects	*toy use↑, fine motor↑, independence↑, throwing↓*		

STEP 2. FOR EACH BEHAVIOR LISTED IN STEP 1, ARE THERE ANY OTHER BEHAVIORS OR SKILLS THAT OCCUR WITH IT? IF "YES," THEN DESCRIBE THE BEHAVIORS THAT GO TOGETHER. THESE BEHAVIORS MAY INCLUDE OTHER EXCESSES OR POSITIVE SKILLS AND NEED NOT BE LIMITED TO THOSE LISTED IN STEP 1.

For group or clustered behaviors, see considerations on page 95.

Our observations suggest that Jerry will usually throw an object after flicking it during free play periods and small group instruction.

Group 1—flicking objects occurs with throwing objects during free time and small group situations.

Jerry also pulls and twists his clothes when engaged in high-level matching tasks (e.g., matching numbers, coins) during one-to-one instruction.

Group 2—pulling and twisting clothes occurs with matching words and numbers, and so forth, during one-to-one instruction.

STEP 3. FOR EACH BEHAVIOR LISTED IN STEP 1, ASK:

Question 1: Would a decrease in this behavior result in a significant decrease in another excess behavior? If yes, then enter the excess that would decrease in Column B of STEP 1. Include an arrow to indicate direction of change.

Since flicking objects occurs immediately prior to throwing objects, we would expect decreases in flicking objects to result in decreases in object throwing. We answer "yes" and enter *throwing* under Column B for flicks objects.

Question 2: Would a decrease in this behavior result in a significant increase in a positive behavior/skill? If yes, then enter the behavior/skill that would increase in Column B of STEP 1. Include an arrow to indicate direction of change.

By decreasing flicking and rubbing objects, we would anticipate both an improvement in fine motor skills (e.g., use of pencil, crayon, paste, etc.) and independent work habits (finishing task with fewer verbal reminders). We answer "yes" and enter *fine motor* and *independence* under Column B for rubs objects and for flicks objects.

Question 3: Would a decrease in this behavior result in an unacceptable increase in another excess behavior? If yes, then enter the excess that would increase in Column C of STEP 1. Include an arrow to indicate direction of change.

Previous attempts to decrease pulling and twisting clothes have resulted in both mild and severe tantrum behavior. We answer "yes" and enter *biting thumbs, head slapping,* and *tantrums,* in Column C for pulls/twists clothes.

Question 4: Would a decrease in this behavior result in an unacceptable decrease in a positive behavior/skill? If yes, then enter the behavior/skill that would decrease in Column C of STEP 1. Include an arrow to indicate direction of change.

Since pulling and twisting clothes allows Jerry to concentrate on the task, we are concerned that decreases in pulling/twisting clothes might result in decreases in Jerry's higher level matching skills. We answer "yes" and enter *matching* in Column C for pulls/twists clothes. We are not sure if Jerry can discriminate between appropriate throwing objects and inappropriate throwing objects. Decreasing object throwing may also decrease ball play. We answer "yes" and enter *ball throwing* in Column C for throws objects.

For flicking and rubbing objects, a toy training program may result in increase in toy play. We answer "yes" and enter *toy use* in Column B for flicks objects and for rubs objects.

For throwing objects, an overcorrection program may result in resistance to the procedure and tantrumming. We answer "yes" and enter *tantrums* in Column C for throws objects.

For pulling/twisting clothes, a redirection program may result in increases in tantrums, which has already been entered under Column C for pulls/twists clothes.

Question 5: Would the intervention I plan to use have any effect on the child's behavior other than changing this behavior? If yes, list positive effects in Column B and negative effects in Column C of STEP 1. Include an arrow to indicate direction of change.

STEP 4. FOR EACH EXCESS BEHAVIOR LISTED IN STEP 1, ASK:

Pulling/twisting clothes serves a self-mediating function for Jerry. It doesn't appear that he has any similar type skill that he could use in place of pulling/twisting clothing. We answer "no" and enter *STOP* in Column D for pulls/twists clothes.

Question 1: Does the child currently have enough skills to engage in appropriate behavior if I eliminate this excess? If no, enter *STOP* and question number in Column D of STEP 1.

For the remaining four behaviors, there are various intervention options available that have demonstrated success: throwing—overcorrection; flicking—toy play plus reprimand; rubbing—reinforcement on a DRI schedule; ear poking—sensory reinforcement on a DRO schedule.

Question 2: Are there interventions available that have demonstrated success in the elimination of this excess? If no, enter *STOP* and question number in Column D of STEP 1.

The average overcorrection time runs 5–10 minutes. During this period, no skill training can take place. With a frequency of 15–20 incidents per day, overcorrection could take 2 hours of instructional time. We answer "yes" and enter *STOP* in Column D for throws objects.

Question 3: Will the intervention I have selected require me to use an inordinate amount of instructional time? If yes, then enter *STOP* and question number in Column D of STEP 1.

Interventions with the remaining behaviors would not result in postponing a needed skill.

Question 4: Would intervening with the excess result in postponing the teaching of a needed skill? If yes, enter *STOP* and question number in Column D of STEP 1.

None of the interventions would appear painful or inhumane to a third party.

Question 5: Could the intervention be considered physically painful or inhumane by a third party? If yes, enter *STOP* and question number in Column D of STEP 1.

NOW ASK:

To answer this question, we consult the information contained in STEP 1 of the Cost-Benefit Analysis. A *STOP* in Column D indicates that either the issue must be satisfactorily resolved or the behavior must be accommodated. Negative effects (i.e., increases in other excesses or decreases in skills) also indicate a need to accommodate the behavior.

IF THE ANSWER IS "NO, THE CHILD CANNOT CHANGE WITHOUT MAJOR COSTS TO CHILD/ PROGRAM," THEN

In Jerry's case, the cost of intervening with throwing objects and pulling/ twisting clothes outweighs the benefits. We choose to accommodate these behaviors. They will be monitored but no program for intervention will be designed.

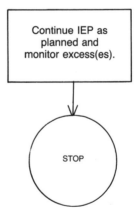

IF THE ANSWER IS "YES, THE CHILD CAN
CHANGE WITHOUT MAJOR COSTS," THEN

For rubbing and flicking objects and ear poking, we will combine them during instructional periods on a gradually extended DRO schedule. Ear phone music will be used as reinforcement for not engaging in the behaviors. We feel that any intervention requiring a more intrusive program could not be justified with respect to instructional time. The DRO interval will be incorporated into Jerry's current fine motor and toy play programs.

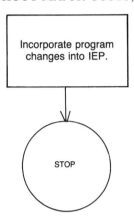

A SUMMARY STATEMENT

All of the decisions or judgments made in this chapter are ones that you have made many times in the past—not necessarily in terms of content (i.e., what to *do),* but in terms of process (what to *think about).* The flow diagram model seems complicated in places only because it formalizes logical steps in decision making that you are already quite accustomed to doing. Anyone working in a real life educational environment knows that the conditions affecting behavior are all interconnected: for example, your choice of sign to teach a student will always be influenced by secondary benefits, so that the sign "I want juice" not only adds to a positive communicative repertoire but also serves to eliminate grabbing and other negative behaviors. You would always, to take another example, think of the costs (instructional time, etc.) of decreasing object flicking when teaching an adolescent a vocational skill versus the benefits (increase in the student's productivity, etc.). All that the decision model does is ensure that these decisions are made in a logical fashion and ensure that one's focus on any particular area of need does not result in the neglect of another concern.

It is important to recognize that a single example, as we have presented here, sets certain limits on the issues that could have been raised and considered. Again, we can only hope that you will focus on the process of judgment and not on the specifics of the solutions suggested. Other children may have very similar behaviors but require quite different strategies; thus, we have argued that *prescriptions* for how to modify excess behavior cannot be derived from the formal experimental literature. Published research studies are a source of hypotheses, not a source of standardized procedures. If your student exhibited one of the behaviors mentioned here but was a severely motorically involved teenager with good receptive language skills, your intervention techniques might be quite indirect, such as teaching a verbal rule or providing an explanation for why the behavior is inappropriate. There are clearly many intervention options.

In the next chapter we have tried to outline some of the major methods of intervention that are appropriate for use in natural environments like school and community settings. We shall provide more examples of how the decision model might be applied to addressing various other intervention needs. As can be seen from the flow diagram, careful decision making might result in our choosing to intervene with some behaviors only informally, that is to say, just modifying some minor aspect of our everyday behavior in order to have an effect on behaviors that are not of critical importance. Other behaviors will have been judged as requiring major changes in the environment, in the curriculum, or in the application of major contingency rules. You might find it beneficial to read over the procedural suggestions of the next chapter before trying to apply the formal model to the unique behaviors that concern you in the students with whom you work.

chapter 5

Integrating Behavioral Interventions in Educational Contexts

In Chapter 3 (and, with the specific example, in Chapter 4), we recommended that whenever a formal intervention to modify an excess behavior was appropriate, one of two "combination" approaches to behavior change should be implemented: (1) an *ecological/ curricular* approach is preferable whenever the teacher is confident that the environment can be rearranged in some way to prevent the occurrence of the behavior while an alternative positive behavior is being taught to the learner; and (2) a *curricular/negative consequences* approach is appropriate for those cases where rearranging the environment does not successfully reduce the behavior. In such cases, occurrences of the excess behavior must be consequated (through an effective but nonintrusive punishment) while, again, an alternative positive behavior is being taught.

In each case, an alternative skill must be taught. This implies a period of time, sometimes lengthy, in which the learner does not yet have the positive alternative in his or her repertoire. Even when it has been mastered under instructional conditions, the new skill may not be reliable or fluent enough to function as an effective alternative for the student. Thus, the clinician must either ecologically prevent the behavior from occurring or, if prevention is not possible, negatively consequate the behavior.

This chapter describes procedures that clinicians can use to implement the intervention decisions they have made. We present specific examples to illustrate the use of ecological, curricular, and negative consequences procedures that are effective and also consistent with the contingencies and ethics of least restrictive educational and community training environments. We also examine several "counterexamples" of more traditional intervention solutions that were developed and applied in institutional and other isolated clinical and laboratory settings. In addition to the ethical issues involved, the way learning principles were translated in these settings has resulted in intervention procedures that are difficult to use in natural educational and community training environments. The nonintrusive alternative strategies recommended here are consistent with the conditions presented by those environments and, based upon our own experiences and recent empirical work in this area, are, therefore, more effective and habilitative in meeting the needs of learners in the community.

INFORMAL TREATMENT PLANS

Throughout the book and particularly in Chapter 4, we have argued that some excess behaviors do not require formal intervention, but that in many of those cases, the behavior may nevertheless be of sufficient concern that the teacher will want to monitor it closely. When a Level II behavior does actually escalate in frequency and intensity to the extent that it outweighs the "costs" associated with intervention (for example, the risk of increasing another excess), the teacher would then want to modify that behavior. Level III behaviors will probably not be as crucial to monitor, but, for example, a parent may begin to express concern over an excess that has previously been dealt with at Level III. For instance, successful community training might result in an increase in joint family activities, such that an excess that the parents had tolerated at home has now become a source of embarrassment or inconvenience in the neighborhood shopping center. In such cases, the teacher may also begin to collect baseline information on these excess behaviors. For all excess behaviors that are not the focus of a formal intervention plan— including those for which potential baseline data are being collected—the teacher does, however, have in effect various "informal" treatment conditions (see Chapter 1). These typically include the overall impact of the systematic instruction of individualized educational objectives as well as basic, positive behavior management strategies. These general management strategies include contingent social reinforcement for work well done and, in many cases, an implicit DRO program in which the teacher would be most likely to distribute verbal praise and preferred activities to students at times when they are not exhibiting excess behavior and are instead engaged in some other particularly appropriate behaviors. The implicit rules influencing the behavior of authority figures (and sometimes of peers) can be defined by three categories as they relate to the target child: (1) response-occurrence contingencies (i.e., how the adult responds when the excess behavior happens), (2) response-nonoccurrence contingencies (i.e., ways of responding when the disruptive

behavior does not occur), and (3) non-contingent social behavior, such as generally increasing positive affect, giving a little more special attention, spending more (or less) time in positive social interactions, and so on.

The DRO schedule, in which reinforcement is delivered contingent upon a predetermined period of nonoccurrence of the excess behavior, is not always effective in applied studies (e.g., Harris & Wolchik, 1979). Rather than thinking of DRO as an intervention technique in and of itself, it is more useful to think of it as a guide to implicit teacher decisions regarding the most appropriate time to reinforce the student. Even if the child had just accomplished some important task, you would be unlikely to deliver reinforcement if the child were engaged in an undesirable behavior at that moment. Social praise, for example, would be provided, for whatever reason, only if the child were *not* actively engaged in the excess behavior at a given moment in time—what Repp, Barton, and Brulle (1983) have called "momentary DRO."

Informal strategies also include systematically ignoring certain types of pupil behavior and delivering mild though negative verbal consequences ("No, don't open the drawer") for other behavior. Such strategies may be generally and informally applied to all excess behavior for which contrary intervention procedures have not been specified, and they may also be extended to those excess behaviors for which more explicit and specific procedures are in place at other times during the day or in addition to the general management strategies. Additionally, it would be fair to conclude that a more serious excess that has been successfully brought under control (e.g., either eliminated altogether or significantly decreased) would then also be effectively maintained at this reduced level by no more extreme intervention procedures than the usual appropriate behavior management practices followed by a good teacher or a consistent parent.

While we are mentioning these everyday methods of praise, reprimand, and verbal direction, it might be worth emphasizing how important it is not to neglect ordinary cognitive techniques of behavior influence. Children learn a good deal of appropriate behavior through verbally expressed rules, which are most effective when parents give reasonable explanations and justifications for the rule. Because severely handicapped children by definition do have limited verbal and cognitive repertoires, we often forget to take the time and effort to articulate the principle behind our efforts at control; sometimes it is simply easier to say "no" or "stop that" than to explain, using whatever symbolic communication system the student has, why a particular behavior is undesirable or inappropriate. In our observations of nonhandicapped peers interacting with severely handicapped children, we have frequently noticed how carefully the peers do explain social rules and conventions; remarks such as "You can't have that now, it's not your turn" help to provide a consistent context for the numerous requirements that society imposes on any student's behavior.

One of the benefits of systematically explaining the justification for some behavior requirement is that it helps the caregiver distinguish between arbitrary rules based on authority ("use a spoon, not your fingers"; "don't run in the hallways") and those that we base on *principles* of concern for self ("brush your teeth after a meal") or others ("don't hit"). Many social rules are based on considerations of age of the child and it is not uncommon for us to tolerate what is clearly age-inappropriate behavior in students who are severely handicapped—for instance, allowing teenagers to interrupt conversations without waiting for an appropriate break. When students are dependent on adult care, we also act toward them in an arbitrary fashion, much as we might control a very young child. We have noticed that we have to remind ourselves not to remove some game or other materials from severely physically involved students, for instance, without first explaining that the activity is over and it is time to move on to some other task.

Students in wheelchairs often get suddenly shunted from one place to another without the simple procedure of explaining where they are being taken and requesting permission to move them. These actions will not only prevent tantrums and other emotional outbursts but also have the potential of decreasing a severely handicapped individual's feelings of helplessness.

In addition to these standard procedures common in natural environments, effective teachers and parents follow a number of implicit ecological principles to prevent excess behavior from arising. Many of these are general arrangements of objects, furniture, and persons, formulated to ensure basic safety. Hence, a teacher of young children would place electrical appliances out of reach and would insist on physical proximity (even holding hands) at street crossings. These informal interventions would be in place for all students, and one might see an exaggeration of the general strategy for an individual student with a particular problem. Thus, a student who typically dashes away unexpectedly would not likely be allowed to cross a street without tight physical and verbal control.

There are wide variations in an individual clinician's management styles. Some teachers and parents may be so highly structured (schedules, level of supervison, and "childproof" arrangements of furniture, objects, and even child-child seating arrangements) that excess behavior appears to be under control. Yet, it is possible to be *too* preventative: pupils may be totally unprepared for the natural stimuli of actual, nonclassroom environments that they will encounter in the community. When this occurs, their excess behavior repertoire changes dramatically whenever the structure is removed. Over time, the result of providing maximum structure and environmental control is actually to restrict the child's ability to ever function acceptably in the real world. At the opposite extreme, other teachers and parents may be so loosely organized and provide such environmental disarray and confusion that it is nearly impossible for students *not* to respond with excess behavior.

These are classic concerns of good teaching and good parenting, of course, and we do not raise them here with the intent of surprising the reader with any new insight on the issues. *But*, it is important to be aware of the expectation that such informal principles of good behavior management should be in place in home and treatment environments as part of the general practices followed by all staff and by caregivers. As we emphasized in Chapter 1, learners should also be experiencing *educative* home, school, and community environments, where there is systematic instruction in functional skills appropriate for and useful to those settings. There is really no justification for imposing isolated *formal* treatment programs to reduce any single excess behavior in the absence of an appropriate educational plan and/or the provision of general environmental conditions, informal as they may seem, which are supportive of positive behavior and learning.

Having discussed these important background principles, we present, in the following sections, the components of each of the major formal intervention approaches, taking the categories of ecological, curricular, and negative consequences one at a time. Before we move into considering these, however, we want to emphasize that our extension of the three categories to particular intervention strategies is somewhat arbitrary. We would expect, for example, that some clinicians might object to including response interruption (i.e., brief physical restraint during instruction, not as a contingent consequence) in the ecological category. Similarly, one could disagree with our including extinction in the negative consequences discussion. We are including these techniques in the categories designated because of the functional implications of the strategy, not because we are in any way arguing for an extension of traditional terminology or differing with standard theoretical assumptions.

ECOLOGICAL STRATEGIES: PREVENTING THE OCCURRENCE OF AN EXCESS

Ecological interventions involve some rearrangement of the conditions under which the excess behavior typically occurs, and can be one of three basic types: (1) the *environmental antecedents* may be modified, including changes in such factors as furniture arrangement, presence of materials, seating vis-à-vis other persons, time schedules, and environmental stimuli such as noise, lighting, and so on; (2) *task-related instructional components* may be changed, including changes in the nature of the task itself (such as making it more functional, more or less difficult, more reinforcing, etc.) and/or the way in which the task is being taught (such as teaching in functional routines and interrelated skill clusters rather than in massed practice trials, changing the performance criteria, etc.); and (3) *response interrruption*—typically a brief physical restraint—may be employed prior to or throughout instructional situations. This latter category should be clearly distinguished from brief physical restraint that is applied as a punishment, that is, implemented contingent upon occurrence of the excess behavior. Response interruption procedures can include the use of a prosthesis, manual restraint, and/or verbal cueing. Each of the three basic types of ecological interventions are covered in more detail and with specific examples.

It is important to realize that different explanations for the occurrence of an excess behavior (see the possibilities presented in Chapter 2) can imply that alternative interventions might be appropriate in varying situations. Consider the examples listed in Table 5.1, which illustrates a process of "generating intervention hypotheses." We have filled in descriptions of five excess behaviors, as well as provided some information regarding the conditions under which each behavior appears to be most problematic. Note that for each of the first three excess behavior descriptions, we have generated three possible explanations (functional analyses, if you will) for the occurrence of the behavior. Each of the explanations demands a different approach to successfully changing the excess behavior. We have listed a "function test" for each explanation (in some cases, involving more than one possible manipulation of the conditions associated with the behavior) that the teacher might use to investigate which condition variable is, in fact, associated with reliable changes in the excess. The teacher can test each of these possible explanations by conducting the function test and observe any changes (or absence of change) in the excess behavior as a result. We have completed the table by generating alternative ecological and curricular intervention strategies that might be employed to produce more permanent positive changes in the excess behavior depending upon the results of the function test. After you have looked over the three examples that we have completed in the table, see if you can complete the table for the last two excess behavior descriptions.

Environmental Antecedents

Ecological modifications that involve environmental antecedents are no doubt quite familiar to most readers. These include placing tempting toys and objects out of reach (see the second excess behavior example in Table 5.1), establishing seating and grouping arrangements so that children who provoke one another will not be in proximity, and so on. Remember to ask yourself whether these modifications are acceptable for a reasonable length of time. For instance, in the fifth example of Table 5.1, the student who grabs food from others could be required to eat far away from the other students; however, that would be quite inappropriate, and forestalls rather than prevents the problems. But if your function test had suggested the child grabs food from one particular student because of the way that student reacted (or did not react!), then moving the target child to another place at the table might be indicated. Another strategy is giving children a chance to rest briefly or quiet down

(for a few seconds or minutes) before and after a stimulating event and before they are expected to attend to a difficult task or one that requires that they listen carefully. We would suggest that by grouping children together on the basis of shared repertoires of multiple behavior problems—as is the case with programs and classrooms for autistic students—we have in fact created a situation with an overload of antecedents likely to generate higher levels of excess behavior. In these settings, all children in the room serve as "poor" models for one another and no "good" models are available.

Manipulating very general antecedents—essentially setting events—can produce significant reductions in excess behaviors without any prior functional analysis of the behaviors. Anne Donnellan (personal communication, February 22, 1984) reports an individual consultation case where a simple manipulation of seating arrangements successfully reduced a child's operant vomiting to a low enough frequency to allow other positive experiences to occur. A functional analysis suggested that the child employed vomiting at the lunch table to obtain teacher attention that was rewarding to the child. In order for the child to realize that this attention would be equally forthcoming from demonstrations of other, appropriate eating behaviors, as well as to reduce the availability of any attention for the vomiting, the first need was to reduce the occurrence of the excess behavior. Donnellan advised the teacher to seat the child in a different position around the table for each meal, and for some unexplained reason, this change in stimulus conditions temporarily interrrupted the vomiting behavior, thus allowing the child to be reinforced for other behaviors. We know of another case where a child's operant vomiting seemed to be similarly maintained by caregiver attention, but the child's *ability* to vomit was obviously facilitated by her manipulation of her milk along with her meal. This child would swallow large gulps of milk (and presumably air) along with her meal, and one could almost see her physiologically preparing herself to

TABLE 5.1

Generating Intervention Hypotheses

Description of excess behavior	Alternative explanations	"Function test"— Will excess decrease if:	Alternative intervention strategies	
			Ecological	Curricular goal/s
After approximately 15 minutes of one-to-one instruction, child tantrums, including crying/screaming, throwing objects, and slipping out of chair onto floor.	1. Child dislikes one-to-one instructional demand situations, a particular teacher, or the task itself.	1.1. Demands are alternated with low-demand interactions. 1.2. Teacher is changed. 1.3. Task is different.	Implement skill cluster instructional formats, vary instructor, and supplement one-to-one with group instruction; instruction on difficult tasks and initial instruction on all tasks occurs after quiet period, followed by preferred activity.	Communication skills needed: "I'm tired"; "Need a break"; "I don't know."
	2. Child tires quickly, loses control after a short period of instructional demands.	2.1. Instructional sessions are shortened, increased gradually to longer periods.		Social skills needed: self-regulation; exit situation; consequate others; cope with negatives.
	3. Task is too difficult, and child cannot cope with stress and errors.	3.1. Task is broken down into smaller steps. 3.2. Another equally important task is taught.		
When walking in the room (or any indoor environment), child "makes the rounds," pushing objects off table surfaces and shelves onto the floor.	1. Child enjoys (is reinforced by) attention from peers and teacher that results from behavior.	1.1 Teacher ignores behavior. 1.2. Teacher says "no." 1.3. Peers are not present in room.	Shelves and table surfaces kept clear wherever possible, child not allowed to walk close to shelves: setting gradually faded to "normal" conditions. Hands may be kept "busy" initially (carrying preferred items, etc.).	Social skills needed: self-regulation (carry things, hands in pockets, etc.).
	2. Child enjoys watching and hearing toys fall onto the floor (i.e., is otherwise bored).	2.1. Floor is carpeted or objects themselves are soft. 2.2. Child busy with novel situation.		Play skills needed: appropriate object-play activity; gross motor activity.
	3. Child needs physical exercise.	3.1. Walking across room occurs *after* recess versus after period of instruction.		

Behavior	Setting events / situations		Interventions		Skills needed
After approximately 10–20 minutes in community training experience, teenager hits a peer and/or begins to yell at others.	1. Teenager cannot tolerate relatively unstructured community setting for more than a few minutes.	1.1. Community experience never exceeds 10–15 minutes duration. 1.2. Supervision and structure is increased.	Transport learner to setting for last 15 minutes of training experience only, gradually increase time, (backward chaining); regroup at site.		Communicate skills needed: "Need a break"; "Stop that." Social skills needed: self-regulation; exit situation; consequate others; cope with negatives.
	2. Peer is making him or her angry.	2.1. Peer is not present, or another peer is present. 2.2. Aversive behavior of peer is identified and changed.			
	3. When peer or others do not respond as she or he wishes, hits and yells to get his or her way.	3.1. Peer taught to respond positively. 3.2. Peer taught to move away.			
Child finger flicks nearly constantly during instruction as well as during free time.	1.	1.1. 1.2.			
	2.	2.1. 2.2.			
	3.	3.1. 3.2.			
Child yells, grabs others' food at lunch.	1.	1.1 1.2.			
	2.	2.1. 2.2.			
	3.	3.1. 3.2.			

vomit. By simply removing the milk and allowing her only small drinks until her meal was finished, she was unable to produce the excess even though her motivation to do so probably remained the same. With the excess temporarily prevented from occurring, it was then possible, as with the first example, to focus the child's attention on the fact that social reinforcement would be equally forthcoming for positive dinnertime behaviors.

Another good example is a study by Bachman and Fuqua (1983) that showed that a brief period of warm-up exercise followed by short distance jogging reduced the frequency of excess behavior in three of the four students. Although the effects were quite modest, these authors point out how much more practical (as well as ethical) it is for a teacher to program periods of PE (physical education) in such a way that the enhanced physical exercise has a beneficial effect on subsequent excess behavior. We would prefer to manipulate the usual PE period rather than schedule a special jogging period, partly because it is important to translate the recommendation into something that is natural and expected in a typical school environment, and partly because there is no real indication of what the causal factor is in such interventions. Was the jogging effective because the child had had an enjoyable experience, or was physically tired, or what? In the absence of such specific knowledge, we are following simple pragmatics—trying something and seeing if it works and continuing it if it does. Under these circumstances, it is especially important that the procedure be natural and clearly beneficial in its own right. Various journal articles have described apparently similar procedures that look very much like forced exercises. Some interpretations of overcorrection, for instance, require the student to run on the spot or do push-ups. These end up being very inappropriate punishment routines associated with a great deal of stress for both teacher and child. If you think of events that are clearly desirable and enjoyable, the setting event change might not be jogging at all (which, as the authors can attest, not all of us enjoy!), but

might be aerobic exercises, dancing, deep relaxation, or any activity worked out with the physical education and recreation instructors.

Task-Related Instructional Components

For children with very limited communication and social skills, excess behaviors may occur in situations where the child is exposed to unreasonable demands and has no other appropriate strategy to modify or escape these aversive events. The tasks they are asked to learn or to do may be too difficult, too easy, or too boring. In the latter situations, such "boring" tasks are very often those tasks that are repetitive and/or result in no apparent critical effects for the child. For example, it is easy to see how a response such as pointing to a red block would quickly lose the interest of an 8-year-old (or a 16-year-old!) child, particularly when this task is practiced over and over, in massed trial format, while requiring the child to remain seated at a table for long periods of time. In developing a model of systematic and structured instruction for handicapped children, we may have lost sight of their biological or physical capacity to learn and to comply while asked to remain physically inactive for long periods of time in high-demand situations. We know that most non-handicapped children will protest sitting and/or complying for extended time periods in uncomfortable situations, so it should not surprise us if a child with multiple and severe handicaps displays an unwillingness if not inability to do so as well. How many programs for non-handicapped children consist of structured one-to-one demand situations as the major instructional method? Highly structured procedures do not even guarantee high levels of social reinforcement. In a 3-year study of teacher-pupil interactions in classrooms serving severely handicapped children ages birth through 8 years of age, the 32 children we observed experienced teacher approval only 18% of the time during one-to-one instruction and 10% of the time during group instruction (Evans & Voeltz, 1982). We are not, of course, suggesting that programs for severely handicapped children should not be data-based, structured, and consistent. But these program characteristics can be achieved in instructional design formats that are appropriate to children's ages and that are facilitative of maintaining their interest and motivation to participate in learning opportunities.

Teachers of severely handicapped children need the opportunity to observe the behaviors (and natural environments) of nonhandicapped peers at each age level. We recall an amusing story that circulated recently among those involved in social integration in Hawaii. An elementary age child with severe handicaps was meticulously prepared by his teacher over a period of months for integration into the school cafeteria for lunch. His skill training program emphasized proper utensil use, staying in his seat, and good table manners. The irony was that when the child was considered ready for the cafeteria, he was so appropriate that he actually appeared out of place at the lunch table in the lunchroom in comparison to the natural behaviors displayed by his nonhandicapped peers. In addition, he was unable to do the many task-related lunchroom skills also needed in that environment but that the teacher—not having used an ecological inventory as the starting point for his program design—had not addressed. These included specifics such as standing in line and busing trays, but also involved negotiating self and materials in an environment that was essentially chaotic! It seems clear that, whatever our wishes and fantasies of rows of eager-to-learn, quiet, compliant, and appropriately behaved children in school settings, regular education has made certain concessions to the realities of characteristics of children.

For children with little or no language and social skills, the only strategy to deal with stressful and boring situations may be to cry, scream, go limp, run away, aggress, self-injure, or engage in whatever other idiosyncratic excess behavior the child has learned to use as an effective way to manipulate others so that a change in the situation is certain to follow. Many ecological modifications will be accu-

rately reflective of a child's capacities to perform a task or tolerate a situation or an environment. Most such modifications also signal a skill-deficit need, such that a more appropriate social/communication strategy must be acquired to allow the child an equally effective positive way to let others know his or her needs in similar future situations. Thus, we recommend that a curricular perspective be combined with an ecological modification to provide for such alternatives. The first and fourth excess behavior examples in Table 5.1 provide examples of possible task-related problems. We have generated alternative explanations, "function tests" for each explanation, and ecological and curricular strategies for the tantrumming example. You might have hypothesized that finger flicking in the fourth example provided sensory input, particularly visual if the child flicked in front of his or her eyes. A test for this hypothesis would be to see whether presenting very visually interesting materials to a child (e.g., a "slinky," a hand-held electronic game, a Sesame Street glove puppet) would hold his or her attention and produce a cessation of the finger flicking. The ecological component would be to use very interesting tasks to reduce finger flicking and the curricular component would be to teach play skills, especially those involving manual manipulation of, or holding onto, objects. Play skills are indicated as an instructional objective, rather than simply any manual skill, because the child finger flicks in *both* instructional and free time settings. This suggests that the flicking is providing general sensory reinforcement (i.e., it is a simple form of "play").

We conducted an experimental investigation of task-related excess behavior by comparing the behavior and task performance of a profoundly retarded 10-year-old boy under two different conditions (Evans & Voeltz, 1982). During a traditional, massed-trial instructional program (one-to-one with a highly qualified special education teacher), this child displayed high levels of object spinning (14% of total time), object dropping (3%), and bolting (4%), and in general his behavior was appropriately on-task only 33% of the time. When his instructional objectives were rewritten into a skill cluster format as illustrated in Figure 5.1, object spinning dropped to 2%, object dropping to nearly zero, and bolting to less than 1% (even though the new instructional situation— with the same teacher—involved some walking around and might therefore have put him into a better position to run away). And, his appropriate on-task behavior jumped to over 64% of the observation intervals.

In this example the child's behavior improved substantially when his teacher restructured the way instruction was delivered. The change ostensibly involved less physical control, depending more upon the natural reinforcements built into the task sequence rather than instructional reinforcers, thus resulting in a significant improvement in his behavior. We have often observed that clinicians are hesitant to involve severely handicapped learners in community-based and nonschool instructional program opportunities if those students exhibit high levels of excess behavior. Instead, such students are exposed to ever-increasing demand situations with more structure and control, to which they are expected to comply in order to demonstrate their ''readiness'' for community environments. While it would be naive of us and an oversimplification of the issues to suggest that all excess behaviors are simply messages that instruction is inappropriate, it is likely to be true in many cases that instructional modifications and access to more interesting, normalized, and thus motivating tasks and environments *will* produce marked changes in behavior, most of which may well be improvements.

Response Interruption

In response interruption procedures, the teacher might use a prosthesis (arm or hand restraints, Velcro straps, mittens, etc.), manual restraint (holding the child's hands down or blocking the child's attempt to move his or her hands), and/or verbal cueing (''Put your hands down, please,'' ''I'm waiting for you to be quiet'') prior to the instructional session or

individual instructional trials. These procedures would be relevant in cases where it is clear that the excess behavior makes it impossible for the learner to attend to instruction or is dangerous and *can* be interrupted through such measures while teaching an alternative skill. It might be helpful to think of such response interruption procedures as analogous to supported sitting and positioning adaptations that would be provided for a child with cerebral palsy during eating, for example, so that the child's attention to and capacity for volitional hand-to-mouth responses, and so on, are not interfered with by the need to exert considerable concentration to simply maintain balance or correct for uncontrollable reflexive reactions. We discuss particular response interruption procedures in more detail and provide specific examples and counterexamples below. Note, however, that as we are using the concept here, response interruption should *not* be thought of as a contingent consequence (either a punishment or, as often happens with children who exhibit self-injurious behavior, a reward). The focus is instead upon interrupting the excess behavior so that it does not occur, or the child's attempt is redirected to the task or activity at hand.

Restraint procedures that inhibit the student's natural range of physical movement have a deleterious effect on development and interfere with skill acquisition goals. The long-term use of such restraints with self-injurious behavior seems to produce an effect that used to be observed frequently in institutional settings where attempts to remove the restraints (arm cuffs, straps, etc.) would result in intensive bursts of the self-injurious behavior that could only be terminated by returning the individual to the restraints. This suggests that the restraint condition had somehow become highly reinforcing (Favell, McGimsey, & Jones, 1978). Recently, however, some approaches to restraint have been described that seem to obviate these undesirable features. Rojahn, Mulick, McCoy, and Schroeder (1978) reported an interesting idea using jackets that had been adapted so that they had large pockets that allowed the individual to exert self-

Program Summation

Domains: Domestic and vocational (self-help, cognitive, language)

Student's position at start of session: seated at snack table

page 1 of 3 pages

Child P

Key: Cue/correction phases
(1) Initial intrusive
(2) + Fading process
Response objective
mass trial practice

Skill cluster A

Teacher/s P, H, EA

Setting snack corner of room, near sink, at table

Materials cup with name, dish drainer, snack (cookie), small toy reinforcer, cloth to wipe table.

	Natural cue	Instructional cue	Prompts/Corrections	Response objective	Reinforcement Natural	Reinforcement Instructional
GOAL:	Cookies on table, snack time plus verbal cue: "(name) [wait for attention], what do you want?"	(1) Teacher stands by drainer, holding cup in view 6 inches above surface, while asking P what he wants. (2) As above, but only pointing to cup. (3) As above, but T increases distance from cup (toward table) on successive days. (4) T sits at table next to P, pointing toward drainer.	(1) T prompts for sign "drink." (2) T models sign "drink."	P signs "drink."	Delayed primary: drink (and cookies)	Social: "Good, you want a drink!"
GOAL:						
GOAL:	"P, get your cup and get a drink of water for snack."	(1) Repeat cues one at a time (while prompting response).	(1a) T physical prompt to drainer, back to seat. (1b) T models taking cup from drainer, gets water from faucet.	P goes to drainer and gets cup, turns on faucet, and gets water in cup. Returns to seat.	Primary: drink of water (after returning to chair)	

FIGURE 5.1. Paul's skill cluster for Phase B observations.

FIGURE 5.1. *(continued)*

Program Summation

Domains: __Domestic and vocational__
__(self-help, cognitive, language)__

Student's position at start of session: __seated at snack table__

page __2__ of __3__ pages

Child __P__

Skill cluster __A__

Key: Cue/correction phases
(1) Initial intrusive
(2) + Fading process
Response objective
[mass trial practice]

Teacher/s __P, H, EA__
Setting __snack corner of room, near sink, at table__
Materials __cup with name, dish drainer, snack (cookie), small toy reinforcer, cloth to wipe table.__

Natural cue	Instructional cue	Prompts/Corrections	Response objective	Reinforcement Natural	Reinforcement Instructional
Teacher holding P's cup with drink.	Verbal cue: "P, what do you want?"	(1) T prompts for sign "drink." (2) T models sign "drink."	P signs "drink."	Primary: drink (and cookies)	Social: smiles, miscellaneous talk
P finishes drink and cup is empty—snack time continuing *NOTE*: REPEAT VARI-ATION OF LAN-GUAGE/COGNITIVE PROGRAM AS NEEDED DURING SNACK TIME	"P, do you want more drink? Get more water."	As above.	P gets more water from faucet.	As above	As above
P finishes snack, snack time over, verbal cue: "All done; put your cup away and clean up."	Repeat detailed cues and provide detailed cues (e.g., "take cup to sink"), one at a time (while prompting response)	T physical prompt.	P takes cup to sink, rinses cup, puts in dish drainer (sink?)..	Delayed preferred activity: ring toy	Social: "Good job, P!"

GOAL:

GOAL:

GOAL:

FIGURE 5.1. (continued)

Program Summation

Domains: Domestic and vocational
　(self-help, cognitive, language)
Student's position at start of session:
　seated at snack table
page 3 of 3 pages

Child P

Skill cluster A

Key: Cue/correction phases
　(1) Initial intrusive
　(2) + Fading process
　Response objective
　mass trial practice

Teacher/s P, H, EA
Setting snack corner of room, near
　sink, at table
Materials cup with name, dish drainer,
　snack (cookie), small toy reinforcer,
　cloth to wipe table.

Natural cue	Instructional cue	Prompts/Corrections	Response objective	Reinforcement	
				Natural	Instructional
Verbal cue: "P, clean up table."	(1) Extra verbal "Get cloth" and physical prompts (2) Extra verbal, plus gestural cues	T physical prompts.	P gets cloth, turns on water and wets cloth, wrings out cloth, cleans table, returns cloth to sink, rinses, etc. Partial: cloth already ready, P gets and cleans table, returns cloth to sink (T rinses).	Preferred activity: ring toy for ___ minutes. Paired social: "Good job, P."	

GOAL: GOAL: GOAL:

restraint during periods when self-injury might be likély. Dorsey, Iwata, Reid, and Davis (1982) used the concept of sensory extinction in designing protective equipment that did not restrict range of motion but that did prevent the individual's activities from being self-injurious. Foam-padded gloves effectively prevented eye gouging and hand biting, and a foam-padded football helmet prevented the injurious features of head hitting. The use of this equipment did reduce self-injurious behavior (defined now as *attempts* at self-injury, of course). Even with improved devices, an effective fading procedure is critical.

Response interruption procedures can be used during instruction, but they might also be most useful in preventing the occurrence of severe behaviors during times when other supervision and intervention is less available or not available at all. Thus, rather than attempting to implement an all-day intervention program to deal with the severe hand biting of a 5-year-old girl, we helped the teacher set up a program that would occur during instructional situations and whenever teacher intervention was realistic. However, the child's arm restraints were kept in place during "down times" such as on the bus, and during other times and in other places where the behavior could not be dealt with systematically. The time in restraints was decreased across the school year so that by the end of the year, they were no longer needed. In another instance involving a severely self-injurious 15-year-old who bites his hands and pushes his fingernails against his head and neck (breaking the skin), wearing mittens and gloves are being faded, but the boy is also allowed to put them on voluntarily when he seems to feel stressed and requests them.

Response interruption can also be applied to dealing with the effects of certain excess behavior. For example, there are many children who for various reasons relating to their disabilities are unable to control their mouth saliva so that they may "drool" continuously in all environments. Rather than denying those students access to environments or waiting until the program to teach them to wipe their mouths regularly is successful, we have seen the use of highly successful and normalized "prostheses" to absorb saliva. A student might be provided with a bandana or scarf to wear around his or her neck (something that is commonly worn by downhill skiers for a similiar reason!). These prostheses should be as normalized as possible: for instance, we did not approve of an upside-down visor that one severely handicapped student was made to wear in a program we once observed. But in extreme cases that involve serious behaviors such as head banging (as well as uncontrolled seizure activity where a child's head must be protected), it is far more important to ensure the child's safety than to be overly concerned about the reaction of the community to a prosthetic device. Persons in the community can be educated to understand the use of such equipment and adaptations, even as we work to decrease the necessity of their use.

CURRICULAR STRATEGIES: TEACHING A POSITIVE ALTERNATIVE

The previous chapter provides guidelines for the selection of an alternative incompatible skill objective that would be incorporated into the student's educational program. We suggested some criteria to use in assessing the *function* of an excess behavior for the individual learner in order to identify an alternative *form* (i.e., a new skill behavior) that would be an equally or even more effective (and, of course, appropriate) means of accomplishing that function. In Chapter 2 we described various theories and research studies of the possible etiologies and functions of excess behavior. In this section, we divide these possible causes of excess behavior into three broad categories of functions, or purposes, and suggest the most relevant alternative skills that might be taught.

1. Some excess behaviors appear to serve *social/communicative* purposes, providing the learner with a "simple" mechanism, often quite effective, to accomplish

functions such as obtaining attention or escaping from and/or avoiding nonpreferred persons, demands, and environments (Carr, 1983).

2. Some excess behaviors may be *self-regulatory,* allowing the learner to adjust arousal levels, block out distracting stimuli, selectively attend to particular activities, and so on.

3. Other excesses may represent *play.* Stereotyped motor movements may be the only form of "entertainment" available to a severely handicapped child who is left to his or her own resources while caregivers attend to other needs in the classroom, for example.

If the clinician suspects that an excess has a *play* function (as might be true for stereotyped mannerisms, for example), the most appropriate alternative curricular objectives would involve the acquisition of play skills, particularly those that can be enjoyed while alone. Wuerch and Voeltz (1982) provide a field-tested menu of leisure materials and validated instructional strategies for individual and dyadic play activities that are age-appropriate and within the skill level capabilities of severely handicapped individuals. For excess behavior with suspected social/communicative and self-regulatory functions, however, explicit curricular guides are not as readily available. For these instances, the teacher will need to formulate hypotheses as to function by careful observation, again, of the conditions under which the behavior occurs. Table 5.2, the Excess Function and Intervention Plan Worksheet will assist the teacher in this process.

Before we discuss the examples in Table 5.2 in more detail, we should emphasize that curriculum-based strategies are not limited solely to instruction in alternative, more appropriate behaviors that have functions basically comparable to the excess behavior. Adaptive alternative skills can be programmed at at least three levels, corresponding to the three major categories of behavior control: setting event, eliciting event, and consequence (or the

purpose/function of the behavior). To illustrate this, consider the example of Wally, a 22-year-old man who had been diagnosed since the age of 4 as autistic. Wally had been involved, on several occasions, in arguments with fellow workers in his vocational training program. During these incidents he had punched and hit the other individuals. Our functional analysis revealed that in each case the arguments had arisen over the other worker not performing a task according to proper procedures. Wally had an exaggerated level of concern over tasks being completed according to the formal procedural rules, and he did not relate to, or interact with, his fellow workers.

The alternative response to yelling at someone and hitting him or her, in terms of serving the function of changing his or her behavior, is to ask him or her by words or signs to stop what he or she is doing, or call over a supervisor and complain. So those were skills we taught Wally to perform. The alternative behavior to the eliciting stimulus—seeing someone make a mistake infuriated Wally—might be to try to stay calm, take a deep breath, and practice brief muscle relaxation; this, too, was taught to Wally. But perhaps the most critical influence on Wally's behavior was the *setting event,* which was his lack of social interaction with fellow workers. Thus, the third curriculum component in his "intervention" plan was to have one of the vocational rehabilitation counselors run a group session (to which he was invited) focusing on social skills such as making new friends, asking for dates, and so on. A leisure skill might be a viable alternative to a self-stimulatory behavior, but a friendship that produces social interaction is the most general background, or setting event, to spending leisure time. Loneliness, jealousy, and other emotional states are sometimes forgotten when working with severely handicapped people, but they are, we believe, quite common setting events for excess behavior. Such states are dealt with by planning natural activities: the adolescent who has been taken shopping for her new clothes is less likely to tear them, the person who is given some pride in his ap-

TABLE 5.2

Excess Function and Intervention Plan Worksheet: A sample for tantrumming with social/communicative intent

Description of excess form	Possible function[a]	Curricular objective	Rationale for objective	Ecological modifications and instructional strategies
1. Becomes irritable, cries, tantrums when shopping in grocery store.	COPE WITH NEGATIVES: Attempts to terminate aversive stimuli with avoidance and protest behavior.	Accompany parent to grocery, shop for up to 6 items, pushing cart through aisles and placing items in cart as parent selects them.	Rather than allowing learner to avoid situation, it is reasonable to train adaptive behavior in successive approximations of "grocery shopping." Ultimate objective would be that learner not only accompany caregiver, but take active role in shopping task.	1.1. Initial training with teacher, in criterion grocery store (one used by parent) 1.2. Training with parent after learner reaches criterion with three other adults (teacher, aide, peer) 1.3. Initial trips for 1–2 items only, time in store limited to 5 minutes; at least one learner-preferred item 1.4. Access to preferred activity after shopping on continuous then variable intermittent schedule 1.5. Six items always to include one learner-preferred item.
2. Cries, yells, and may hit peer who consistently takes away favorite toy.	PROVIDE NEGATIVE FEEDBACK: Escalates negative affect to stop a disapproved behavior by peer.	Avoid situations likely to result in conflict by: (1) playing with favorite toy when peer is not present; and (2) putting toy away if/when peer approaches.	Learner should be allowed to play with toy without inappropriate peer instructions; objectives are feasible for learner's existing social skill level. Ultimate objective would be that learner provide verbal correction (vocal/signed "stop that") to peer for intrusions, and follow up with putting toy away if necessary.	1.1. Learner prompted with verbal cue and visual (toy) when peer is not present, fading to verbal only, during free time. 1.2. Learner prompted to put toy away in safe place when peer enters room *and* approaches, faded to putting toy away when peer appears. 1.3. Learner is cued that extra free time with toy will be provided later, and commitment kept by teacher. 1.4. Materials/peer play, with another toy and peer/s, should be implemented as mastery of initial objective occurs.

| 3. After approximately 15 minutes of instruction, tantrums—including screaming, throwing objects, and slipping out of chair onto floor.[b] | LEAVE-TAKING/EXIT: Engages in avoidance and protest behavior to stop teacher demands and performance requirements. | After 10–15 minutes of working, will sign request to stop (i.e., "Need a break"), and will return for 10 more minutes of work after 2-minute break. | Learner has no socially acceptable strategy to signal need for a workbreak.

Ultimate objective would be to "normalize" patterns of work-leisure to those typical of vocational, home, and other settings, and to incorporate normalized degrees of choice in existing task demands, postponing work until later, and so on. | 1.1. Work sessions initially restricted to 8 minutes, after which learner prompted to sign "Need a break" and given 1–2 minutes respite prior to no more than 5 additional minutes of working.
1.2. Prompting withheld until after 10 minutes or until "pretantrum" signals occur, at which point learner prompted to sign "Need a break," and so on.
1.3. If tantrum occurs, teacher ignores outburst and resumes task demands when tantrum subsides, prompting "Need a break" sign after 2 additional minutes of work. |

[a] From *The Assessment of Social Competence*, by Meyer, Reichle, McQuarter, Evans, Neel, and Kishi (1983).
[b] See also Table 5.1.

pearance through social reinforcement is less likely to injure his face, and the child whose dressing and toileting privacies are respected is less likely to engage in public masturbation, digging behavior, or stripping of clothing.

In Table 5.2, we have taken a typical excess behavior, tantrums, and provided three different situation descriptions of that behavior that can be analyzed to suggest possible functions of the tantrumming for the learner in each case. As we have emphasized throughout, it is possible for a single excess behavior (in this case, tantrums) to serve multiple functions for an individual learner, and it is highly probable that the "same" excess behavior does serve different functions in different learners. We have identified three different functions for the three sample excess descriptions. These are, of course, hypotheses supported by consistent patterns of excess behavior in certain types of situations. In each instance, rather than seeing the intervention task as one of simply decelerating tantrums, the learner needs assistance coping with difficult situations as well as specific, socially appropriate (but equally effective!) strategies to accomplish the intended function. We have written a possible instructional objective in each case, a rationale for that objective as well as a "future" goal, and provided a series of intervention phases and ecological modifications that might be tried. We encourage you to use the Excess Function and Intervention Worksheet to follow this procedure whenever an intervention decision supports behavior change, and have provided a blank worksheet in Appendix B.

Carr and Durand (in press) have presented evidence that for many students, self-injurious behavior may be used to accomplish one of two functions, each of which would have completely different implications for the design of effective intervention strategies to change what might appear to be identical forms of the behavior. In Figures 5.2 and 5.3, we have provided two different examples of the decisions that might be made to modify hand biting in an autistic teenager. In Figure 5.2, the teacher has conducted a functional analysis and hypoth-

esized that Jeffrey bites his hands in certain situations that he appears to dislike in order to attract her exclusive attention and interact with her instead of continuing the task. In the other example (Figure 5.3), the teacher has determined that Jeffrey bites his hands to get out of particular environments and put an end to performance demands on certain tasks. In either case, Jeffrey's hand biting is a severe behavior that has resulted in considerable permanent scarring and continuously open sores on his hands, and the behavior has thus been determined to be a high priority for intervention. He bites his hands most severely during "prevocational" training and at lunch time, both of which seem to be activities that he dislikes and that are associated with a long history of conflict and compliance demands. Jeffrey, who is 16, is also an example of a child who engages in self-restraint: he will wrap his hands in a towel or in his jacket or place them in his back pockets whenever he seems to be anxious, and, failing some restraint procedure, once he is anxious, the behavior rapidly escalates to a level where he no longer seems in control of his behavior.

In the example presented in Figure 5.2, an ecological/curricular procedure has been designed to keep to a minimum any teacher attention for hand biting. Since Jeffrey does not pay particular attention to one of the educational assistants, this person was selected to interrupt any hand biting attempts (rather than the teacher) and to stay directly behind Jeffrey during the meal rather than being in his view; she was to interrupt any hand biting attempts without saying a word. At the same time, the teacher would be providing Jeffrey with considerable social/verbal reinforcement, in the form of appropriate positive mealtime conversation, on a DRO schedule, that is, contingent upon the nonoccurrence of hand biting attempts. The teacher also encouraged Jeffrey and his peers to interact at the table. A contingent negative consequence that could be added to this program would be for the teacher to literally turn her face and body away from Jeffrey for a set time interval (10 seconds)

Implement ecological/curricular component.

↓

Incorporate skills into IEP planning of curriculum objectives.

↓

STEP 1.   IN COLUMN A, LIST THE LIFE/HEALTH-THREATENING BEHAVIOR(S).
          IN COLUMN B, LIST THE BEHAVIOR(S) OR STIMULUS EVENT(S) THAT SIGNAL(S) THE ONSET
          OF THE TARGET EXCESS BEHAVIOR.

A	B
Hand biting	Loud vocalizations followed by hands-to-mouth and biting

STEP 2.   DESCRIBE IN DETAIL THE SKILL TO BE TAUGHT AND THE PROCEDURE TO BE USED.

Natural cue	Mealtimes: food in serving dishes and empty individual plate.
Verbal cue	"Put your knife and fork down." "Ask to leave the table."
Task description	Jeffrey is expected to dish out own food from serving dishes, pass dishes to peers, cut food and eat bite-sized food portions "European-style"; he should signal when finished by asking to leave the table.
Prompting procedure	1) Shadowing—educational assistant stands behind Jeffrey and "shadows" his hands and arms, blocking hand-to-head movement. 2) Modeling—peers and teacher model serving and passing food, and appropriate eating. 3) Verbal prompt—"Are you finished? Ask to leave the table."

STEP 3.   IN Part A, DESCRIBE THE EVENTS THAT APPEAR TO BE MAINTAINING THE EXCESS
          BEHAVIOR. IN Part B, DESCRIBE THE REINFORCING EVENTS TO BE USED THAT MIGHT
          SUCCESSFULLY COMPETE WITH THE EVENTS DESCRIBED IN Part A.

Part A   Hand biting results in Jeffrey being removed from the table with a great deal of teacher attention.

Part B   Contingent upon asking "May I leave the table?" Jeffrey is allowed to "bus" his dishes and then go
         to the leisure area and listen to records. Hand biting will not result in teacher attention or removal
         from the table by any adult.

STEP 4.   DESCRIBE IN DETAIL THE PREVENTION TECHNIQUE TO BE EMPLOYED.

Jeffrey is expected to eat at the table for gradually increasing amounts of time in a "backward-chaining" type
procedure. He will also serve himself and pass serving dishes to others throughout the meal, thus involving his
hands in other activities.

(continued)

FIGURE 5.2.   Sample ecological/curricular component for self-injurious hand biting: Performing an atten-
tion-getting function. (Note that Jeffrey is 16 years old and, since the "prevocational" training task has been
judged inappropriate, another goal is needed in the vocational domain to replace the previous one. The new
goal should, of course, involve an activity that does not provoke extreme negative reactions from Jeffrey.)

STEP 5.   DESCRIBE ANY CHANGES TO THE ENVIRONMENT THAT WILL BE NEEDED.

Food must be served "family style" at the table, not in pre-served trays, and so on. Jeffrey comes to the table for initially short periods of time only, and is kept "working" on another task by the EA while the other children eat most of their meal; timing is planned so that he joins the group for the time period he can handle, at which point lunch is done and everyone leaves the table. Through a "fading" process, he joins the group earlier and earlier until he finally starts the meal at the same time. A preferred tape of rock music is kept in the leisure area, and he may listen to this tape after lunch.

STEP 6.   DESCRIBE ANY CHANGES NOT INCLUDED IN STEPS 1–5 THAT WOULD BE NEEDED FOR PROGRAM SUCCESS.

After much consideration, the team decides that the "prevocational" task will probably never be a success experience for Jeffrey, and the activity is dropped from his program. Alternative community-based vocational training will be implemented in a service profession rather than production (e.g., serving as an attendant in a video arcade).

STEP 7.   IN THE SPACE PROVIDED, WRITE THE NEW CURRICULUM OBJECTIVE. THEN, INCORPORATE OBJECTIVE INTO IEP.

1.   Jeffrey will participate in a 20-minute "family-style" meal, serving his own portion, interacting with others to pass serving bowls and communicate socially, and eat his own meal appropriately with no occurrence of hand biting. He will signal when finished by asking "May I leave the table?" and, given permission, will leave the table, "bus" his dishes, and move to the leisure area.

NEXT, teach skills and prevent excess.

↓

THEN, after skill mastery, fade prevention.

IN THE SPACE PROVIDED, INDICATE THE PROCEDURE FOR FADING THE PREVENTION COMPONENT.

Level 1.   Jeffrey joins the lunch group for the final 5 minutes of lunch only; the EA is continuously available to "shadow" his arms and hands, blocking from behind any attempt by Jeffrey to move his hands to his face.

Level 2.   Jeffrey's length of time at the lunch table is systematically lengthened, with the EA still shadowing.

Level 3.   Jeffrey's length of time at lunch begins with the group, with the EA close by but involved in other activities.

Level 4.   Jeffrey's lunch time is entirely with the group, and the EA available for the group.

FIGURE 5.2. *(continued)*

whenever he *did* hand bite, and, in fact, spend this time talking positively with another student. This negative consequence would be added if it became apparent that the effort to prevent the behavior from occurring (the "shadowing" by the aide) and to replace it with an alternative (positive mealtime be-

haviors and conversation to attract the teacher's social attention) are not sufficient to change the behavior.

In the example presented in Figure 5.3, an ecological/curricular procedure has also been designed for hand biting behavior; however, in this case, the behavior does not seem to be

Implement ecological/curricular component.

↓

Incorporate skills into IEP planning of curriculum objectives.

↓

STEP 1.   IN COLUMN A, LIST THE LIFE/HEALTH-THREATENING BEHAVIOR(S).
IN COLUMN B, LIST THE BEHAVIOR(S) OR STIMULUS EVENT(S) THAT SIGNAL(S) THE ONSET OF THE TARGET EXCESS BEHAVIOR.

A	B
Hand biting	Loud vocalizations followed by hands-to-mouth and biting

STEP 2.   DESCRIBE IN DETAIL THE SKILL TO BE TAUGHT AND THE PROCEDURE TO BE USED.

Natural cue	Mealtimes: food on "tv table" in front of casual chair in a solitary eating area, with music playing at a low volume from the tape recorder.
Verbal cue	"That looks like lunch, Jeffrey. I'll see you later."
Task description	Jeffrey is taken to the solitary eating area and the teacher leaves the area.
Prompting procedure	The eating area must be a place where no task demands have been or will be made while Jeffrey is in this program. No one should interrupt him and he should be allowed to decide for himself when he will finish and leave the area.

STEP 3.   IN Part A, DESCRIBE THE EVENTS THAT APPEAR TO BE MAINTAINING THE EXCESS BEHAVIOR. IN Part B, DESCRIBE THE REINFORCING EVENTS TO BE USED THAT MIGHT SUCCESSFULLY COMPETE WITH THE EVENTS DESCRIBED IN Part A.

Part A   Hand biting results in Jeffrey being removed from the task demand and instructional environment.

Part B   Jeffrey is allowed to eat alone with no instructions from the teacher. There will be no one present who would be associated either with making these demands or intervening with the hand-biting. Jeffrey enjoys being alone and listening to the music and also likes the food.

STEP 4.   DESCRIBE IN DETAIL THE PREVENTION TECHNIQUE TO BE EMPLOYED.

Jeffrey's isolation from other people during mealtime will gradually be reduced through a systematic desensitization procedure. A nonfamiliar adult (someone who has never been associated with task demands) will appear near the eating area when Jeffrey is nearly finished eating, will appear earlier and earlier, and will finally join Jeffrey in the area with a meal of his or her own.

(continued)

FIGURE 5.3.   Sample ecological/curricular component for self-injurious hand biting: Performing a task-avoidance function. (Note that Jeffrey is 16 years old and, since the "prevocational" training task has been judged inappropriate, another goal is needed in the vocational domain to replace the previous one. The new goal should, of course, involve an activity that does not provoke extreme negative reactions from Jeffrey.)

STEP 5. DESCRIBE ANY CHANGES TO THE ENVIRONMENT THAT WILL BE NEEDED.

Jeffrey must be able to eat his meal separate from the other students and adults. Through the desensitization procedure described above, a noninstructional person will gradually be introduced into the situation. A preferred tape of rock music is made available to him only at this time.

STEP 6. DESCRIBE ANY CHANGES NOT INCLUDED IN STEPS 1–5 THAT WOULD BE NEEDED FOR PROGRAM SUCCESS.

After much consideration, the team decides that the ''prevocational'' task will probably never be a success experience for Jeffrey, and the activity is dropped from his program. Alternative community-based vocational training will be implemented in an environment where he can work alone most of the time rather than receive instructions from another person.

STEP 7. IN THE SPACE PROVIDED, WRITE THE NEW CURRICULUM OBJECTIVE. THEN, INCORPORATE OBJECTIVE INTO IEP.

[The final objective will be identical to the one indicated in Figure 5.2. However, it is anticipated that it may take considerably longer to accomplish this objective than in the previous example.]

NEXT, teach skills and prevent excess.

THEN, after skill mastery, fade prevention.

IN THE SPACE PROVIDED, INDICATE THE PROCEDURE FOR FADING THE PREVENTION COMPONENT.

Level 1. Jeffrey is left completely alone during his (preferred food) lunch, with music playing.

Level 2. The noninstructional adult appears close to the eating area toward the end of Jeffrey's lunch time, after he has eaten most of his meal. This individual pays no attention to Jeffrey, but is engrossed in eating his or her own meal from his or her own tv table.

Level 3. The noninstructional adult gradually increases the amount of time spent eating close to the eating area until she or he is present for all of Jeffrey's lunch time.

Level 4. The noninstructional adult moves his or her tv table closer to Jeffrey's day by day, until they are touching.

Level 5. A small table replaces the two tv tables for eating lunch, with the noninstructional person continuing to eat lunch with Jeffrey.

Level 6. The noninstructional person introduces conversation into the lunch time, making certain that none of this conversation could be interpreted as either demands or questions.

Level 7. The small table is moved closer and closer to the larger table and eating area used by the rest of the class, until finally Jeffrey is eating at the larger table with his peers.

FIGURE 5.3. (continued)

motivated by the social attention from the teacher but, in fact, seems designed to allow Jeffrey to stop doing a task or put an end to demands from someone else regarding his behavior. If the self-injurious behavior seemed to be serving this *task-avoidance* function, contingent social attention will probably have no impact upon the behavior, and as long as he is required to remain in the situation he considers to be aversive, his self-injury will be high. In such a case, it may be necessary to remove the student from all situations where self-injury occurs and gradually reintroduce task performance demands into situations where self-injury is under control. In both of our examples, we have determined that the "prevocational" training program can easily be dropped in favor of another, community-based vocational training program more reflective of tasks that Jeffrey would be willing to do and thus be more likely to become job possibilities. But Jeffrey must obviously participate in eating meals, so another procedure must be identified for this situation. Our example essentially allows Jeffrey to eat alone initially, thus removing all visible (person) stimuli who might represent task performance demands, and gradually introduce the presence of other persons back into the mealtime situation.

NEGATIVELY CONSEQUATING AN EXCESS AND REINFORCING ITS ABSENCE

In many cases, it is simply not possible to prevent an excess behavior from occurring or to allow it to occur while an alternative skill is being taught. The behavior may be so dangerous that it must be rapidly decelerated immediately. Other behaviors may occur in such a way that they actually do interfere with the learner's ability to respond to instruction—including learning an alternative incompatible skill. In some cases, we can successfully apply the suggestions provided in the ecological section to restructure the environment to prevent the behavior from occurring and/or restrain it when it does occur. In other cases, these ecological efforts will fail, and a deceleration program must be implemented along with the effort to teach a new skill.

Throughout our decision model and this text, we have used the term *negative consequences* rather than *punishment* to describe the procedures that we would recommend whenever ecological and curricular approaches alone are not sufficient to decelerate a serious

excess behavior. The term "punishment" is clearly associated, in the public mind, with the use of verbal and physical aversive, corporal punishment (e.g., spanking), and in general the more intrusive consequences that the TASH resolution (see Table 3.1) seeks to eliminate from children's educational programs. As professionals well read in the applied behavior analysis literature, clinicians are well aware that the technical term "punishment" simply refers to any contingent consequence that decreases the behavior that it follows; thus, the term ought to be a neutral one as such consequences would usually be idiosyncratic to the individual. In fact, there is considerable evidence that many intended "corporal punishment" procedures may even be reinforcing to individuals (e.g., child abuse victims, over time, are said to respond in this way to continued parental verbal and physical abuse). Yet we feel that the vernacular definition of the term "punishment" is so firmly rooted in our language system (for years before we take our first course in behavior modification) that a more neutral term is needed to preclude any misinterpretation that this model supports the use of the kinds of *intrusive* interventions challenged by the TASH resolution. Thus we use the term *negative consequences* to signify the use of a contingent nonintrusive punishment, that is, one that successfully reduces the behavior that it follows but is *not* associated with any of the five characteristics of intrusive interventions (see Table 3.1).

It is sometimes necessary for the caregiver to respond promptly to extremely disruptive behavior during instructional situations or at home. One of the classic ironies in dealing with such behavior is that those actions that usually terminate or control the behavior in the short term (grabbing the child by the arm, physical restraint, shouting, or harshly reprimanding, etc.) often do not reduce the future probability of the behavior. Caregivers, however, get reinforced for these responses because of their immediate effectiveness; Patterson (1976) refers to this as the "coercive trap" in his work on aggressive children. Nevertheless, in instances where behaviors are harmful to the student or those around him, some reaction is needed. This response should be carefully defined and standardized. Such a specification is a potentially important decision, but it is not an intervention plan. It is important to separate the actions one takes in an "emergency" (to prevent harm) from planned interventions, even when the latter are quite informal, natural reactions to a situation. Emergency procedures might require restraint, for instance, which cannot be relied upon as a program in its own right.

When one considers the patterns of social interaction that take place in any school, home, or work environment, the delivery of social consequences for an excess behavior does not typically involve a new "treatment," but instead consists of rearranging and standardizing the social reactions that would otherwise occur. As the consequences become more intrusive or time demanding, more careful planning is needed. For instance, you might ignore a child who throws one of your test items on the floor because your major goal is to continue administering the psychological assessment. Conversely, you might require the child to go and retrieve the item, which would be a fairly standard, natural, and brief consequence not seriously interfering with your own goal of finishing the testing. If, however, you were to impose an overcorrection procedure that takes 5 minutes to implement, your strategy would have significant impact on the various activities that you might otherwise conduct with other children. Such an intervention must be carefully planned and justified according to the guidelines proposed in Chapters 3 and 4 so that the major purposes of an educational program are maintained.

Sometimes we go to great lengths to plan sophisticated "punishment" procedures such as overcorrection or timeout, and forget that other features of our program or placement environment that might have provided natural consequences have been eliminated by the "artificiality" of the specialized treatment setting. (This is somewhat analogous to the process of adding vitamins to flour from which all natural nutrients have been removed!). For example, nonhandicapped peers provide simple, natural, and unequivocal negative consequences to unacceptable behavior that might be exhibited by a child. Handicapped learners who attempt to engage in various excess behaviors in the presence of nonhandicapped peers would be exposed to these natural consequences on a (theoretically effective) variable schedule. As part of an integration project in which handicapped and nonhandicapped teenagers were prepared to engage in leisure-time interactions with one another, we have videotaped two such examples in which, in each case, a highly aggressive severely handicapped teenager displayed clear intent and posturing to attack a nonhandicapped peer. The intended "hits" did not occur, as the child dramatically withdrew each threat following a clear message from the nonhandicapped student (through body posture and facial expression) that such behavior would not be tolerated. Such natural contingencies will not be a major component of the experiences of severely handicapped learners placed in restrictive—and thus highly predictable—segregated programs. Sometimes, to pursue this point a little further, very caring and "helpful" nonhandicapped peers and persons in the community will suspend their usual strategies to deal with the excess behavior of a handicapped child. For example, nonhandicapped youngsters do not allow other children to take toys away, pull their hair, hit them, not give them their turn on an activity, and so on, and yet may tolerate these behaviors from a severely handicapped peer. Similarly, customers in a store may allow someone with an obvious handicapping condition to move ahead of them in line rather than expecting the individual to wait his or her turn. And often when we visit classrooms for severely handicapped students we are expected by the staff to respond positively when approached with hugs and handshakes by these students, when, as strangers, these initiatives are usually inappropriate and should be ignored and avoided. In each of these situations, the nonhandicapped individuals involved must be reassured that the *educative* reaction to inappropriate behavior by a severely handicapped child is to display an adaptive *negative consequence* similar to how each of us would react to such behavior by anyone else.

The case of Wally that we described earlier provides another example. By referring Wally to a consultant psychologist, the vocational program director had not followed through with the widely known standard rule for all employees: behavior that could endanger the safety and well-being of other employees usually would result automatically in a brief suspension and loss of pay. By allowing the natural consequence of suspension without pay to occur for Wally as it would for anyone else, he would be learning to respond to the natural contingencies available to maintain work behavior in actual employment situations. Being squirted with ice water, having a cover put over one's head, or being removed to a timeout room are not at all typical of school or workplace disciplinary procedures.

As we noted in Chapter 3, there are certain principles that must be adhered to whenever a *negative consequence* is put into effect. First, as already explained, we do not include use of the full range of possible punishment options that have been proposed by some as effectively reducing behavior. The reader should refer again to Chapter 4 (pages 86–87) regarding consent and review procedures whenever a clinician wishes to implement a procedure that exceeds standard practice. And, of course, the use of any negative consequence or extinction procedure requires that some type of differential reinforcement schedule is in place. By combining a curricular intervention with the use of a contingent negative consequence, we would be virtually guaranteeing that at least DRI would occur. Yet, early on in the teaching of an incompatible or alternative positive skill, the student may not exhibit enough of that new behavior to receive much reinforcement. While this problem is addressed to some extent by initially reinforcing prompted occurrences of the skill, this reinforcement schedule may

still not be rich enough. And, since the instructional situation is by definition a *demand* situation, the level of reinforcement may not adequately compensate for learner perceptions that the session itself is an aversive situation. Furthermore, differentially reinforcing just one other alternative behavior would not permit a naturally occurring contingency of reinforcement for nonoccurrence of the excess.

Go back for a moment to the tantrum descriptions provided in Table 5.2. Suppose that you do not share our curricular orientation to the solution of excess behavior problems. In the case of the first tantrumming example, the parents come to the IEP meeting with you and tell you that changing this behavior would be very important to them. They have another child—a younger, preschool age child—and cannot leave the two children home alone without a sitter when they go on outings to the grocery store, and so on. While they occasionally do shop alone, the mother and father enjoy cooking and shopping together whenever possible. Sometimes a sitter is available, but that option is expensive, and the parents are not well-to-do. If their handicapped child cannot be taken along on shopping trips without making the activity miserable for everyone involved, they themselves are deprived— possibly for a period of years—of one of their favorite joint activities.

In the framework of more traditional behavior modification practices, the parents would most likely be provided with a carefully detailed *consequence manipulation* procedure that had been consistently demonstrated to be highly effective in reducing similar behaviors in other learners in the school environment. They might, for example, be trained in a timeout procedure in which the learner is taken to the car for 5 minutes contingent upon a tantrum in the store. Or, they might be trained to deliver an overcorrection procedure in which the learner is made to walk nicely up and down an aisle contingent upon protest and tantrum behaviors. They might even follow Lovaas's (1981) suggestion to simply spank their child. Such consequence manipulation procedures, if implemented correctly and consistently, can be effective in decelerating excess behavior. However, these procedures were developed for and validated in the privacy of clinical settings and the home. Not only are these environments isolated from public scrutiny, they contain few distracting stimuli. Consequence manipulation procedures were also generally carried out under one-to-one instructional conditions, often with additional therapists and observers present to assist with and monitor the program. The reality is that such interventions are not readily transportable to the conditions of criterion community environments. Even the experimental literature on excess behavior acknowledges the limitations of existing consequation technologies in failing to maintain improvements over time. Kelly and Drabman (1977), for example, report that though an overcorrection procedure had successfully reduced behavior in the short run, the procedure was too exhausting and difficult to implement by other staff and was soon abandoned—with the behavior increasing once again.

How then could this student's parents reasonably be expected to implement timeout or overcorrection or physical punishment in the grocery store setting? Even if they could, would they *want* to, or would the intervention itself be as unpleasant to them as was the tantrumming? In community settings, one must also consider the responses of shoppers and others to both the tantrums and the intervention procedure. These responses (staring, comments, a report to the local child protective agency, etc.) may be so aversive to the parents that the procedures are simply unworkable. Also, the reactions of others to a procedure such as timeout may actually be reinforcing to the child. We could, of course, "solve" the problem by retreating from the situation. The parents could stop taking the child to the grocery store, we could exclude the child from community training experiences, and ultimately, from "normalized" environmental participation opportunities. We have used this restrictive and exclusionary approach to deal

with the problems presented by severely handicapped learners for some time and not achieved lasting behavior change, nor have we succeeded in reducing the eventual institutionalization of these individuals. Consequences manipulation procedures are time consuming and require staffing resources beyond those available in community environments. Most importantly, however, such procedures are no substitute for training alternative prosocial behaviors that are adaptive to those current and future environments. We do admit the occasional necessity to use a negative consequences procedure where a behavior must be decelerated to enable the teacher to teach an alternative. But this strategy is a last, not first, choice because it is both costly as well as noneducative.

Rather than teaching parents how to "punish" the child in the grocery shopping example, the ecological and curricular approach described in Table 5.2 is preferable because it is not only educative but is far more likely to be possible for the parents to do. By successively approximating "criterion grocery shopping," the child can acquire the skills to tolerate longer shopping sessions with more items. These procedures emphasize for the child that grocery shopping can be rewarding, since the initially low task performance demands are accompanied by obtaining a preferred food item. Then, if these procedures are not sufficient and the child continues to tantrum, removal from the store *would* clearly signal removal from the reward, that is, the preferred food item.

A SUMMARY STATEMENT

In this chapter we have attempted to supplement the formal decision model with suggestions illustrating how interventions themselves can be designed. This is not a complete account of all possible intervention techniques nor an overview of principles of behavior analysis and modification. As stated in the introduction to this book, we expect teachers, psychologists, and other clinicians to be familiar with the principles of learning and motivation upon which behavior modification has been based. However, it is always incumbent on the clinician to translate these principles into a program that suits the needs of the individual student. Deciding how to design and implement a behavioral program requires careful consideration of principles that are not clearly articulated in clinical textbooks and research reports describing behavioral interventions. Some of the principles highlighted in this chapter are: (1) ensuring that planned interventions are natural, that is, age-appropriate and relying on the contingencies of social and material rewards that might be found in the ordinary environment; (2) interweaving formal and informal intervention decisions and plans; and (3) emphasizing the acquisition of positive alternative skills as the most central technique for reducing excess behaviors.

The most important *general* principle described in this chapter is the importance of designing interventions that fit naturally into the everyday activities of the classroom environment, or, more broadly, the instructional environment that also includes community, work, as well as other settings. The ideas expressed are only suggestive in keeping with our notion that you will have to make numerous decisions based on the special circumstances of your educational environment. However, our distinction of ecological, curricular, and negative consequences strategies should help you in making those decisions. This is especially true as you realize that those three strategies are *always* used in combination: in the formal flow diagram we combine ecological/curricular and curricular/negative consequences, but it is possible (indeed, likely) that all three might be required to meet the needs of particular individuals. Interventions, however designed, always get modified, adjusted, and fine-tuned on a day-to-day basis. It is this process of continued evaluation that we feel will ultimately provide the best assurance that effective and permanent interventions are merged into the natural contingencies of children's experiences. In the final chapter, we outline the kinds of evaluation procedures that can be used by clinicians to determine, on an individual child basis, whether or not the interventions implemented have accomplished the intended purpose of meaningful behavior change.

chapter 6

Educational Validity and Evaluating Interventions

In the first chapter of this book, we stated that it was not our intent to provide a guide to plan for children's skill acquisition needs. Yet, as should be clear by now, our guide to decision making for the remediation of children's excess behaviors is integrally tied to decisions as to which skills a child will be taught in his or her school program. A general theme of our approach is to emphasize that children's behaviors are interrelated in complex but, fortunately, predictable ways. By anticipating that the various behaviors in a child's repertoire are somehow dependent upon and/or have an impact on one another, clinicians can begin to accumulate information that will facilitate maximum positive behavior change in the most efficient way. We must begin to appreciate the overwhelming evidence that indicates that whenever we decrease a behavior or teach a child a new skill, other *unplanned* changes also occur. Some of these are referred to as collateral effects, that is, additional positive benefits that were associated with a change in the target behavior we had intended to modify. Others are labeled side effects, as in cases where the decrease in a negative behavior has been accompanied by an increase in another, equally negative behavior. Sometimes when we teach a child a certain skill, we are pleased to find not only that the child uses that skill where we hoped it would occur, but that the skill has generalized to a variety of appropriate situations and environments.

Baer (1981) has commented that perhaps we refer to "generalization" as a concept we have invented for our expectation that we can avoid teaching each isolated target behavior in each natural situation in the various environments in which that behavior is needed. We expect that most children will take what they have learned in the classroom and, gradually, be capable of adapting that behavior outside the classroom to the natural situations where it is relevant. Thus, nonhandicpped fourth graders are viewed as being able to benefit from separate instructional sessions concentrated in each of the traditional academic areas (math, reading, social studies, etc.), and put these things together to somehow "generalize" or synthesize the different component skills to live, work, and recreate in the community. Severely handicapped children seem less able to synthesize skills taught in isolation into natural sequences of behavior outside the classroom. A recently accepted approach to this instructional problem has been, quite rightly, to emphasize that the more severely handicapped a child is, the more important it is to teach sequences of behavior (not isolated responses) where we want them to occur, and not simply expect them to generalize from school to the community.

But, quite frankly, we would simply not have enough time to teach children with severe handicaps everything needed for the natural environment if we did have to provide explicit instruction for every instance of a functional behavior. Nor could we predict all relevant responses that will be needed. For children with severe handicaps, then, it is important to take seriously any evidence that some skills are more powerful or useful than others and should thus be given priority as educational goals. Guess and Noonan's (1982) *critical skill* and Wahler's (1975) *keystone behavior* concepts reflect this idea that there are certain target behaviors that are particularly crucial to maximum participation in everyday life. Such behaviors are said to produce multiple benefits in return for instructional planning, either because they are somehow pivotal skills needed for the development of other important skills or because they are associated with multiple uses in a variety of current situations. And there is considerable evidence that some behaviors do lead to multiple behavior changes in the child's repertoire (Meyer et al., in press; Voeltz & Evans, 1982). Thus, we must begin to plan for maximum behavior change.

With regard to excess behavior, it is particularly crucial that we do not make things worse by eliminating behavior without regard to the functions of the behavior. When this happens, teachers often find that the behavior simply reappears as soon as the program ends, or it is replaced by another, equally negative behavior problem, or its reduction is associated with the loss of certain positive behaviors as well. In many cases, reportedly effective intervention strategies have no impact on a student's negative behaviors. As we have emphasized again and again, this is undoubtedly because even though we judge the behavior to be deviant or "maladaptive," the particular excess serves a general purpose for that child in dealing wilth the environment. To the adult observer, there is another, better, more posi-

tive way, but for the child with few skills and less ability to appreciate the value of social conventions and so on, the excess is working. Finally, while there is increasing recognition of this relationship between excess behavior and the absence of skills, we have not yet fully appreciated the implications of this for educational programs. We are convinced that simply implementing DRI (teaching a new skill to replace an excess) will, in the long run, be equally ineffectual in preparing severely handicapped learners for participation in community environments unless some rather drastic habilitative reforms are implemented. It makes little sense to teach a child to play with a toy to replace finger flicking if that child generally has no access to that toy and continues to spend the majority of his or her free time in restricted, nonhabilitative environments with only other severely handicapped persons as companions. Practically speaking, we know by now that behaviors do not improve by removing children from the community environment. Though we protest that the "less restrictive" environment is unable and ill-equipped to deal with serious and multiple needs, it seems logical that if we are able to generate the resources, equipment, staff, and programs to serve these children elsewhere (e.g., in "special" schools and in residential facilities and institutions) we could reassign those efforts to provide assistance in the natural environment. Surely, severely handicapped learners will find the reinforcers available to them in the community far more motivating than those that have been available to them in artifical and intrusive classroom and hospital settings. Perhaps the multiple stimuli and consequences that characterize the community—including numerous persons in those environments—are less likely to support aberrant behavior precisely because the child's intent will not be interpreted correctly in most cases. In contrast, parents and teachers who are intensively interacting with the same child for months and years became "trained" by that child to respond to failures to perform (by prompting and helping) and to disruptive, aggressive, and self-stimulatory or self-injurious behavior (by giving the child what she or he wants or leaving him or her alone).

While there is as yet an incomplete empirical database for community-based intervention, the components can be logically derived and specified and are now being systematically investigated (Horner, Meyer, & Fredericks, in press). In the interim, we recommend that children's programs can begin by reflecting the standard of the "criterion of the least dangerous assumption" (Donnellan, 1984). This criterion holds that until we do have longitudinal data regarding the impact of various educational interventions upon children's outcomes, we should implement programs that seem least likely to interfere with the student's eventual ability to function in the community. Intrusive interventions that remove students from conventional environments and control their behavior through increasingly artificial and aversive strategies do not meet this criterion. Such practices are almost certain to result in the development of an adult who cannot interact in everyday situations and who requires severe measures to maintain even a minimal positive repertoire in what is essentially a deviant (restrictive) environment. In addition, people and services within the community will have had no opportunity to develop the skills and support networks needed to accept and interact with that handicapped individual.

For these reasons, then, we would argue that any effort to modify a child's behavior should be constructed within the framework of an appropriate program and setting characteristics. This means that the evaluation of an intervention will require more than the standard behavior modification method of monitoring baselines derived from daily frequency data. This chapter provides a brief overview of the kinds of evaluation data needed to support the *educational valildity* of a child's educational program and the success of program outcomes. We shall suggest various evaluation procedures and sample measures that can be used to address each of three important components of educational validity (Voeltz & Evans, 1983):

1. Is the planned behavior change meaningful?
2. Has behavior change occurred as a function of the intervention?
3. Did the educational intervention occur as specified in the educational plan?

The evaluation procedures will be closely tied to the child's skill acquisition goals. Our approach to monitoring the occurrence of an excess behavior, therefore, is to do so in the context of skill acquisition programming and to consider its impact upon any other behaviors that are already in the child's repertoire or might subsequently emerge.

EMPIRICAL AND SOCIAL VALIDITY

Imagine for a moment that you are a legislator who has to choose which model program will receive funding that would enable many local school districts in your state to implement that program. Two model programs are described for you, and each program illustrates its effectiveness by telling the state legislature the kinds of gains made by students in the program. Both programs present carefully documented, objective data on student progress. A highlight of Program A's accomplishments is that an autistic child learned to walk on a balance beam. A child with cerebral palsy from Program B, on the other hand, is learning to use a communication board. Without being given any further information, which educational outcome would seem most valuable to you? Why?

We can make some judgments about the importance of program outcomes by collecting information on the social and empirical validity of a behavior change. *Social validity* refers to the relative value that different persons would place on the behavior. (The term is also used to characterize judgments by whether or not the intervention technique is acceptable and whether the degree of change is significant. See Wolf [1978] for a discussion of these issues.) The social validity of a goal can be established by evidence that persons in a position to affect the child's opportunities and experiences (parents, teachers, nonhandicapped peers, employers, etc.) see the goal as one that is meaningful to them. We could judge the meaningfulness of different programs by simply polling groups of these *significant others* and having them rate or rank the programs on different criteria such as effectiveness, appropriateness, and so on. Sometimes, the value attached to a goal by one of these constituent groups will be very closely related to how well a child will do if he or she attains the skill. For example, if we wish to train teenage learners to work in a supermarket chain, and ask the managers and supervisors of those stores to list for us the skills they value most in an employee, it is likely that those skills are relevant to how well the teenager would eventually do on the job if she or he learned them. If the only persons determining the value of particular behaviors are unfamiliar with the environments for which the behaviors are being trained, judgment errors are more likely to result. We suspect that this "isolation" of some teachers of severely handicapped students from the community environments that are typically part of teenagers' everyday experiences could partially explain why adolescents continue to be taught how to stack plastic rings, assemble puzzles, and manipulate pegboards in special education. We could determine that ring stacking is a socially valid activity if we were able to find a large group of teachers willing to agree that this is a meaningful skill for adolescents with severe handicaps. Thus, social validity is not a sufficient criterion for judging the importance of an outcome—it must be supported with empirical evidence that the student's accomplishments will help produce the best possible long-term outcome. By adding the criterion of *empirical validity,* it would be difficult to justify classroom instruction in ring stacking beyond preschool.

Empirical validity refers to the need for evidence that a particular accomplishment will make a difference in the ability of an individual to participate in current and future community environments and activities. Empirical validity can be established by the immediate effects of learning a skill; for example, learning to grasp objects will allow the child to participate in many daily activities independently whereas these activities would otherwise be inaccessible to or would have to be done for the learner (e.g., pick up a toy, hold a sandwich to eat it, pull off a sock). Empirical validity can also be supported by evidence that the goal attainment produces a ripple effect: because the child can manipulate a video-game joystick, she or he is now able to participate in playing video games, which in turn increases her or his interactions with siblings and peers, leading to increases in social and communicative skills, and so on. Empirical validity also refers to long-term outcomes that might be established by follow-up data on graduates: a program that can report that a high percentage of its graduates are employed would be considered empirically valid in comparison to a program for similar students whose graduates are largely unemployed.

In Table 6.1, we have summarized various criteria that have been offered to assist teachers, parents, and others in judging the empirical and social validity of educational goals. Think back to the example described earlier in this chapter of the legislator who had to choose among several model programs. Can you tell specifically why one outcome (learning to use a communication board) seems more valid than the other (learning to walk on a balance beam)? Now read the following descriptions of program outcomes and judge these behavior changes according to the criteria listed in Table 6.1.

Missy

Missy is 8 years old and has been diagnosed autistic. Missy is extremely disruptive and spends a great deal of her time in school either running away from her chair (especially during one-to-one and group instruction) and finger flicking. At the end of the school year, Missy's teacher reports that there has been some improvement in her "bolting" behavior (she now

TABLE 6.1.   Empirical and social validity evaluation questions

Normalization

1. Is the activity age-appropriate?
2. Will attainment of the skill be useful in integrated environments?
3. Will nonhandicapped peers view the learner positively if they see him or her engage in this activity?
4. Is this an activity the learner can access both when she or he is alone and with others?
5. Will the learner be able to access this activity, once taught, without direct supervision?
6. Will the activity be longitudinally appropriate, across the lifespan?
7. Do the learner's parents value this activity?
8. Is the activity accessible in a variety of places and throughout the year?

Individualization

1. Can this activity be used at both low and high skill levels?
2. Can any need for assistance on the activity be accomplished by involving nonhandicapped persons in the natural, community environment?
3. Can the activity be adapted or modified with needed prosthetic devices?
4. Does the learner enjoy this activity?
5. Does the activity involve the performance of one or more critical skills?
6. Will the activity enhance personal development (physical benefits)?

Environmental

1. Will this activity continue to be available to the learner in the future?
2. Is the activity reasonably safe?
3. Will this activity be noxious to others in the learner's environment?
4. Can the activity continue to be accessed at reasonable cost?
5. Can instruction on this activity be provided in the relevant criterion situations and environments?
6. Will the learner's natural environment (home, etc.) continue to support the use of this activity?

runs away only once or twice per 15-minute session, as compared to five or six times at the beginning of the year), and she will follow instructions to put her "hands down" and stop flicking when the teacher asks her to do so, though she will start flicking again after a minute or so. Her parents report that they still cannot take Missy on family outings, to the grocery store, and so on, because of the problems and embarrassment presented by these two behaviors. But Missy has learned to look at the teacher briefly when told "Look at me," she can point to the colors red and green for both pictures and three-dimensional objects, she can assemble a four-piece interlocking puzzle, and sign "eat" at snack and lunch time in order to obtain portions of her food.

Janna

Janna is 16 years old, has a seizure disorder, and is diagnosed severely retarded. She has no leisure time skills other than to spend her time rocking back and forth in her chair. She seems

uninterested in materials and, in fact, often tantrums if she is expected to engage in fine motor tasks for any period of time. She is enrolled in a vocational training program in which she sits at a table and sorts nuts and bolts into separate bins, placing them into plastic bags when the sorting is completed. Her teacher is hopeful that Janna will be able to work in a sheltered workshop by the time she is 21, though she currently would not qualify as her behavior on task is so disruptive and she requires constant supervision to keep working. Janna has learned to correctly sort the workshop materials, and will fill the plastic bags without a specific cue to do so when she is finished sorting. She then tries to leave the table.

Tommy

Tommy is 8 and is said to be autistic-like. He has received both speech therapy and occupational therapy for the current school year in addition to attending a special education class.

In speech therapy, he is learning to label pictures of a cup and a toothbrush, though he has not made much progress on this objective. He often runs away from his chair, so the speech therapist uses a velcro strap around his waist and the chair back to keep him at his seat. He does not resist this procedure (or run away). In occupational therapy, since Tommy has low muscle tone and little strength in his hands, he spends about 10 minutes each day being pulled around on a low cart with wheels by holding, with his hands, onto a wooden dowel that is held by the therapists to pull him up and down the hallway. This procedure is intended to strengthen his thumbs, as he must hold onto the dowel in order to be pulled down the hall. Tommy has been able to spontaneously sign "more" and then "eat" in sequence to request food for nearly 3 years. Recently, he has been using this sign sequence whenever anyone asks him to sign anything. The teacher is trying to teach Tommy to sign "more" and then "music" so she plays a guitar or other instrument for a few seconds, then prompts him to sign in order to get her to continue playing. He likes the music and seems to try hard, but for several months has continued to sign "more eat" instead. Tommy does not play with any other children, but he has learned to sit at a table in the classroom during group art instruction; he must be guided by a full-time aide, however, to actually participate in the art activity. For next year's IEP, his instructional team wants to continue working on current programs as they feel he needs more time to learn the skills involved.

How would you judge the "outcomes" being accomplished for the children described in the above sections? Missy has learned to discriminate red and green in the classroom, and perhaps you judged this to be an important skill since this might be useful in street crossing. But according to the criteria in Table 6.1, we cannot *infer* that this discrimination skill is useful unless Missy actually demonstrates its use in the situation where we think it is important: crossing streets. There is no evidence that Missy's teacher is attempting to implement the discrimination training in actual situations, nor do we have any indication that Missy has generalized the skill on her own. Signing "eat" seems like a valuable skill, though again the situation in which this is occurring does not reflect criterion situations in the home environment. One is unlikely to be required to sign "eat" for each bit of food at the table; instead, the spontaneous use of this sign would be appropriate to request a snack at an appropriate time of the day when food is not readily available to the child without asking for it. And while the reduction in bolting and finger flicking is promising, we cannot tell if these behaviors are simply being controlled by the teacher or if there is a systematic effort to replace them with other skills. Perhaps assembling the four-piece puzzle could be viewed as a play skill to replace the finger flicking during free time, but we could identify a number of other appropriate play activities that might accomplish the same purpose and have a far greater "ripple" effect. Thus, in Figure 6.1, we have provided a comparison rating of puzzle assembly and learning to play a computer game (e.g., "Simon") with a non-handicapped peer. As you can see, the Simon activity seems far more likely to result in multiple benefits for Missy in comparison to puzzle assembly.

Can you generate similar evaluations for the program outcomes reported in Janna's and Tommy's cases? Clearly, Janna dislikes the vocational task selected for her. Is it likely that this training will ever result in a productive, marketable skill given her current reaction to the activity? Instead, Janna's teacher might attempt to locate a service-oriented task in a community setting that allows Janna to move about, and provides Janna's program with an opportunity to also teach her the related social skills that would be needed for a job. And Tommy could participate in a variety of *functional* tasks that would be equally capable of increasing his hand grasp strength (pulling open his milk carton at lunch, using an ice cream scoop, opening bureau drawers, opening the peanut butter jar, pulling the zipper on

Figure 6.1.

Activity Selection Checklist[a]

Normalization: A concern for selecting activities that have social validity and will facilitate normalized domestic living, leisure, vocational and community integration, as well as provide opportunities for movement toward increasingly complex interactions.

		Peer play with electronic game	Solitary play with puzzle
1.	*Age-appropriateness:* Is the activity something a nonhandicapped peer would do and/or enjoy?	(Yes) No	(Yes) No
2.	*Integration:* Does the activity occur in criterion environments that include the presence and involvement of nonhandicapped persons?	(Yes) No	Yes (No)
3.	*Acceptability/attractability:* Is the activity considered acceptable/desirable by nonhandicapped persons who are likely to be present in the specific environment?	(Yes) No	(Yes) (No)
4.	*Flexibility:* Can the activity be accessed by the individual alone as well as in a group?	(Yes) No	(Yes) No
5.	*Degree of supervision:* Can the activity be used with little to no caregiver supervision without major modifications?	(Yes) No	(Yes) No
6.	*Longitudinal application:* Can the activity be used with little to no caregiver supervision without major modifications?	(Yes) No	(Yes) (No)
7.	*Caregiver preferences:* Is use of the activity appropriate across the lifespan, particularly for the adolescent and adult?	(Yes) No	Yes (No)
8.	*Multiple applications:* Is the activity useful for a variety of current and/or future environments? (Including seasonal considerations?)	(Yes) No	Yes (No)

Normalization area of concern score: 8   3

Individualization: Concern related to meeting the unique needs and interest of the individual learner.

		Peer play with electronic game	Solitary play with puzzle
1.	*Skill level flexibility:* Can the activity accommodate low- to high-entry skill levels without major modifications?	(Yes) No	Yes (No)
2.	*Participation access:* Can the activity be accessed independently or through minimal use of partial participation, preferably involving persons available in the natural environments?	(Yes) No	(Yes) No
3.	*Prosthetic capabilities:* Can the activity be adapted to varying handicapping conditions (sensory, motor, behavior) through normalized means?	(Yes) No	(Yes) No
4.	*Learner preferences:* Is the activity something of interest to the learner that she or he would enjoy doing or be willing to do in order to access other benefits?	(Yes) No	Yes (No)
5.	*Skill level development:* Does the activity provide an opportunity to develop one or more critical skills?	(Yes) No	(Yes) No
6.	*Personal development:* Will the activity enhance personal development (e.g., physical benefits)?	(Yes) No	Yes (No)

Individualization area of concern score: 6   3

(continued)

147

FIGURE 6.1. (continued)

Environmental: Concerns related to logistical and physical components of activities in current and future environments.

	Peer play with electronic game	Solitary play with puzzle
1. *Availability:* Is the activity likely to be available, both now and in the future, in the environments the learner can access?	(Yes) No	(Yes) No
2. *Longevity:* Is the activity likely to remain available for a reasonable period of time (e.g., for materials: likely to last without need for major repair or parts replacement for at least a year)?	(Yes) No	(Yes) No
3. *Safety:* Is the activity safe, within normalized "risk taking" limits (e.g., would not pose a serious/unacceptable risk for the learner and others in the environment?)	(Yes) No	(Yes) No
4. *Noxiousness:* Is the activity *not* likely to be overly noxious (noisy, space consuming, distracting) to others in the learner's environment?	Yes (No)	(Yes) No
5. *Expense:* Can the activity be accessed at reasonable cost (e.g., materials are priced reasonably or have multiple uses; transportation costs reasonable, etc.)?	(Yes) No	(Yes) No
6. *Minimal interference:* Can the activity be programmed effectively for performance in criterion environments through available/feasible instructional opportunities?	(Yes) No	(Yes) No
7. *Support/willingness:* Will persons in the environment provide opportunities for the individual to engage in the activity?	(Yes) No	(Yes) No
Environmental area of concern score:	6	7
Total Score (number of items circled "yes"):	20	13

21

"From Meyer, McQuarter, and Kishi (1984); reprinted by permission.

his jacket, etc.). While identifying a cup and a tooth brush seems to represent functional skills, in the natural environment one is seldom asked to verbally label these objects (as opposed to getting and using them). Tommy's speech therapist and teacher should work together to identify actual verbal (signing) behavioral responses that would meet the criteria listed in Table 6.1 for Tommy. What modifications might you make in the group art activity described for Tommy?

Each of the questions in Table 6.1 can be asked *before* planning an instructional program, and should be used to assign skill acquisition goal priorities for the IEP. Thus, by using the "Activities Selection Checklist" form illustrated in Figure 6.1, Missy's teacher could support the selection of one activity goal rather than another to provide Missy with a new skill to replace an excess behavior in her repertoire. Remember that the flowchart model described throughout this book should be used to support the validity of any intervention plan designed to decelerate an excess behavior—finger flicking in Missy's example. Since changing this excess behavior involves teaching Missy alternative skills, the "Activities Selection Checklist" allows the teacher to go further than simply identifying an alternative, incompatible skill; the next step prior to instruction is to establish that this new skill is meaningful in its own right. We would want to justify the acquisition of this skill not only because it is associated with a reduction in finger flicking, but because the skill itself implies new competence on Missy's part that would be valued by persons in her environment and in the community.

An additional social validity question involves the *significance* of the behavior change. This question can be asked in reference to both the decrease in an excess behavior and the increase in the performance of a new skill. At one time, interventionists were satisfied with criterion performance of a new skill during instruction; the student was considered to have mastered the skill if she or he could respond correctly to the teacher's cue 80% of the time

on 3 consecutive days of instruction, for example. Based upon evidence that children could meet this criterion of "mastery" in the instructional situation and yet not demonstrate use of the skill in the relevant, noninstructional community environments and situations, mastery criteria now include evidence of generalization. Instruction does not cease and mastery is not attained until the clinician can establish that the child uses the new skill spontaneously and correctly in the community (see Evans & Brown, 1984). Thus, for skill acquisition goals, the significance of the behavior change is part of the goal-setting process: if we agree that the goal is meaningful (through a process to address the evaluation questions listed in Table 6.1) and the new skill occurs in the natural environment following instruction, the behavior change is agreed to be significant as well as meaningful.

Also related to the social validity question is the determination of whether the reduction in the occurrence of an excess behavior is significant. How does one establish the significance of a reduction in the occurrence of an excess behavior? At the beginning of the academic year, Missy's teacher reported that she ran away approximately 5–6 times per 15-minute instructional session. At the end of the year, she "bolted" only once or twice during this same length of time. Is this a significant behavior change? We have already suggested that the behavior change might not be significant if this reduction in running away is simply the result of increased teacher control over Missy. However, from a statistical perspective, this decrease in bolting would be considered to be significant. From a clinical perspective, we must evaluate the change in view of its effect upon Missy's performance in criterion community environments and situations. Clinically, we would be optimistic about this improvement rather than satisfied since the caregivers in Missy's environment will no doubt experience the same difficulties with her regardless of whether she runs away once or twice or four or five times during a period of time. While fewer times seem less "aversive" for parents and teachers, the consequence of running away even once—for Missy's safety, and so forth, in community settings—are as serious as doing so more often. Thus, a significant behavior change will actually be parallel to a significant change in the acquisition of a new skill: Missy must demonstrate "mastery" (i.e., a near-zero rate of running away) in the natural environment before intervention can cease.

A final component of educational validity involves evidence of multiple, unplanned behavior change as a result of a planned behavior change. This phenomenon is well established (Voeltz & Evans, 1982) and has considerable significance for interventions with excess behavior. You will recall that in Chapter 4, a cost-benefit analysis was required to consider multiple effects as one makes intervention decisions. In Table 6.2, we have summarized several examples of multiple effects that have been reported in intervention studies designed to decelerate different excess behaviors; some of these effects are positive (benefits) and some are negative (costs).

Now look at the examples provided in Table 6.3. Note that for each of the excess behaviors listed, we have suggested a possible alternative skill and indicated those behaviors that the teacher or parent felt were related in some way to the occurrence of their listed excess behavior. For example, finger flicking might typically occur while the child is rocking in his or her chair, and while the child is engaging in these excess behaviors he or she is not attending to the task or playing with the available toys. The teacher might decide that appropriate toy play would be a logical alternative skill to teach, and by looking at the hypothesized behavioral interrelationships might expect a decrease in rocking, an increase in attending to the activity, and an increase in positive peer interactions to accompany a successful modification of this child's finger flicking. But the child also frequently breaks toys and other materials, so another possible "side effect" of teaching that child to interact more often with toys might be an increase in the destruction of those toys. In this case, we would most likely judge the potential benefits to outweigh the possible cost involved, but it would probably be helpful to carefully monitor any increase in destructive behavior with materials and attempt to prevent this from occurring. By formulating hypotheses regarding possible behavioral interrelationships—based upon your own intuitions regarding which behaviors seem to occur together or in the absence of one another—you can not only try to plan for multiple positive behavior changes but you can be watchful for (and intervene early with) possible negative effects as well. We suggest that whenever you have decided to intervene with an excess behavior you should complete this Excess Behavior Intervention Evaluation Input form for the planned target behavior. In addition to formulating your own hypotheses regarding how the target behavior might be related to other behaviors in the child's repertoire, you should ask the child's parents or caregivers whether they have noticed these behaviors occurring together, following one another, or in place of one another. A blank version of this form for your use in monitoring possible multiple behavior changes is included in Appendix B.

CHANGE AS A FUNCTION OF THE INTERVENTION

To determine the effectiveness of any intervention program, we need to document that the target behavior has changed significantly as a function of that program. This requires, at the very least, that we are able to report *baseline* and *acquisition* performance levels that differ from one another in a positive direction. Researchers who publish intervention studies are required not only to document this difference in behavior, but also to demonstrate that the change can be attributed to the planned intervention through procedures designed to establish experimental control. This "control" is demonstrated by evidence that whenever the intervention is not in effect, the behavior occurs at baseline rates, intensity, and/or dura-

TABLE 6.2.

Concurrent Behavior Changes in Studies Intervening with a Target Excess Behavior

Intended target behavior (study)	Benefits: concurrent positive behavior changes	Costs: concurrent negative behavior changes	Comments
Various self-stimulatory behaviors (Linscheid & Cunningham, 1977)	Increase in social behavior (one child).	Increase in aggression toward therapists. Decrease in social behavior (another child).	Authors also monitored appropriate toy play, but this did not occur.
Banging objects (Pendergrass, 1972)	Increase in looking. Decrease in biting own hands and lips.	Decrease in responding, touching, and speaking.	
Plate spinning, hand flapping (Rincover, Cook, Peoples, & Packard, 1979)	Increase in appropriate play (one child).	Decrease in appropriate toy play following initial increase; also, finger flapping returned to baseline levels at follow-up (another child).	Toy play was also trained along with program to reduce self-stimulatory behaviors.
Climbing on bookcase; rocking (Risley, 1968)	Increase in eye contact and imitative clapping.	Increase in climbing on chair.	There was training to increase eye contact prior to treatment to decrease climbing.
Self-stimulation (Romanczyk, 1977)	Increase in social approach behavior and toy play		
Temper tantrums (Sailor, Guess, Rutherford, & Baer, 1968)	Increase in quantity of vocal imitation.	Decrease in quality of vocal imitation.	
Inappropriate talking (Sajwaj, Twardoz, & Burke, 1972)	Increase in speech to children and in cooperative play.	Decrease in task-appropriate group behavior. Increase in disruptive behavior.	Authors subsequently successfully reduced the inappropriate group behaviors.
Inappropriate object manipulation (Wells, Forehand, Hickey, & Green, 1977)	Decrease in mouthing and inappropriate hand movements (one child). Increase in toy play.	Increase in mouthing and inappropriate hand movements (one child).	Since the overcorrection procedure consisted of manually guided toy play, this is a direct (not a "side") effect.
Noncompliance, out-of-seat behavior, inappropriate object manipulation (Whitman, Hurley, Johnson, & Christian, 1978)	Decrease in physical aggression and in cries and screams.	Decrease in "gleeful vocalizations."	

TABLE 6.3.

Excess Behavior Intervention Evaluation Input

Excess behavior	Alternative skill needed	Potentially related excess behaviors/skills[a]	Possible benefits	Possible costs
Finger flicking	Appropriate toy play	Rocking (+) Attending to activity (−) Destruction of materials (−)	Decrease in rocking Increase in attending and activity performance	Increase in destruction of materials
Hitting peers	Social/communication skills for specific intents Activity-related skills	Smiling, laughing (+) Vocalizing (+) Spitting at peers (+) Attending to activity (−)	Decrease in spitting Increase in attending to activity	Decrease in positive social behaviors (vocalizing, etc.)
Crying, tantrumming	Appropriate requesting to "take a break" Appropriate turn-taking	Hitting peers (+) Task errors (+) Running away (−)	Increase in positive peer interactions Increase in task performance "Generalized" leave taking, turn taking skills	Increase in running away Unwillingness to continue working on task for more than a few minutes

[a]For each potentially related behavior, a (+) indicates a positive relationship (the behaviors seem to "go together") and a (−) indicates a negative relationship (one behavior seems to occur when the other is not occurring).

tion. These experimental procedures thus require: (1) a description of the target behavior, objectively defined so that an outside observer would agree with us that the behavior is or is not occurring at any given point in time (this has been discussed briefly in Chapter 2); (2) a strategy to measure or count the behavior, again, objectively defined so that an outside observer would agree with us regarding how much of the behavior is occurring; and (3) a report of instances during which the intervention is and is not occurring, with evidence that the behavior improves only when the intervention is in place or has succeeded in having an effect. We agree on the importance of these first two requirements for use by teachers, and, while concurring that the third is also crucial to establish the efficacy of instructional programs, we present strategies that teachers can use to meet the third requirement that differ from those established for use by researchers.

The third requirement for establishing experimental control requires instances during which the intervention will or will not be in place. These different instances can be comparisons among *children* (e.g., a clinician shows that the 10 children who used Curriculum A made more gains on a test than the 10 children who used a control Curriculum B). With *group* comparisons like this, a pretest versus posttest design is generally sufficient to establish the effectiveness of one procedure rather than another, assuming that the two groups are similar to one another (and various experimental ''rules'' have been followed to support this claim that they were similar prior to instruction). Thus, these two groups would all take a pretest of their skill level, and repeat this same (or a parallel) measure as a posttest following instruction on one of the two curricula being compared.

Because severely handicapped children exhibit such heterogeneity and because programs must be individualized for these students, such group comparisons are seldom appropriate in evaluations of instructional effectiveness. Instead, within-subject research methodology is more likely to be employed, where the behaviors of one student are compared *within that student across treatment phases*. Multiple baseline, simultaneous treatment, and reversal designs are examples of procedures whereby intervention researchers establish that the behavior change is a function of their treatment or instructional procedures. Many teacher training programs, particularly those in the area of severe handicapping conditions, emphasize competency in the use of single-subject research methodology as an essential component of successful teaching (e.g., Snell, 1983). We have argued elsewhere that use of these designs is not generally necessary and may not even be appropriate for use by teachers to evaluate the day-to-day effectiveness of their instructional programs for students (Voeltz & Evans, 1983). Briefly, because single-subject designs require that the subject serve as his or her own control, the effects of a ''successful'' intervention must be highly specific to a single targeted behavior and to the instructional situation. In essence, we can demonstrate such experimental control only if behaviors fail to have ripple effects, that is, they fail to have a generalized effect on other situations (with other persons, etc.), settings, and behaviors. The multiple baseline and simultaneous treatment designs rely upon failures of generalization, and the reversal design relies upon failures of maintenance in order to demonstrate experimental control. If, in contrast, teachers accept responsibility to demonstrate *generalized* responding (in all relevant community situations) that *maintains* over time, these standard within-subject designs will not work for us.

In addition, these designs also fail to meet the practicing teacher's actual needs as an empirically guided professional (as an applied, not a basic, scientist). The teacher needs to be able to determine whether an intervention is working on a day-to-day basis, not after the fact. This requires monitoring the effects of an intervention (including curricula) on the pupil's performance from day to day given efficacy data on the pupil's performance. The teacher cannot wait until a preset treatment phase is ended, unable to alter an intervention plan once it is implemented, but must be an active decision maker, continually adjusting and re-adjusting intervention strategies and educational programs (cf. Evans, 1982). This does not imply that teachers are less than basic scientists in the sense that they unfortunately are forced to allow their standards of evidence, inference, and attribution of causal effects to be lower because of the demands of the real world. Their needs as practicing clinicians are different. A recommendation for alternative "interactive" (cf. Cronbach et al., 1980) evaluation procedures that are more relevant to the needs of educators and other clinicians is not an apology for the absence of scientific rigor. Educators require an evaluation model that allows continuous adjustment of the program based upon both knowledge of the current program and short- and long-term pupil outcomes.

The A-B Design

A standard quasi-experimental design that actually describes what clinicians most often do is the A-B design. This is a simple time series analysis, with several data probes of the behavior conducted before and during (as well as after) instruction in the multiple (relevant) situations and environments. A change in behavior from *A* (baseline) to the *B* (intervention) phase should be sufficient to establish that change has occurred. However, an A-B design is not considered to be an acceptable way to demonstrate experimental control (that the change in behavior during the *B* phase can be attributed to the intervention) since there could be various alternative explanations for the improvements in the pupil's repertoire that could have little to do with the planned "treatment." "History" is the most likely of the plausible alternative explanations for behavior change (Kazdin, 1981). We would maintain that with a severely handicapped child in a special education classroom where the teachers and caregivers communicate regularly, it is unlikely that something influential enough to account for a significant behavior change could go unnoticed. Where behavior shows a steady pat-

tern of expected change associated in time with the intervention and that student's typical response to a skill training program, we would consider this to be sufficient demonstration of the intervention's effects. The strongest evidence of the effectiveness of any skill training program would still probably be replications of those effects across children.

Daily or frequent probe (e.g., two to three times weekly) record keeping can reveal suspected performance variations such as hypothesized performance decrements after vacation, seasonal or cyclical changes, and so on, and can provide valuable archival data regarding the natural history of behavioral or cognitive difficulties exhibited by a particular child. We recommend that parents and teachers exchange objective, anecdotal notes between school and home on a regular basis (e.g., a daily class record, supplemented by a "diary" going back and forth from school to home) to monitor pupil performance. Figure 6.2 provides a sample (probe) skill acquisition performance record that is useful to monitor the acquisition of multiple skills (and the occurrence of excess behaviors) being instructed in a skill cluster format. Note that this particular form also requires a record of the number of planned sessions that were actually conducted; this is a component of *educational integrity,* which is the final evaluation issue discussed later in this chapter. In addition to this systematic record of pupil performance during instruction, a spiral-bound notebook (a "diary" record) should be circulated between the school and the home to share what parents and the instructional staff consider to be meaningful changes in the learner's behavior as well as differences in environmental conditions that might have an impact of how the learner performs.

Thus far, we have not discussed the possible effects of medication upon students' behavior and skill acquisition performance. As most teachers are no doubt aware, many if not most of their students will have medication prescribed for them at one time or another in their school careers. As mentioned in Chapter 2, these medications are typically prescribed to

Skill Acquisition and Excess Behavior Record
(2-Week Sample)

Student __Missy__

Skill cluster __Peer play with Simon game__

Excess (A) __bolting__ (C) __pulling hair (others)__

(B) __finger flicking__ (D) _____

Level of Assistance Key	
I = Independent	FP = Full physical
V = Verbal prompt	X = Partial participation
PP = Partial physical	

Date and teacher's initials[a]

Steps in Activity Sequence

Steps	LM 9/8	IE 9/10	IE 9/14	LM 9/15	LM 9/17	% Correct
10. Wave "bye" when peer leaves.	10ᵛ	10ᵛ	10ᴾᴾ	10ᵛ	10	0
9. Signs "want to play" for turn.	9ᶠᴾ	9ᶠᴾ	9ᴾᴾ	9ᴾᴾ	9ᵛ	0
8. Attends to Simon and other child's play.	8̶	8ᵛ	8̶	8̶	8̶	80
7. Relinquishes turn to peer.	7ᶠᴾ	7ᶠᴾ	7ᶠᴾ	7ᴾᴾ	7ᴾᴾ	0
6. Attends to turn and maintains play.	6̶	6ᵛ	6̶	6ᵛ	6̶	60
5. Presses panel to activate Simon.	5̶	5̶	5̶	5̶	5̶	100
4. Tolerates physical assistance to reach Simon.	4̶	4̶	4̶	4̶	4̶	100
3. Points to Simon (or _____) when asked by peer to select toy.	3ᶠᴾ	3ᶠᴾ	3ᴾᴾ	3ᵛ	3ᵛ	0
2. Smiles, eye contact with peer (at least once at imitation).	2ᵛ	2̶	2̶	2̶	2̶	80
1. Walks to peer at play area.	1ᴾᴾ	1ᵛ	1ᵛ	1̶	1̶	40

X̄ Day

Excess Behavior Tally

Note: Place an X in box to indicate that no data collection occurred.

	9/8	9/10	9/14	9/15	9/17	X̄ Day
A	//	0	/	/	0	80
B	⊬⊬ //	X	⊬⊬ ///	///	//	5
C	//	/	/	0	/	/
D	—	—	—	—	—	NA

% Correct

Check of planned instructional opportunities (/ = completed)

Week of: __9/6 – 9/10__

	M	T	W	Th	F	% Completed
A.M.	9/6	9/7		9/9	9/10	50
P.M.	9/6		9/8			100

Week of: __9/13 – 9/17__

	M	T	W	Th	F	% Completed
A.M.	9/13		9/15	9/16		67
P.M.		9/14	9/15		9/17	33

Average % of sessions completed: | 58 | %

---

[a] These are probe data collection sessions that should be scheduled in advance of each 2-week period of time from among the total *planned* instructional sessions listed at the right of the data sheet.

FIGURE 6.2.

control seizure disorders and to regulate the pupil's behavior and, it is sometimes suggested, ability to learn. Ironically, though the presumed effects of these medications are likely to be observed by the teacher and the parent who are the adults who interact with the student for the majority of the day, systematic sharing of information regarding the pupil's behavior seldom occurs. To attempt to correct this situation, Brulle, Barton, and Foskett (1983) have designed a behavioral record to monitor the possible effects of medication on pupil behavior (see Figure 6.3). We recommend that in addition to following the implementation guidelines recommended by the Council for Exceptional Children (1977) that ensure that relevant adults are informed of procedures and potential side effects, the teacher should draft an individualized version of this form, in consultation with the child's parents and the physician prescribing the medication, in order to monitor the effects of a pharmacological intervention. This is especially important as the teacher will also be simultaneously implementing various behavioral and instructional intervention programs to change pupil behavior, and will need information to judge whether behavior change (or the absence of behavior change) can be attributed to the direct and/or indirect effects of classroom procedures.

Problem Solving

Tharp (1981) has described "personal knowing" as valid input into educational decision making, and "data guidance" as an additional metamethod involving the use of daily observation, criterion-referenced testing, and other similar sources of information needed to interpret the effects of interventions on children. Teachers working with severely handicapped students will often have to make adjustments in individualized programs, perhaps even daily in extreme cases. Multiple time-series probes over time, graphed as they are collected, would allow ready diagnosis of a program that is not working. Figure 6.2 allows for this combination of periodic time-series performance data and graphing of performance patterns. But the teacher will be able to make accurate decisions based upon such information only if she or he regularly collects comparable acquisition and behavioral data across programs and students over time. The teacher will be able to judge whether or not a program should be modified based upon pupil performance only if she or he has *personal knowledge* of both the typical acquisition curve by similar students on that skill and the typical response of that student to similar programs. If the resultant acquisition

curve differs from the teacher's personal knowledge with similar skills and similar students, she or he would have a good basis for making a change in the program.

Whenever significant behavior changes do occur, teachers can rule out alternative explanations by simple tests of their hypothesis that the intervention has caused the behavior change. For example, if the physical arrangement of the room was changed at the same time that the intervention was implemented, the teacher could probe the student's performance in an environment similar to the previous physical arrangement but with the new intervention in place. The teacher could also probe the learner's behavior in the new environment without the intervention. If a decrease in performance occurs when the environment is changed regardless of the intervention, but the behavior improves again in the new environment even without the intervention, the teacher has clear data that ecological variables are exerting control over the behavior, not the intervention procedures.

EDUCATIONAL INTEGRITY

Almost all traditional and behavioral assessments used in educational programs focus on student performance and behavior. However, many of the intervention procedures described in the behavioral literature really refer to changes in the clinician's behavior. Adoption of any specific educational program plan alters the existing ecological system in the classroom. Thus, in addition to the planned "treatment," there are numerous other setting variables already in place that could be contributing in important ways to positive and negative pupil outcomes. An otherwise effective instructional program might be ineffective in a classroom that includes multiple distracting stimuli and nontreatment "contingencies" (such as several other highly disruptive peers who might reinforce the target behavior regardless of teacher efforts to ignore it). And an otherwise ineffective instructional program might appear to be extremely bene-

Medication Data Collection/Communication Form

Patient Information   Name: _____ Birth Date: _____ C.A.: _____ School: _____

Case Manager/Teacher: _____ Physician: _____   DATA COLLECTION MODE

MEDICATION: _____ DATE INITIATED: _____   F = Frequency recording

DOSAGE: (a) _____ (b) _____ (c) _____   D = Duration recording

ADMIN. INTERVAL: (a) _____ (b) _____ (c) _____   M = Momentary time sampling

Date of Observation																				
Time of Observation — Start																				
Time of Observation — Finish																				
Admin. Interval																				
Dosage																				
Time most recent admin.																				
BEHAVIORS 1.																				
BEHAVIORS 2.																				
BEHAVIORS 3.																				
BEHAVIORS 4.																				

Description of Target Behaviors   *Physician Comments:*

1.

2.

3.   *Observer Comments:*

4.

FIGURE 6.3.   (From Brulle, Barton, & Foskett, 1983; reprinted by permission.)

ficial simply because of the amount of learning time devoted to that program in comparison to another program that does not seem to be working. Teacher affect, physical arrangements, daily activities, and social conditions are a few of the additional environmental variables that will influence the educational process.

Interventions described in the research literature are seldom perfectly replicable. This is so either because, for sake of brevity, the researcher did not describe all the essential components of the intervention, or failed to identify the critical components and/or "background" setting characteristics under which the intervention was implemented. For example, the majority of available intervention research has actually been conducted not in public schools, but in rarified laboratory classrooms or other specialized, highly staffed settings. Thus, we should probably not be surprised when we fail to achieve the same dramatic gains under realistic community conditions. We should also remember that these significant results are most typically reported *only* under highly controlled and artificial intervention conditions so that the kinds of changes we need to document in community environments will actually be quite different. If we are to recommend that a particular intervention procedure or curriculum component should be implemented by public schools, we should be able to provide data indicating that the program was field tested—and was successful—in similar classroom situations. Teachers should look for evidence that a program was validated with learners similar to their own but, perhaps even more importantly, was also implemented under conditions similar to those of an integrated public school and various natural community environments that are a reality for their students.

Teachers should also value information on their own instructional behavior as a primary source of data to make needed changes in programs for their students. Rather than viewing observation of teaching in classrooms as strictly teacher evaluation procedures (sources of evidence that a particular teacher is "good" or "bad"), they should be seen as the source of valuable information regarding variability in the child's performance under different instructional conditions. It is not uncommon for consultants to observe teachers following technically sound procedures but to display some subtle component of implementation that could be responsible for the lack of success with a particular student. Figure 6.4 is a sample Anecdotal/Functional Analysis Observation Record that teachers can use to problem solve whenever a learner's performance is not proceeding as planned. This sample record parallels the objective data record provided in Figure 6.2 to monitor a learner's performance during a skill cluster instructional program for establishing an interactive play skill. By watching the child while she or he is engaged in the activity, the teacher can attempt to identify subtle social influences on the child's behavior, including contingencies in the peer interaction that might not have been previously identified but that might now be controlling the behaviors. Such an anecdotal record can be useful as a self-evaluation taken throughout one's teaching career, and can yield significant information to add to child assessment data in the design of individualized programs.

Instructional team members should periodically take turns observing one another in the conduct of intervention programs in order to do a functional analysis. This is especially important when a program does not appear to be working. When this occurs, the teacher should either videotape his or her instruction to watch later, or, if this is not possible, ask another adult (the educational assistant, physical therapist, etc.) to watch the instruction of the program. A key component of this evaluation procedure is to conduct the observation and compare the actual behaviors being displayed with the written program description. Occasionally, an ineffectual program can be explained by the presence of an extra-stimulus prompt that is being idiosyncratically and inadvertently provided during an instructional session (e.g., the child is expected to sign

Anecdotal/Functional Analysis Observation Record

Student _____   Date of observation _____

By whom: _____

Steps in activity sequence:	What occurred (what _____ did, peer did, problems with materials, etc.)	Comments by observer	Summary, changes, and so on, by teacher
10. Waves "bye" when peer leaves			
9. Signs "want to play" for turn			
8. Attends to Simon play by peer			
7. Relinquishes turn to peer			
6. Attends to turn and maintains play			
5. Presses panel to activate Simon			
4. Tolerates physical assistance to reach toy			
3. When asked by peer to select toy, points to choice			
2. Smile/eye contact with peer/s			
1. Approach/move wheelchair			

FIGURE 6.4.

"cookie," and the teacher delivers the intended verbal cue "What do you want?" along with an unintended physical prompt—holding and releasing the child's hands prior to each opportunity to respond).

Another lack of educational integrity that could explain limited student progress is simply insufficient instructional time. In addition to a faithful representation of the intended written program plan, educational integrity is also dependent upon the quantity of learning opportunities—whether or not a program is occurring often enough for learning to occur. If you look back at Figure 6.2 you will note that this data recording sheet also requires that, at the beginning of each 2-week time period, the teacher should record planned instructional sessions and mark these off after they have occurred. It is not atypical for less than half of the planned instructional sessions to actually occur. Large amounts of program time may be sacrificed for field trips, movies, and other special events not incorporated into children's programs and thus not serving as learning opportunities. Children's programs are also often preempted due to seizures, illness, "bad days," impressions that the child is too tired, and so on. Even though interruption of instructional sessions might (or might not be) justified, it is important to know how often the program sessions have been precluded before deciding that a program is not working. Using the format illustrated in Figure 6.2, a teacher can tell at a glance that this session has only occurred a certain percentage of the times planned. If a program has not occurred often enough as planned, the first "revision" for a program that is not working might simply be to ensure that a higher percentage of planned instructional sessions will take place as intended.

Ultimately, a concern for educational integrity must involve specifying precisely the procedures and programs that seem to lead to favorable outcomes across large numbers of severely handicapped learners. Assessing pupils' accomplishments without accompanying information on what their programs were like will not give us all the data we need. The written documentation provided by the individual children's IEPs and various Program Summation Sheets (see pp. 123–125, 199) will be important beginnings toward accumulating knowledge of what kinds of experiences lead to what kinds of gains by learners with severe handicapping conditions.

A SUMMARY STATEMENT

For many years now, the standard accepted method for evaluating interventions with severely handicapped students (and indeed most individuals exhibiting significant behavioral problems) has been the individual baseline, derived from periodic observations of the frequency of a given behavior. Undoubtedly this methodology has served our field well. Documented changes in specific target behaviors have provided unequivocal evidence for the general efficacy of numerous techniques. Also, the single-subject experimental design takes into account the uniqueness of the handicapped individual's behavior and allows for students who are research subjects to serve as their "own control." The formal charting of behavior change provides for an unusual degree of objectivity in practical, everyday educational environments. A number of useful texts exist that explain to teachers and other professionals how to do observation, recording, charting, and graphing of behavior (e.g., Gaylord-Ross & Holvoet, 1984). Teachers of severely handicapped students are expected to have the competencies of the applied scientist, in much the same way as practicing psychologists are admonished to be "empirical clinicians" (Barlow, 1981). In some precision teaching methods, graphing progress is carefully embedded in the recording of success or failure on every trial. Systematic data gathering is a prerequisite for carrying out a formal functional analysis of excess behavior.

However, there are some limitations to this approach, particularly if we use it uncritically. As explained in this chapter, judging whether an intervention is successful or the most promising approach that could have been used requires more than documentation that a particular target behavior has changed in frequency. As an *evaluation* approach, the charting of individual responses leaves much to be desired. It will not answer the question of whether the change documented is clinically or educationally significant; it will not answer the question of what other collateral effects (good or bad) have taken place; it will not answer the question of whether the intervention strategy itself was appropriate, humane, and in keeping with philosophical or legal assumptions regarding the handicapped child's rights. As we have stressed repeatedly throughout this book, these issues require consideration of various other factors, which in turn require that we use our very best judgment as educators, psychologists, and other professionals. It is the purpose of this book to aid that judgment process and to emphasize that the design of successful interventions requires many decisions, not just the application of some previously documented technique. We have tried to avoid the writing of a prescriptive manual, concentrating instead on the principles of the detective work that we feel is so necessary to solve severe behavioral difficulties in handicapped students.

Gathering data on a regular basis in an applied situation provides a clear and objective guide to the decision making strategies being proposed. Formal information on a student is only of use if it actually contributes to the decisions that must be made by the professional and the parents. If a new skill is increasing in frequency or an excess behavior is steadily declining, you have good cause to continue with your educational program. But severely handicapped students' behaviors can be quite erratic, some changes are very slow, and sometimes long periods of little or no progress can be encountered. This concern has been most carefully addressed by Haring and White (1981) who suggested how one might compare actual progress with expected progress (the "celeration" baseline) and redesign the program if the information obtained shows that the

discrepancy became considerable. This is a decision model based on feedback from objective data and we heartily endorse the suggestion in principle.

In our experience, however, gathering detailed observational data suitable for charting onto meaningful baselines is really quite difficult to achieve in many natural school and community educational settings. Even in a discrete trial format we have noticed some interesting difficulties. For example, we observed one teacher who was dutifully keeping trial-by-trial data on one of our research students, and when she would turn away from the child to record on her data sheet after each trial, the child would burst into an intense episode of hand flapping and finger flicking. Collecting continuous data is a considerable task for the teacher and, in fact, inserts brief intervals of "down time" for the child who is left waiting while the teacher records data. If program modifications can be made on the basis of regularly scheduled, *periodic* (not continuous) data probes, this data collection strategy could also be viewed as being far less disruptive to teaching and learning. This is not in any way intended to diminish the importance of collecting objective data on pupil performance and behavior. Instead, in this chapter we have made various suggestions as to how information can be gathered that will be most relevant to the actual decisions that have to be made—in the context of public school and community training settings.

In addition to emphasizing the use of information, we have provided examples of how nontraditional types of information can and should be gathered in order to determine the educational validity of your activities. In some cases, these data will provide measures that are actually better—or more representative of the issues of concern—than supposedly highly objective baselines. For instance, a social validity check that the student's aggressive behaviors are reduced, and socially appropriate behaviors increased to the point that other children in the playground do not avoid him or her, might be more significant than a reported percentage decrease in frequency of aggression. In some cases, the measures are not necessarily more accurate portrayals, but are practical, and do not require inordinate amounts of teacher, parent, or clinician time. Our suggestions here are closely in tune with those proposed by Nelson (1981) for practicing clinical psychologists and consultants. For instance, we can sometimes estimate change by indirect measures. A reduction in hand mouthing might be deduced from observations of a lessening in skin rashes and the callouses and raw spots on a student's hands.

None of the suggestions in this chapter should be interpreted as a move away from the scientific heritage that has been the hallmark of behavioral interventions with severely handicapped students. We believe very strongly that the field should maintain its empirical orientation and hope that this book will encourage special educators and behavioral psychologists and other clinicians to continue to influence each other for the benefit of those students who are most in need of our best instructional technologies. We have quite often been critical of established methods in this book, but have always tried to offer constructive alternative recommendations. These alternative suggestions are not uniquely our own, but are con-

sistent with the exctiting new ideas being expressed by many persons working in this area. By striving to implement and validate an instructional technology to operationalize these ideas, we will be able to advance not only our knowledge base but also the quality of life of severely handicapped individuals. And that should be, after all, the ultimate intent of our efforts.

Essentially, the approach and strategies outlined in this book have been for our intended primary audience—you, the teachers and clinicians who are providing the direct services. But it is also hoped that our comments and recommendations, along with the growing empirical literature in this area, will have a stimulating effect on researchers who are reporting outcome studies and pioneering new methods of intervention. We have not disguised our concern that traditional behavior modification techniques, both in their design (see Chapter 5) and in their evaluation (see this chapter) have become constrained by an emphasis on documenting behavior change with insufficient regard for the broader educational and social implications for the lives of severely handicapped individuals. It is our hope that this book will stimulate both practice and research toward this extended goal.

References

Bachman, J. E., & Fuqua, R. W. (1983). Management of inappropriate behaviors of trainable mentally impaired students using antecedent exercise. *Journal of Applied Behavior Analysis, 16*, 477–484.

Baer, D. M. (1981, November). *Promoting generalization of treatment effects with children: Issues and strategies.* Paper presented at the 15th Annual Convention of the Association for the Advancement of Behavior Therapy, Toronto.

Barlow, D. H. (1981). On the relation of clinical research to clinical practice: Current issues, new directions. *Journal of Consulting and Clinical Psychology, 49*, 147–155.

Baumeister, A. A. (1978). Origins and control of stereotyped movements. In C. E. Meyers (Ed.), *Quality of life in severely and profoundly mentally retarded people: Research foundations for improvement* (pp. 353–384). Washington, DC: American Association on Mental Deficiency.

Baumeister, A. A., & Forehand, R. (1971). Effects of extinction of an instrumental response on stereotyped body rocking in severe retardates. *Psychological Record, 21*, 235–240.

Baumeister, A. A., MacLean, W. E., Kelly, J., & Kasari, C. (1980). Observational studies of retarded children with multiple stereotyped movements. *Journal of Abnormal Child Psychology, 8*, 501–521.

Berkson, G. (1983). Repetitive stereotyped behaviors. *American Journal of Mental Deficiency, 88*, 239–246.

Bijou, S. W., & Baer, D. M. (1961). *Child development: Vol. 1. A systematic and empirical theory.* New York: Appleton-Century-Crofts.

Borthwick, S. A., Meyers, C. E., & Eyman, R. K. (1981). Comparative adaptive and maladaptive behavior of mentally retarded clients of five residential settings in Western states. In R. H. Bruininks, C. E. Meyers, B. B. Sigfor, & K. C. Lakin (Eds.), *Deinstitutionalization and community adjustment of mentally retarded people* (pp. 351–359). Washington, DC: American Association on Mental Deficiency.

Brown, L., Nietupski, J., & Hamre-Nietupski, S. (1976). The criterion of ultimate functioning and public school services for severely handicapped students. In M. A. Thomas (Ed.), *Hey, don't forget about me: Education's investment in the severely, profoundly and multiply handicapped* (pp. 2–15). Reston, VA: Council for Exceptional Children.

Brulle, A. R., Barton, L. E., & Foskett, J. J. (1983). Educator/physician interchanges: A survey and suggestions. *Education and Training of the Mentally Retarded, 18*, 313–317.

Carr, E. G. (1983, May). *The social motivation of self-injurious behavior.* Paper presented at Self-Injurious Behavior—A National Conference, King of Prussia, PA.

Carr, E. G. (in press). Behavioral approaches to language and communication. In E. Schopler & G. Mesibov (Eds.), *Current issues in autism: Vol. 3. Communication problems in autism.* New York: Plenum Publishing Corp.

Carr, E. G., & Durand, V. M. (in press). The social-communicative basis of severe behavior problems in children. In S. Reiss & R. Bootzin (Eds.), *Theoretical issues in behavior therapy.* New York: Academic Press.

Carr, E. G., Newsom, C. D., & Binkoff, J. A. (1976). Stimulus control of self-destructive behavior in a psychotic child. *Journal of Abnormal Psychology, 4*, 139–153.

Carr, E. G., Newsom, C. D., & Binkoff, J. A. (1980). Escape as a factor in the aggressive behavior of two retarded children. *Journal of Applied Behavior Analysis, 13*, 113–129.

Cataldo, M. F., & Harris, J. (1982). The biological basis for self-injury in the mentally retarded. *Analysis and Intervention in Developmental Disabilities, 2*, 21–39.

Colman, R., Frankel, F., Ritvo, E., & Freeman, B. J. (1976). The effects of fluorescent and incandescent illumination upon repetitive behavior in autistic children. *Journal of Autism and Childhood Schizophrenia, 6,* 157–162.

Corbett, J. A., & Cambell, H. J. (1981). Causes of self-injurious behavior. In P. Mittler (Ed.), *Frontiers of knowledge in mental retardation: Vol. 2. Biomedical aspects* (pp. 285–292). Baltimore: University Park Press.

Council for Exceptional Children. (1977). Development and use of policies regarding administration of prescribed medication to children. *Exceptional Children, 43,* 251.

Cronbach, L. J., Ambron, S. R., Dornbusch, S. M., Hess, R. D., Hornik, R. C., Phillips, D. C., Walker, D. F., & Weiner, S. S. (1980). *Toward reform of program evaluation: Aims, methods, and institutional arrangements.* San Francisco: Jossey-Bass.

Davidson, P. W., Kleene, B. M., Carroll, M., & Rockowitz, R. J. (1983). Effects of Naloxone on self-injurious behavior: A case study. *Applied Research in Mental Retardation, 4,* 1–4.

Derer, K. R., & Hanashiro, R. (1982). *Behavior intervention index* (Tech. Rep. No. 9). Honolulu: University of Hawaii Behavioral Systems Intervention Project.

Donnellan, A. M. (1984). The criterion of the least dangerous assumption. *Behavioral Disorders, 9,* 141–150.

Donellan, A. M., Anderson, J. L., & Mesaros, R. A. (in press). An observational study of stereotypic behavior and proximity related to the occurrence of autistic child/family member interactions. *Journal of Autism and Developmental Disorders.*

Dorsey, M. F., Iwata, B. A., Reid, D. H., & Davis, P. A. (1982). Protective equipment: Continuous and contingent application in the treatment of self-injurious behavior. *Journal of Applied Behavior Analysis, 15,* 217–230.

Durand, V. M. (1982). A behavioral/pharmacological intervention for the treatment of severe self-injurious behavior. *Journal of Autism and Developmental Disorders, 12,* 242–251.

Edelson, S. M., Taubman, M. T., & Lovaas, O. I. (1983). Some social contexts of self-destructive behavior. *Journal of Abnormal Child Psychology, 11,* 299–312.

Evans, I. M. (1971). Theoretical and experimental aspects of the behaviour modification approach to autistic children. In M. Rutter (Ed.), *Infantile autism: Concepts, characteristics and treatment* (pp. 229–251). London: Churchill Livingstone.

Evans, I. M. (1982). Behavioral assessment. In E. C. Walker (Ed.), *Handbook of clinical psychology: Theory, research and practice* (pp. 391–419). Homewood, IL: The Dorsey Press.

Evans, I. M. (in press). Individual behavioral repertoires as systems: Towards a heuristic model of clinical judgment in assessment. *Behavioral Assessment.*

Evans, I. M., & Brown, F. (1984). *Assessment of competencies in special education students: An analysis for administrators and policy makers.* Binghamton: Project SPAN, SUNY.

Evans, I. M., & Voeltz, L. M. (1982). *The selection of intervention priorities in educational programming of severely handicapped preschool children with multiple behavior problems.* (Final Report, Grant No. G00-790-1960). Honolulu: University of Hawaii Departments of Psychology and Special Education.

Evans, I. M., & Wilson, F. E. (1983). Behavioral assessment as decision making: A theoretical analysis. In M. Rosenbaum, C. M. Franks, & Y. Jaffe (Eds.), *Perspectives on behavior therapy in the eighties* (pp. 35–53). New York: Springer Publishing Co.

Falvey, M., Brown, L., Lyon, S., Baumgart, D., & Schroeder, J. (1980). Strategies for using cues and correction procedures. In W. Sailor, B. Wilcox, & L. Brown (Eds.), *Methods of instruction for severely handicapped students* (pp. 109–133). Baltimore: Paul H. Brookes Publishing Co.

Favell, J. E., Azrin, N. H., Baumeister, A. A., Carr, E. G., Dorsey, M. F., Forehand, R., Foxx, R. M., Lovaas, O. I., Rincover, A., Risley, T. R., Romanczyk, R. G., Russo, D. C., Schroeder, S. R., & Solnick, J. V. (1982). The treatment of self-injurious behavior. (AABT Task Force Report, Winter, 1982). *Behavior Therapy, 13,* 529–554.

Favell, J. E., McGimsey, J. F., & Jones, M. L. (1978). The use of physical restraint in the treatment of self-injury and as positive reinforcement. *Journal of Applied Behavior Analysis, 11,* 225–241.

Favell, J. E., McGimsey, J. F., & Schell, R. M. (1982). Treatment of self-injury by providing alternative sensory activities. *Analysis and Intervention in Developmental Disabilities, 2,* 83–104.

Ford, A., Brown, L., Pumpian, I., Baumgart, D., Nisbet, J., Schroeder, J., & Loomis, R. (1984). Strategies for developing individualized recreation and leisure programs for severely handicapped students. In N. Certo, N. Haring, & R. York (Eds.), *Public school integration of severely handicapped students: Rational issues and progressive alternatives* (pp. 245–275). Baltimore: Paul H. Brookes Publishing Co.

Forehand, R., & Baumeister, A. A. (1976). Deceleration of aberrant behavior among retarded individuals. In M. Hersen, R. M. Eisler, & P. M. Miller (Eds.), *Progress in behavior modification: Vol. 2* (pp. 223–278). New York: Academic Press.

Gaylord-Ross, R. (1980). A decision model for the treatment of aberrant behavior in applied settings. In W. Sailor, B. Wilcox, & L. Brown (Eds.), *Methods of instruction for severely handicapped students* (pp. 135–158). Baltimore: Paul H. Brookes Publishing Co.

Gaylord-Ross, R., & Holvoet, J. (1984). *Teaching severely handicapped children and youth.* Boston: Little, Brown & Co.

Gilliam, J. E., & Coleman, M. C. (1981). Who influences IEP committee decisions? *Exceptional Children, 47,* 642–644.

Gold, M. W. (1972). Stimulus factors in skill training of the retarded on a complex assembly task: Acquisition, transfer and retention. *American Journal of Mental Deficiency, 76,* 517–526.

Goldstein, S., Strickland, B., Turnbull, A. P., & Curry, L. (1980). An observational analysis of the IEP conference. *Exceptional Children, 46,* 278–286.

Guess, D., & Helmstetter, E. (in press). Skill cluster instruction and the Individualized Curriculum Sequencing Model. In R. H. Horner, L. H. Meyer, & H. D. Fredericks (Eds.), *Education of learners with severe handicaps: Exemplary service strategies.* Baltimore: Paul H. Brookes Publishing Co.

Guess, D., & Noonan, M. J. (1982). Curricula and instructional procedures for severely handicapped students. *Focus on Exceptional Children, 14,* 1–12.

Haring, N. G., & White, O. R. (1981). *Field-initiated research studies of compliance behavior in severely handicapped.* Annual Report 1980–1981. (Grant No. G00-800-1915). Seattle: University of Washington.

Harris, S. L., & Wolchik, S. A. (1979). Suppression of self-stimulation: Three alternative strategies. *Journal of Applied Behavior Analysis, 12,* 185–198.

Hawkins, R. P. (1975). Who decided that was the problem? Two stages of responsibility for applied behavior analysts. In W. S. Wood (Ed.), *Issues in evaluating behavior modification* (pp. 195–214). Champaign, IL: Research Press.

Heads, T. B. (1978). Ethical and legal considerations in behavior therapy. In D. Marholin, II (Ed.), *Child behavior therapy* (pp. 416–433). New York: Gardner Press.

Hobbs, N. (1975). *Issues in the classification of children* (Vols. 1–2). San Francisco: Jossey-Bass.

Horner, R. H., & Budd, C. M. (1983). *Teaching manual sign language to a nonverbal student: Generalization and collateral reduction of maladaptive behavior.* Unpublished manuscript. University of Oregon, Eugene.

Horner, R. H., Meyer, L. H., & Fredericks, H. D. (Eds.). (in press). *Education of learners with severe handicaps: Exemplary service strategies.* Baltimore: Paul H. Brookes Publishing Co.

Hung, D. W. (1978). Using self-stimulation as a reinforcement for autistic children. *Journal of Autism and Childhood Schizophrenia, 8,* 355–369.

Hutt, S., & Hutt, C. (1968). Stereotypy, arousal and autism. *Human Development, 11,* 277–286.

Janis, I., & Mann, L. (1977). *Decision making: A psychological analysis of conflict, choice, and commitment.* New York: The Free Press.

Kanfer, F. H., & Nay, W. R. (1982). Behavioral assessment. In G. T. Wilson & C. M. Franks (Eds.), *Contemporary behavior therapy: Conceptual and empirical foundations* (pp. 367–402). New York: The Guilford Press.

Kazdin, A. E. (1980). Acceptability of alternative treatments for deviant child behavior. *Journal of Applied Behavior Analysis, 13,* 259–273.

Kazdin, A. E. (1981). Drawing valid inferences from case studies. *Journal of Consulting and Clinical Psychology, 49,* 183–192.

Kelly, J. A., & Drabman, R. S. (1977). The modification of socially detrimental behavior. *Journal of Behavior Therapy and Experimental Psychiatry, 8,* 101–104.

Koegel, R. L., Egel, A. L., & Dunlap, G. (1980). Learning characteristics of autistic children. In W. Sailor, B. Wilcox, & L. Brown (Eds.), *Methods of instruction for severely handicapped students* (pp. 259–301). Baltimore: Paul H. Brookes Publishing Co.

Krantz, P. J., & Risley, T. R. (1977). Behavioral ecology in the classroom. In S. G. O'Leary & K. D. O'Leary (Eds.), *Classroom management: The successful use of behavior modification* (pp. 349–366). New York: Pergamon Press.

LaVigna, G. W., & Donnellan, A. M. (in press). *Alternatives to punishment: Non-aversive strategies for solving behavior problems.* New York: Irvington Press.

Linscheid, T. R., & Cunningham, C. E. (1977). A controlled demonstration of the effectiveness of electric shock in the elimination of chronic infant rumination. *Journal of Applied Behavior Analysis, 10,* 500.

Lovaas, O. I. (1967). A behavior therapy approach to the treatment of childhood schizophrenia. In J. P. Hill (Ed.), *Minnesota symposia on child development* (pp. 108–159). Minneapolis: University of Minnesota Press.

Lovaas, O. I. (1981). *Teaching developmentally disabled children: The ME book*. Baltimore: University Park Press.

Lovaas, O. I., Koegel, R. L., Simmons, J. Q., & Long, J. S. (1973). Some generalization and follow-up measures on autistic children in behavior therapy. *Journal of Applied Behavior Analysis, 6,* 131–165.

Maisto, C. R., Baumeister, A. A., & Maisto, A. A. (1978). An analysis of variables related to self-injurious behavior among institutionalized retarded persons. *Journal of Mental Deficiency Research, 22,* 27–36.

Martin, R. (1975). *Legal challenges to behavior modification: Trends in schools, corrections, and mental health*. Champaign, IL: Research Press.

Mayhew, G. L., & Harris, F. C. (1978). Some negative side effects of a punishment procedure for stereotyped behavior. *Journal of Behavior Therapy and Experimental Psychiatry, 9,* 245–251.

Meyer, L. H., Evans, I. M., Wuerch, B. B., & Brennan, J. M. (in press). Monitoring the collateral effects of leisure skill instruction: A case study in multiple-baseline methodology. *Behaviour Research & Therapy*.

Meyer, L. H., McQuarter, R. J., & Kishi, G. S. (1984). Assessing and teaching social interaction skills. In W. Stainback & S. Stainback (Eds.), *Integration of severely handicapped students with their nonhandicapped peers: A handbook for teachers*. Reston, VA: Council for Exceptional Children.

Meyer, L. H., Reichle, J., McQuarter, R. J., Evans, I. M., Neel, R. S., & Kishi, G. S. (1983). *Assessment of social competence (ASC): A scale of social competence functions*. Minneapolis: University of Minnesota Consortium Institute.

Neel, R. S. (1983, November). *Assessment of communication form and function in children with autism*. Paper presented at the annual meeting of the Association for Persons with Severe Handicaps, San Francisco, CA.

Neel, R. S., Billingsley, F. F., McCarty, F., Symonds, D., Lambert, C., Lewis-Smith, N., & Hanashiro, R. (1983). *Teaching autistic children: A functional curriculum approach*. Seattle: University of Washington College of Education.

Nelson, R. O. (1981). Realistic dependent measures for clinical use. *Journal of Consulting and Clinical Psychology, 49,* 168–182.

Nelson, R. O. (in press). Behavioral assessment in the school setting. In T. R. Kratochwill (Ed.), *Advances in school psychology: Vol. 4*. Hillsdale, NJ: Lawrence Erlbaum Associates.

Nishioka-Evans, V., Hadden, C. K., Kraus, D.,

Johnson, J., Fredericks, H. D., & Toews, J. W. (1983). *The Teaching Research curriculum for mildly and moderately handicapped adolescents and adults: Taxonomy and assessment*. Monmouth, OR: Teaching Research.

Norton, G. R., Austen, S., Allen, G. E., & Hilton, J. (1983). Acceptability of time-out from reinforcement procedures for disruptive child behavior: A further analysis. *Child & Family Behavior Therapy, 5,* 31–41.

Ornitz, E. M. (1971). Childhood autism—a disorder of sensorimotor integration. In M. Rutter (Ed.), *Infantile autism: Concepts, characteristics and treatments* (pp. 50–68). London: Churchill Livingstone.

Ornitz, E. M., & Ritvo, E. R. (1968). Perceptual inconstancy in early infantile autism. *Archives of General Psychiatry, 18,* 76–98.

Patterson, G. R. (1976). The aggressive child: Victim and architect of a coercive system. In A. Hamerlynck, E. J. Mash, & L. C. Handy (Eds.), *Behavior modification and families* (pp. 267–317). New York: Brunner/Mazel.

Pendergrass, V. E. (1972). Timeout from positive reinforcement following persistent, high-rate behavior in retardates. *Journal of Applied Behavior Analysis, 5,* 85–91.

Plummer, S., Baer, D. M., & LeBlanc, J. M. (1977). Functional considerations in the use of procedural time out and an effective alternative. *Journal of Applied Behavior Analysis, 10,* 689–705.

Rachlin, H. (1980). *Behaviorism in everyday life*. Englewood Cliffs, NJ: Prentice-Hall.

Reichle, J., & Keogh, W. (in press). Beginning to communicate: Intervention strategies. In R. H. Horner, L. H. Meyer, & H. D. Fredericks (Eds.), *Education of learners with severe handicaps: Exemplary service strategies*. Baltimore: Paul H. Brookes Publishing Co.

Renzaglia, A., & Bates, P. (1983). Teaching socially appropriate behavior: In search of social competence. In M. E. Snell (Ed.), *Systematic instruction of the moderately and severely handicapped* (2nd ed.) (pp. 314–356). Columbus, OH: Charles E. Merrill Publishing Co.

Repp, A. C., Barton, L. E., & Brulle, A. R. (1983). A comparison of two procedures for programming the differential reinforcement of other behaviors. *Journal of Applied Behavior Analysis, 16,* 435–445.

Rimland, B. (1964). *Infantile autism: The syndrome and its implications for a neural theory of behavior*. New York: Appleton-Century-Crofts.

Rincover, A. (1978). Sensory extinction: A procedure for eliminating self-stimulatory behavior in developmentally disabled children. *Journal of Abnormal Child Psychology, 6,* 299–310.

Rincover, A., Cook, R., Peoples, A., & Packard, D. (1979). Sensory extinction and sensory reinforcement principles for programming multiple adaptive behavior change. *Journal of Applied Behavior Analysis, 12,* 221–233.

Rincover, A., & Devany, J. (1982). The application of sensory extinction procedures to self-injury. *Analysis and Intervention in Developmental Disabilities, 2,* 67–81.

Risley, T. R. (1968). The effects and side effects of punishing the autistic behaviors of a deviant child. *Journal of Applied Behavior Analysis, 1,* 21–34.

Robinson, C. C., & Robinson, J. H. (1983). Sensorimotor functions and cognitive development. In M. E. Snell (Ed.), *Systematic instruction of the moderately and severely handicapped* (2nd ed.) (pp. 227–266). Columbus, OH: Charles E. Merrill Publishing Co.

Rojahn, J., Mulick, J. A., McCoy, D., & Schroeder, S. R. (1978). Setting effects, adaptive clothing, and the modification of head banging and self-restraint in two profoundly retarded adults. *Behavioral Analysis and Modification, 2,* 185–196.

Romanczyk, R. G. (1977). Intermittent punishment of self-stimulation: Effectiveness during application and extinction. *Journal of Consulting and Clinical Psychology, 45,* 53–60.

Romanczyk, R. G., Kistner, J. A., & Plienis, A. (1982). Self-stimulatory and self-injurious behavior: Etiology and treatment. In J. J. Steffen & P. Karoly (Eds.), *Autism and severe psychopathology: Advances in child behavioral analysis and therapy: Vol. 2* (pp. 189–254). Lexington, MA: D. C. Heath & Co.

Rosenthal, R., & Jacobson, L. (1968). *Pygmalion in the classroom: Teacher expectations and pupils' intellectual development.* New York: Holt, Rinehart & Winston.

Runco, M. A., Charlop, M. H., & Schreibman, L. (in press). The occurrence of autistic children's self-stimulation as a function of novel versus familiar stimulus conditions. *Analysis and Intervention in Developmental Disabilities.*

Russo, D. C., Carr, E. G., & Lovaas, O. I. (1980). Self-injury in pediatric populations. In J. M. Ferguson & C. B. Taylor (Eds.), *The comprehensive handbook of behavioral medicine* (pp. 183–201). New York: Spectrum Publications.

Russo, D. C., Cataldo, M. F., & Cushing, P. J. (1981). Compliance training and behavioral covariation in the treatment of multiple behavior problems. *Journal of Applied Behavior Analysis, 14,* 209–222.

Sailor, W., Guess, D., Rutherford, G., & Baer, D. M. (1968). Control of tantrum behavior by operant techniques during experimental verbal training. *Journal of Applied Behavior Analysis, 1,* 237–243.

Sajwaj, T., Twardoz, S., & Burke, M. (1972). Side effects of extinction procedures in a remedial preschool. *Journal of Applied Behavior Analysis, 5,* 163–175.

Sanford, A. R. (1971). *Learning Accomplishment Profile (Chapel Hill Training Outreach Project).* (Available from Kaplan School Supply Corp., 600 Jonestown Road, Winston-Salem, NC 27103.)

Schuler, A. L. (1980, August). *Communicative intent and aberrant behavior.* Paper presented at the Council for Exceptional Children's Topical Conference on the Seriously Emotionally Disturbed, Minneapolis.

Singh, N. N., Manning, P. J., & Angell, M. J. (1982). Effects of an oral hygiene punishment procedure on chronic rumination and collateral behaviors in monozygous twins. *Journal of Applied Behavior Analysis, 15,* 309–314.

Snell, M. E. (Ed.). (1983). *Systematic instruction of the moderately and severely handicapped* (2nd ed.). Columbus, OH: Charles E. Merrill Publishing Co.

Sulzer-Azaroff, B., & Mayer, G. R. (1977). *Applying behavior analysis procedures with children and youth.* New York: Holt, Rinehart & Winston.

Sulzer-Azaroff, B., & Reese, E. P. (1982). *Applying behavior analysis: A program for developing professional competence.* New York: Holt, Rinehart & Winston.

Tharp, R. G. (1981). The metamethodology of research and development. *Educational Perspectives, 20,* 42–48.

Tharp, R. G., & Wetzel, R. J. (1969). *Behavior modification in the natural environment.* New York: Academic Press.

The Association for Persons with Severe Handicaps. (1981, November). Resolution on intrusive interventions. *TASH Newsletter, 7*(11), 1–2.

Turnbull, A. P. (1983). Parent-professional interactions. In M. E. Snell (Ed.), *Systematic instruction of the moderately and severely handicapped* (2nd ed.) (pp. 18–43). Columbus, OH: Charles E. Merrill Publishing Co.

VanDeventer, P., Yelinek, N., Brown, L., Schroeder, J., Loomis, R., & Gruenewald, L. (1981). A follow-up examination of severely handicapped graduates of the Madison Metropolitan School District from 1971–1978. In L. Brown, D. Baumgart, I. Pumpian, J. Nisbet,

A. Ford, R. Loomis, & J. Schroeder (Eds.), *Curricular strategies that can be used to transition severely handicapped students from school to nonschool and postschool environments* (pp. 45–63). Madison: Madison Metropolitan School District.

Voeltz, L. M. (1982). Effects of structured interactions with severely handicapped peers on children's attitudes. *American Journal of Mental Deficiency, 86,* 380–390.

Voeltz, L. M., & Evans, I. M. (1982). The assessment of behavioral interrelationships in child behavior therapy. *Behavioral Assessment, 4,* 131–165.

Voeltz, L. M., & Evans, I. M. (1983). Educational validity: Procedures to evaluate outcomes in programs for severely handicapped learners. *The Journal of the Association for the Severely Handicapped, 8*(1), 3–15.

Voeltz, L. M., Evans, I. M., Derer, K. R., & Hanashiro, R. (1983). Targeting excess behavior for change: A clinical decision model for selecting priority goals in educational contexts. *Child & Family Behavior Therapy, 5,* 17–35.

Voeltz, L. M., Evans, I. M., Freedland, K., & Donellon, S. (1982). Teacher decision making in the selection of educational priorities for severely handicapped children. *Journal of Special Education, 16,* 179–198.

Wahler, R. G. (1975). Some structural aspects of deviant child behavior. *Journal of Applied Behavior Analysis, 8,* 27–42.

Wahler, R. G., & Fox, J. J. (1980). Solitary toy play and time out: A family treatment package for children with aggressive and oppositional behavior. *Journal of Applied Behavior Analysis, 13,* 23–39.

Weeks, M., & Gaylord-Ross, R. (1981). Task difficulty and aberrant behavior in severely handicapped students. *Journal of Applied Behavior Analysis, 14,* 449–463.

Wells, K. C., Forehand, R., Hickey, K., & Green, K. D. (1977). Effects of a procedure derived from the overcorrection principle on manipulated and nonmanipulated behaviors. *Journal of Applied Behavior Analysis, 10,* 679–687.

White, O. R., & Haring, N. G. (1980). *Exceptional teaching* (2nd ed.). Columbus, OH: Charles E. Merrill Publishing Co.

Whitman, T. L., Hurley, J. D., Johnson, M. R., & Christian, J. G. (1978). Direct and generalized reduction of inappropriate behavior in a severely retarded child through a parent-administered behavior modification program. *AAESPH Review, 3,* 68–77.

Whitman, T. L., Sciback, J. W., & Reid, D. H. (1983). *Behavior modification with the severely and profoundly retarded: Research and application.* New York: Academic Press.

Witt, J. C., Elliott, S. N., & Marten, B. K. (1984). Acceptability of behavioral interventions used in classrooms: The influence of amount of teacher time, severity of behavior problem, and type of intervention. *Behavioral Disorders, 9,* 95–104.

Wolf, M. M. (1978). Social validity: The case for subjective measurement, or how applied behavior analysis is finding its heart. *Journal of Applied Behavior Analysis, 11,* 203–214.

Wuerch, B. B., & Voeltz, L. M. (1982). *Longitudinal leisure skills for severely handicapped learners: The Ho' onanea curriculum component.* Baltimore: Paul H. Brookes Publishing Co.

Zentall, S. S., & Zentall, T. R. (1983). Optimal stimulation: A model of disordered activity and performance in normal and deviant children. *Psychological Bulletin, 94,* 446–471.

The Flowchart
Task Book

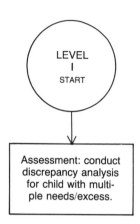

STEP 1.   LIST SOME LEAST RESTRICTIVE ENVIRONMENTS IN WHICH THE CHILD
            CAN FUNCTION.

    _____   _____

    _____   _____

    _____   _____

STEP 2.   LIST SOME FUTURE LEAST RESTRICTIVE ENVIRONMENTS IN WHICH
            THE CHILD COULD FUNCTION.

    _____   _____

    _____   _____

    _____   _____

STEP 3.   FOR EACH ENVIRONMENT LISTED IN STEP 1, IDENTIFY THE SKILLS
            THAT THE CHILD HAS THAT ALLOW HIM OR HER TO PARTICIPATE.

    _____

    _____

    _____

    _____

    _____

STEP 4.   FOR EACH ENVIRONMENT LISTED IN STEP 2, IDENTIFY THE SKILLS
THAT WOULD ALLOW THE CHILD TO PARTICIPATE.

_____

_____

_____

_____

_____

STEP 5.   FOR EACH SKILL FROM STEP 4 THAT HAS BEEN SELECTED FOR
INSTRUCTION, CONDUCT A DISCREPANCY ANALYSIS.

In Column A, list what a nonhandicapped similar age peer does.
In Column B, place a + (plus) if the handicapped student can perform the step and
a − (minus) if the handicapped student cannot perform the step.
In Column C, write what the handicapped child does if she or he cannot perform the
step.

Environment _____ Skill _____   Environment _____ Skill _____

A	B	C		A	B	C

STEP 6.   LIST THE EXCESS BEHAVIORS DISPLAYED BY THE CHILD THAT
CREATE A DISCREPANCY IN THE PERFORMANCE OF THE SKILLS
IDENTIFIED IN STEP 5.

_____   _____   _____   _____   _____

_____   _____   _____   _____   _____

_____   _____   _____   _____   _____

IF THE ANSWER IS "NO, DISCREPANCIES ARE NOT LIFE/HEALTH-THREATENING," THEN

Rule out identifying
excess behaviors
as priorities.

NEXT, GO ON AND

Plan and prioritize
curriculum
objectives (IEP).

NOW,

GO TO
LEVEL
II.

See page 183.

IF THE ANSWER IS "YES, A LIFE/HEALTH-THREATENING DISCREPANCY DOES EXIST," THEN LIST THE BEHAVIOR(S) AND THE POSSIBLE RESULTS.

Behavior   Results

_____   _____

_____   _____

FOR EACH BEHAVIOR IDENTIFIED AS LIFE/HEALTH-THREATENING, ASK:

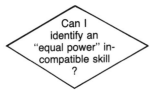

IF THE ANSWER IS "NO, AN 'EQUAL POWER' IN-COMPATIBLE SKILL CANNOT BE IDENTIFIED," THEN GO TO THE DRO QUESTION ON PAGE 174.

IF THE ANSWER IS "YES, AN 'EQUAL POWER' IN-COMPATIBLE SKILL CAN BE IDENTIFIED," THEN ASK:

IF THE ANSWER IS "YES, THE EXCESS CAN BE PRE-VENTED WHILE TEACHING THE SKILL," THEN

IMPLEMENT ECOLOGICAL/CURRICULAR COMPONENT.   See page 177.

IF THE ANSWER IS "NO, THE EXCESS BEHAVIOR CANNOT BE PREVENTED," THEN ASK:

IF THE ANSWER IS "YES, SKILL TRAINING CAN BE CONDUCTED SIMULTANEOUSLY WITH EFFORTS TO DECREASE EXCESS," THEN

IMPLEMENT CURRICULAR/ NEGATIVE CONSEQUENCES COMPONENT.

See p. 180

IF THE ANSWER IS "NO, SKILL TRAINING CANNOT BE CONDUCTED SIMULTANEOUSLY WITH EFFORTS TO DECREASE EXCESS," THEN ASK:

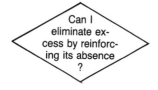

IF THE ANSWER IS "YES, THE EXCESS CAN BE ELIMINATED BY REINFORCING ITS ABSENCE," THEN

Implement DRO procedure.

NEXT, GO TO ALTERNATIVE SKILL QUESTION ON PAGE 176.

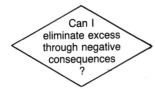

Level I: Negative Consequences (pp. 73–74)

IF THE ANSWER IS "NO, THE EXCESS CANNOT BE ELIMINATED BY REINFORCING ITS ABSENCE," THEN ASK:

STOP:
REEVALUATE
DECISIONS/
CONSULTA-
TION. GO TO
LEVEL II.

IF THE ANSWER IS "NO, THE EXCESS CANNOT BE ELIMINATED WITH A NEGATIVE CONSEQUENCES PROCEDURE," THEN

See page 183.

IF THE ANSWER IS "YES, THE EXCESS CAN BE ELIMINATED WITH A NEGATIVE CONSEQUENCES PROCEDURE," THEN

Implement DRO +
negative consequences
procedure.

See negative consequences considerations, page 181, STEP 5.

NEXT,

Fade negative
consequences
and maintain DRO
procedure.

FOLLOWING THE IMPLEMENTATION OF DRO OR DRO + NEGATIVE CONSE-
QUENCES, ASK:

IF THE ANSWER IS "NO, AN 'EQUAL POWER' AL-
TERNATIVE SKILL CANNOT BE IDENTIFIED," THEN

See page 183.

IF THE ANSWER IS "YES, AN 'EQUAL POWER' AL-
TERNATIVE SKILL CAN BE IDENTIFIED," THEN

Plan curriculum
objective and
implement DRI.

NEXT,

Plan and prioritize
curriculum
objectives (IEP).

NOW,

See page 183.

```
┌─────────────────────────────┐
│ IMPLEMENT ECOLOGICAL/       │
│ CURRICULAR COMPONENT.       │
└─────────────────────────────┘
              │
              ▽
┌─────────────────────────────┐
│   Incorporate skills        │
│   into IEP planning of      │
│   curriculum objectives.    │
└─────────────────────────────┘
```

STEP 1. IN COLUMN A, LIST THE LIFE/HEALTH-THREATENING BEHAVIOR(S). IN
         COLUMN B, LIST THE BEHAVIOR(S) OR STIMULUS EVENT(S) THAT
         SIGNAL(S) THE ONSET OF THE TARGET EXCESS BEHAVIOR.

          A   B

_____   _____

                                                _____

_____   _____

                                                _____

STEP 2. DESCRIBE IN DETAIL THE SKILL TO BE TAUGHT AND THE PROCEDURE TO
         BE USED.

            Natural   Verbal
                 cue _____   cue _____

Task description _____

                               _____

        Prompting
        procedure _____

                               _____

                               _____

STEP 3.   IN Part A, DESCRIBE THE EVENTS THAT APPEAR TO BE MAINTAINING
          THE EXCESS BEHAVIOR. IN Part B, DESCRIBE THE REINFORCING
          EVENTS TO BE USED THAT MIGHT SUCCESSFULLY COMPETE WITH
          THE EVENTS DESCRIBED IN Part A.

          Part A   _____

                   _____

          Part B   _____

                   _____

STEP 4.   DESCRIBE IN DETAIL THE PREVENTION TECHNIQUE TO BE
          EMPLOYED.

          _____

          _____

          _____

STEP 5.   DESCRIBE ANY CHANGES TO THE ENVIRONMENT THAT WOULD BE
          NEEDED.

          _____

          _____

          _____

STEP 6.   DESCRIBE ANY CHANGES NOT INCLUDED IN STEPS 1–5 THAT WOULD
          BE NEEDED FOR PROGRAM SUCCESS.

          _____

          _____

          _____

STEP 7.   IN THE SPACE PROVIDED, WRITE THE NEW CURRICULUM OBJECTIVE;
          THEN, INCORPORATE OBJECTIVE INTO IEP.

          _____

          _____

          _____

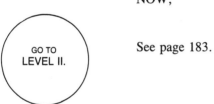

NEXT,

THEN,

IN THE SPACE PROVIDED, INDICATE THE PRO-
CEDURE FOR FADING THE PREVENTION
COMPONENT.

Level   Procedure

1. _____

2. _____

3. _____

4. _____

NOW,

See page 183.

```
┌─────────────────────────┐
│ IMPLEMENT CURRICULAR/    │
│ NEGATIVE CONSEQUENCES    │
│ PROCEDURE.               │
└─────────────────────────┘
            │
            ▼
┌─────────────────────────┐
│ Incorporate skills       │
│ into IEP planning of     │
│ curriculum objectives.   │
└─────────────────────────┘
```

STEP 1.   ENTER THE LIFE/HEALTH-THREATENING BEHAVIOR(S) IN THE SPACE
          PROVIDED.

          _____   _____

STEP 2.   DESCRIBE IN DETAIL THE SKILL TO BE TAUGHT AND THE PROCEDURE
          TO BE USED.

                    Natural   Verbal
                       cue _____   cue _____

          Task description _____

               Prompting   _____
               procedure   _____
                            _____
                            _____

STEP 3.   IN Part A, DESCRIBE THE EVENTS THAT APPEAR TO MAINTAIN THE
          EXCESS BEHAVIOR; IN Part B, DESCRIBE THE REINFORCING EVENTS
          TO BE USED THAT MIGHT SUCCESSFULLY COMPETE WITH THE
          EVENTS DESCRIBED IN Part A.

          Part A _____
                  _____

          Part B _____
                  _____

STEP 4.   DESCRIBE IN DETAIL THE NEGATIVE CONSEQUENCES PROCEDURE TO BE USED.

_____

_____

STEP 5.   FOR THE NEGATIVE CONSEQUENCES TECHNIQUE IN STEP 4, ANSWER THE FOLLOWING QUESTIONS:

Question 1:	Does the technique avoid the use of physical pain?	YES	NO
Question 2:	Would a "third party" consider the technique humane?	YES	NO
Question 3:	Is the technique one that can be legally used within the community?	YES	NO
Question 4:	Have the proper consent forms been obtained from parents/guardians?	YES	NO
Question 5:	Is the technique sufficiently brief to be implemented without interfering with programming?	YES	NO

A "NO" ANSWER TO *ANY* OF THESE QUESTIONS REQUIRES THE SELECTION OF AN ALTERNATIVE NEGATIVE CONSEQUENCES TECHNIQUE.

IF ALL OF THESE QUESTIONS RECEIVED A "YES" ANSWER, THEN BEGIN STEP 6.

STEP 6:   DESCRIBE ANY CHANGES NOT INCLUDED IN STEPS 1–5 THAT WOULD BE NEEDED FOR PROGRAM SUCCESS.

_____   _____

STEP 7:   IN THE SPACE PROVIDED, WRITE THE NEW CURRICULUM OBJECTIVE; THEN, INCORPORATE OBJECTIVE INTO IEP.

_____

_____

_____

NEXT,

Teach skills and consequate excess.

THEN,

After skill mastery, fade negative consequences.

IN THE SPACE PROVIDED, INDICATE THE PROCEDURE FOR FADING THE NEGA-
TIVE CONSEQUENCES COMPONENT.

Level   Procedure

  1. _____

  2. _____

  3. _____

  4. _____

  5. _____

  6. _____

  7. _____

NOW,

See page 183.

Identify remaining
high-priority
excess concerns.

LIST ALL EXCESS BEHAVIORS NOT CONSIDERED ON LEVEL I.

_____   _____   _____   _____

_____   _____   _____   _____

_____   _____   _____   _____

_____   _____   _____   _____

THEN, FOR EACH EXCESS BEHAVIOR LISTED, ASK:

IF THE ANSWER IS "YES, THE EXCESS DOES INTER-FERE WITH LEARNING," THEN ENTER THE BE-HAVIOR UNDER STEP 1 OF THE COST-BENEFIT ANALYSIS ON PAGE 185.

IF THE ANSWER IS "NO, THE EXCESS DOES NOT INTERFERE WITH LEARNING," THEN ASK:

IF THE ANSWER IS "YES, THE EXCESS IS LIKELY TO BECOME SERIOUS," THEN ENTER THE BEHAVIOR UNDER STEP 1 OF THE COST-BENEFIT ANALYSIS ON PAGE 185.

IF THE ANSWER IS "NO, THE EXCESS IS NOT LIKELY TO BECOME SERIOUS," THEN ASK:

IF THE ANSWER IS "YES, THE EXCESS IS DANGER-
OUS TO OTHERS," THEN ENTER THE BEHAVIOR
UNDER STEP 1 OF THE COST-BENEFIT ANALYSIS ON
PAGE 185.

IF THE ANSWER IS "NO, THE EXCESS IS NOT
DANGEROUS," THEN ASK:

IF THE ANSWER IS "YES, THE EXCESS IS OF GREAT
CONCERN TO CAREGIVERS," THEN ENTER THE BE-
HAVIOR UNDER STEP 1 OF THE COST-BENEFIT
ANALYSIS ON PAGE 185.

IF THE ANSWER IS "NO, THE EXCESS IS NOT OF
GREAT CONCERN TO CAREGIVERS," THEN GO TO
SKILL TRAINING PROGRAM ON PAGE 187.

IF THE ANSWER TO ANY OF THE PREVIOUS QUES-
TIONS WAS "YES," THEN CONDUCT A COST-
BENEFIT ANALYSIS FOR THAT EXCESS BEHAVIOR.

COST-BENEFIT ANALYSIS:

```
Estimate costs and
benefits of behavior
      change.
```

STEP 1.   IN COLUMN A, LIST THE EXCESS BEHAVIORS THAT RECEIVED A
          "YES" ANSWER TO ANY OF THE FIRST FOUR QUESTIONS OF LEVEL II:

| Behaviors | Positive effects | Negative effects |
A	B	C
_____	_____	_____
_____	_____	_____
_____	_____	_____
_____	_____	_____
_____	_____	_____
_____	_____	_____

STEP 2.   FOR EACH BEHAVIOR LISTED IN STEP 1, ARE THERE ANY OTHER BE-
          HAVIORS OR SKILLS THAT OCCUR WITH IT? IF "YES," THEN DE-
          SCRIBE THE BEHAVIORS THAT GO TOGETHER. THESE BEHAVIORS
          MAY INCLUDE OTHER EXCESSES OR POSITIVE SKILLS AND NEED NOT
          BE LIMITED TO THOSE LISTED IN STEP 1.

          _____

          _____

          _____

STEP 3.   FOR EACH EXCESS BEHAVIOR LISTED IN STEP 1, ASK:

          Question 1: Would a decrease in this behavior result in a significant decrease in
                         another excess behavior? If yes, then enter the excess that would de-
                         crease in Column B of STEP 1. Include an arrow to indicate direc-
                         tion of change.

          Question 2: Would a decrease in this behavior result in a significant increase in a
                         positive behavior/skill? If yes, then enter the behavior/skill that
                         would increase in Column B of STEP 1. Include an arrow to indicate
                         direction of change.

Question 3:   Would a decrease in this behavior result in an unacceptable increase in another excess behavior? If yes, then enter the excess that would increase in Column C of STEP 1. Include an arrow to indicate direction of change.

Question 4:   Would a decrease in this behavior result in an unacceptable decrease in a positive behavior/skill? If yes, then enter the behavior/skill that would decrease in Column C of STEP 1. Include an arrow to indicate direction of change.

Question 5:   Would the intervention I plan to use have any effect on the child's behavior other than changing this behavior? If yes, list positive effects in Column B and negative effects in Column C of STEP 1. Include an arrow to indicate direction of change.

NOW ASK:

IF THE ANSWER IS "YES, THE COSTS OUTWEIGH THE BENEFITS," THEN

See page 189.

IF THE ANSWER IS "NO, THE COSTS DO NOT OUT-WEIGH THE BENEFITS," THEN ASK:

IF THE ANSWER IS "YES, THE EXCESS CAN BE PRE-VENTED," THEN

Design skill training program and monitor excess behavior(s).

NEXT,

Incorporate skill(s) into IEP.

NOW,

See page 189.

IF THE ANSWER IS "NO, THE EXCESS CANNOT BE PREVENTED WHILE TEACHING IEP OBJECTIVES," THEN ASK:

IF THE ANSWER IS "YES, AN 'EQUAL POWER' IN-COMPATIBLE SKILL CAN BE IDENTIFIED," THEN

Incorporate skill(s) into IEP.

NOW,

GO TO LEVEL III.

See page 189.

Level II: DRO ± Negative Consequences (p. 100)

IF THE ANSWER IS "NO, AN 'EQUAL POWER' IN-COMPATIBLE SKILL CANNOT BE IDENTIFIED," THEN ASK:

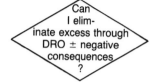

IF THE ANSWER IS "NO, THE EXCESS CANNOT BE ELIMINATED THROUGH DRO ± NEGATIVE CONSE-QUENCES," THEN

See page 189.

IF THE ANSWER IS "YES, THE EXCESS CAN BE ELIM-INATED THROUGH DRO ± NEGATIVE CONSE-QUENCES," THEN

NOW,

See page 189.

188

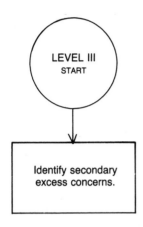

LIST ALL BEHAVIORS THAT WERE IDENTIFIED IN STEP 1 OF THE ASSESSMENT SECTION THAT HAVE NOT BEEN CONSIDERED ON LEVELS I AND II.

_____ _____ _____ _____

_____ _____ _____ _____

FOR EACH BEHAVIOR LISTED, ASK:

IF THE ANSWER IS "YES, THE EXCESS IS NOT IMPROVING OR IS GETTING WORSE," THEN ENTER THE BEHAVIOR UNDER STEP 1 OF THE COST-BENEFIT ANALYSIS ON PAGE 191.

IF THE ANSWER IS "NO, THE EXCESS IS IMPROVING OR GETTING BETTER," THEN ASK:

IF THE ANSWER IS "YES, THE EXCESS HAS BEEN A PROBLEM FOR SOME TIME," THEN ENTER THE BEHAVIOR UNDER STEP 1 OF THE COST-BENEFIT ANALYSIS ON PAGE 191.

IF THE ANSWER IS "NO, THE EXCESS HAS NOT BEEN A PROBLEM OVER TIME," THEN ASK:

IF THE ANSWER IS "YES, THE EXCESS DOES DAM-AGE MATERIALS," THEN ENTER THE BEHAVIOR UNDER STEP 1 OF THE COST-BENEFIT ANALYSIS ON PAGE 191.

IF THE ANSWER IS "NO, THE EXCESS DOES NOT DAMAGE THE MATERIALS," THEN ASK:

IF THE ANSWER IS "YES, THE EXCESS DOES INTER-FERE WITH COMMUNITY ACCEPTANCE," THEN EN-TER THE BEHAVIOR UNDER STEP 1 OF THE COST-BENEFIT ANALYSIS ON PAGE 191.

IF THE ANSWER IS "NO, THE EXCESS DOES NOT INTERFERE WITH COMMUNITY ACCEPTANCE," THEN ASK:

IF THE ANSWER IS "YES, OTHER BEHAVIOR WOULD IMPROVE IF THIS EXCESS IMPROVED," THEN ENTER THE BEHAVIOR UNDER STEP 1 OF THE COST-BENEFIT ANALYSIS ON PAGE 191.

IF THE ANSWER IS "NO, AN IMPROVEMENT IN THIS BEHAVIOR WOULD NOT RESULT IN IMPROVEMENT IN OTHER BEHAVIORS," THEN

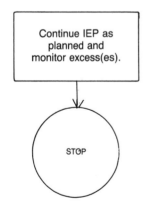

IF THE ANSWER TO ANY OF THE PREVIOUS QUES-TIONS WAS "YES," THEN CONDUCT A COST-BENEFIT ANALYSIS FOR THAT EXCESS BEHAVIOR.

COST-BENEFIT ANALYSIS

STEP 1.   IN COLUMN A, LIST THE BEHAVIORS THAT RECEIVED A "YES" AN-
SWER FOR ANY OF THE FIRST FIVE QUESTIONS OF LEVEL III.

Behaviors	Positive effects	Negative effects	Program effects
A	B	C	D
_____	_____	_____	_____
_____	_____	_____	_____
_____	_____	_____	_____
_____	_____	_____	_____
_____	_____	_____	_____

STEP 2.   FOR EACH BEHAVIOR LISTED IN STEP 1, ARE THERE ANY OTHER BE-
HAVIORS OR SKILLS THAT OCCUR WITH IT? IF "YES," THEN DE-
SCRIBE THE BEHAVIORS THAT GO TOGETHER. THESE BEHAVIORS
MAY INCLUDE OTHER EXCESSES OR POSITIVE SKILLS AND NEED NOT
BE LIMITED TO THOSE LISTED IN STEP 1.

_____

_____

_____

STEP 3.   FOR EACH BEHAVIOR LISTED IN STEP 1, ASK:

Question 1:   Would a decrease in this behavior result in a significant decrease in
another excess behavior? If yes, then enter the excess that would decrease in Column B of STEP 1. Include an arrow to indicate direction of change.

Question 2:   Would a decrease in this behavior result in a significant increase in a
positive behavior/skill? If yes, then enter the behavior/skill that
would increase in Column B of STEP 1. Include an arrow to indicate
direction of change.

Question 3:   Would a decrease in this behavior result in an unacceptable increase
in another excess behavior? If yes, then enter the excess in Column
C of STEP 1. Include an arrow to indicate direction of change.

Question 4:   Would a decrease in this behavior result in an unacceptable decrease in a positive behavior/skill? If yes, then enter the behavior/skill that would decrease in Column C of STEP 1. Include an arrow to indicate direction of change.

Question 5:   Would the intervention I plan to use have any effect on the child's behavior other than changing this behavior? If yes, list positive effects in Column B and negative effects in Column C of STEP 1. Include an arrow to indicate direction of change.

STEP 4.   FOR EACH EXCESS BEHAVIOR LISTED IN STEP 1, ASK:

Question 1:   Does the child currently have enough skills to engage in appropriate behavior if I eliminate this excess? If no, enter *STOP* and question number in Column D of STEP 1.

Question 2:   Are there interventions available that have demonstrated success in the elimination of this excess? If no, enter *STOP* and question number in Column D of STEP 1.

Question 3:   Will the intervention I have selected require me to use an inordinate amount of instructional time? If yes, enter *STOP* and question number in Column D of STEP 1.

Question 4:   Would intervening with the excess result in postponing the teaching of a needed skill? If yes, enter *STOP* and question number in Column D of STEP 1.

Question 5:   Could the intervention be considered physically painful or inhumane by a third party? If yes, enter *STOP* and question number in Column D of STEP 1.

NOW ASK:

IF THE ANSWER IS "NO, THE CHILD CANNOT CHANGE WITHOUT MAJOR COSTS TO CHILD/ PROGRAM," THEN

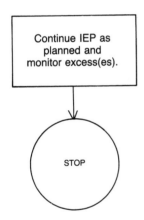

IF THE ANSWER IS "YES, THE CHILD CAN CHANGE WITHOUT MAJOR COSTS," THEN

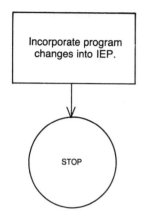

appendix B

Blank Forms
and Data Sheets

Behavioral Techniques Consent and Review Procedures: Checklist

Child's name _____ Teacher's name _____

School setting _____ Date begun _____ Review date _____

Directions: For each of the intervention techniques listed below under each group, check those that are in use for this child. For Groups B through D, an individual procedure entry is required for each technique, with a copy of the intervention program attached.

	Technique[a]	Check if used	Consent and review procedure followed
GROUP A	Positive reinforcement Social disapproval Token economy (positive S^R only) Timeout I (within view) Extinction of non-health-threatening behaviors Graduated guidance Redirection Response cost I (removal of toy, etc.) Modeling		
GROUP B	Timeout II (removed from view or room) Response cost II (restriction from activity) Overcorrection Restitution Positive practice Token economy (with response cost)		
GROUP C	Required relaxation Response cost III (removal of food tray) Timeout III (timeout room)		
GROUP D	Contingent use of physical restraint Extinction of health-threatening behavior Application of noxious behavior Satiation Contingent physically intrusive stimuli		

[a]For Group A, consent may be obtained through standard consent forms at school entry. For Groups B through D, approval of client, parent or guardian, and agency's human rights committee is required. Heads includes a last group of intrusive and highly aversive procedures (e.g., slapping, shock, food deprivation, contingent extremely cold room temperatures) that require approval of an agency administrator, a behavior analysis expert consultant, state agency director, and the state human rights committee. As these are generally illegal and clearly inappropriate for use in habilitative programs with children, we have not included them in the checklist.

Generating Intervention Hypotheses

Description of excess behavior	Alternative explanations	"Function test"— Will excess decrease if:	Alternative intervention strategies	
			Ecological	Curricular goal/s

Excess Function and Intervention Plan Worksheet: _____

Description of excess form	Possible function[a]	Curricular objective	Rationale for objective	Ecological modifications and instructional strategies

[a]From *The Assessment of Social Competence*, by Meyer, Reichle, Evans, Neel, and Kishi (1983).

Program Summation

Domains: _____

Student's position at start of session: _____

page ____ of ____ pages

Child _____

Key: Cue/correction phases
(1) Initial intrusive
(2) + Fading process
Response objective
mass trial practice

Skill cluster _____

Teacher/s _____
Setting _____
Materials _____

Natural cue	Instructional cue	Prompts/Corrections	Response objective	Reinforcement	
				Natural	Instructional
GOAL:					
GOAL:					
GOAL:					

199

Excess Behavior Intervention Evaluation Input

Excess behavior	Alternative skill needed	Potentially related excess behaviors/skills[a]	Possible benefits	Possible costs

[a] For each potentially related behavior, a (+) indicates a positive relationship (the behaviors seem to "go together") and a (−) indicates a negative relationship (one behavior seems to occur when the other is not occurring.)

Activity Selection Checklist[a]

Normalization: A concern for selecting activities that have social validity and will facilitate normalized domestic living, leisure, vocational and community integration, as well as provide opportunities for movement toward increasingly complex interactions.

1.	*Age-appropriateness:* Is the activity something a nonhandicapped peer would do and/or enjoy?	Yes No	Yes No
2.	*Integration:* Does the activity occur in criterion environments that include the presence and involvement of non-handicapped persons?	Yes No	Yes No
3.	*Acceptability/attractability:* Is the activity considered acceptable/desirable by nonhandicapped persons who are likely to be present in the specific environment?	Yes No	Yes No
4.	*Flexibility:* Can the activity be accessed by the individual alone as well as in a group?	Yes No	Yes No
5.	*Degree of supervision:* Can the activity be used with little to no caregiver supervision without major modifications?	Yes No	Yes No
6.	*Longitudinal application:* Is use of the activity appropriate across the lifespan, particularly for the adolescent and adult?	Yes No	Yes No
7.	*Caregiver preferences:* Is the activity valued by caregivers?	Yes No	Yes No
8.	*Multiple applications:* Is the activity useful for a variety of current and/or future environments? (Including seasonal considerations?)	Yes No	Yes No

Normalization area of concern score: 8

Individualization: Concern related to meeting the unique needs and interest of the individual learner.

1.	*Skill level flexibility:* Can the activity accommodate low- to high-entry skill levels without major modifications?	Yes No	Yes No
2.	*Participation access:* Can the activity be assessed independently or through minimal use of partial participation, preferably involving persons available in the natural environments?	Yes No	Yes No
3.	*Prosthetic capabilities:* Can the activity be adapted to varying handicapped conditions (sensory, motor, behavior) through normalized means?	Yes No	Yes No
4.	*Learner preferences:* Is the activity something of interest to the learner that she or he would enjoy doing or be willing to do in order to access other benefits?	Yes No	Yes No
5.	*Skill level development:* Does the activity provide an opportunity to develop one or more critical skills?	Yes No	Yes No
6.	*Personal development:* Will the activity enhance personal development (e.g., physical benefits)?	Yes No	Yes No

Individualization area of concern score: 6

(continued)

Activity Selection Checklist[a] *(continued)*

Environmental: Concerns related to logistical and physical components of activities in current and future environments.

1. *Availability:* Is the activity likely to be available, both now and in the future, in the environments the learner can access?	Yes	No	Yes	No
2. *Longevity:* Is the activity likely to remain available for a reasonable period of time (e.g., for materials: likely to last without need for major repair or parts replacement for at least a year)?	Yes	No	Yes	No
3. *Safety:* Is the activity safe, within normalized "risk taking" limits (e.g., would not pose a serious/unacceptable risk for the learner and others in the environment?)	Yes	No	Yes	No
4. *Noxiousness:* Is the activity *not* likely to be overly noxious (noisy, space consuming, distracting) to others in the learner's environment?	Yes	No	Yes	No
5. *Expense:* Can the activity be accessed at reasonable cost (e.g., materials are priced reasonably or have multiple uses, transportation costs reasonable, etc.)?	Yes	No	Yes	No
6. *Minimal interference:* Can the activity be programmed effectively for performance in criterion environments through available/feasible instructional opportunities?	Yes	No	Yes	No
7. *Support/willingness:* Will persons in the environment provide opportunities for the individual to engage in the activity?	Yes	No	Yes	No

Environmental area of concern score: 7

Total Score (number of items circled "yes"): 21

[a]From Meyer, McQuarter, and Kishi (1984); reprinted by permission.

Skill Acquisition and Excess Behavior Record
(2-Week Sample)

Student _____

Skill cluster _____

Excess (A) _____ (C) _____

     (B) _____ (D) _____

Level of Assistance Key

I = Independent	FP = Full physical
V = Verbal prompt	X = Partial participation
PP = Partial physical	

Date and teacher's initials[a]

Steps in Activity Sequence

10. _____

9. _____

8. _____

7. _____

6. _____

5. _____

4. _____

3. _____

2. _____

1. _____

10	10	10	10	10
9	9	9	9	9
8	8	8	8	8
7	7	7	7	7
6	6	6	6	6
5	5	5	5	5
4	4	4	4	4
3	3	3	3	3
2	2	2	2	2
1	1	1	1	1

% Correct

Check of planned instructional opportunities (/ = completed)

Week of: _____

%
Com-
pleted

	M	T	W	Th	F
A.M.					
P.M.					

Week of: _____

%
Com-
pleted

	M	T	W	Th	F
A.M.					
P.M.					

X̄ Day

Excess Behavior Tally

Note: Place an X in box to indicate that no data collection occurred.

A					
B					
C					
D					

Average % of sessions completed: [____] %

[a] These are probe data collection sessions that should be scheduled in advance of each 2-week period of time from among the total *planned* instructional sessions listed at the right of the data sheet.

Medication Data Collection/Communication Form

Patient Information   Name: _____ Birth Date: _____ C.A.: _____ School: _____

Case Manager/Teacher: _____ Physician: _____   DATA COLLECTION MODE

MEDICATION: _____ DATE INITIATED: _____   F = Frequency recording

DOSAGE: (a) _____ (b) _____ (c) _____   D = Duration recording

ADMIN. INTERVAL: (a) _____ (b) _____ (c) _____   M = Momentary time sampling

Date of Observation																					
Time of Observation	Start																				
	Finish																				
Admin. Interval																					
Dosage																					
Time most recent admin.																					
BEHAVIORS 1.																					
2.																					
3.																					
4.																					

Description of Target Behaviors   *Physician Comments:*

1.

2.

3.   *Observer Comments:*

4.

(From Brulle, Barton, and Foskett (1983); reprinted by permission.)

Anecdotal/Functional Analysis Observation Record

Student _____   Date of observation _____

By whom: _____

Steps in activity sequence:	What occurred (what _____ did, peer did, problems with materials, etc.)	Comments by observer	Summary, changes, and so on, by teacher
10. _____ _____			
9. _____ _____			
8. _____ _____			
7. _____ _____			
6. _____ _____			
5. _____ _____			
4. _____ _____			
3. _____ _____			
2. _____ _____			
1. _____ _____			

Index